PHILOSOPHY AND

Can philosophy enable us to lead better lives through a systematic understanding of our human nature? John Cottingham's thought-provoking study examines the contrasting approaches to this problem found in three major phases of Western philosophy. Starting with attempts of Plato, Aristotle and the Stoics and Epicureans to cope with the recalcitrant forces of the passions, he moves on to examine the fascinating and hitherto little-studied moral psychology of Descartes, and his effort to integrate the physical and emotional aspects of our humanity into a rational blueprint for fulfilment. He concludes by analysing the insights of modern psychoanalytic theory into the human predicament, arguing that philosophy neglects them at its peril if it hopes to come to terms with the complex relationship between reason and the emotions. Lucid in exposition and unusually wide-ranging in scope, *Philosophy and the good life* provides a fresh and challenging perspective on moral philosophy and psychology for students and specialists alike.

PHILOSOPHY AND THE GOOD LIFE

Reason and the passions in Greek,
Cartesian and psychoanalytic ethics

JOHN COTTINGHAM

University of Reading

CAMBRIDGE UNIVERSITY PRESS

PUBLISHED BY THE PRESS SYNDICATE OF THE UNIVERSITY OF CAMBRIDGE
The Pitt Building, Trumpington Street, Cambridge CB2 1RP, United Kingdom

CAMBRIDGE UNIVERSITY PRESS
The Edinburgh Building, Cambridge CB2 2RU, United Kingdom
40 West 20th Street, New York, NY 10011–4211, USA
10 Stamford Road, Oakleigh, Melbourne 3166, Australia

First published 1998

Typeset in 11/12½ pt Baskerville [VN]

A catalogue record for this book is available from the British Library

Library of Congress cataloguing in publication data

Cottingham, John, 1943–
Philosophy and the good life: reason and the passions in Greek,
Cartesian, and psychoanalytic ethics / John Cottingham.
p. cm.
Includes bibliographical references and index.
ISBN 0 521 47310 1. (hardback) – ISBN 0 521 47890 1 (paperback)
1. Ethics. 2. Conduct of life. 3. Reason. 4. Emotions – Moral
and ethical aspects. 5. Ethics, Ancient. 6. Descartes, René,
1596–1650 – Ethics. 7. Psychoanalysis and philosophy.
8. Psychoanalysis – Moral and ethical aspects. I. Title.
BJ1531.C68 1998
170–dc21 98–27898 CIP

ISBN 0 521 47310 1 hardback
ISBN 0 521 47890 1 paperback

Transferred to digital printing 2002

For MLC, MGC and JLC

Contents

Acknowledgements

A considerable portion of the work for this book was completed during my tenure of the Radcliffe Fellowship in Philosophy in 1993–4, and I should like to express my grateful thanks to the Radcliffe Trustees for their support.

In various places in the book, I have drawn on material from previously published articles: 'The Cartesian Legacy', in the *Proceedings of the Aristotelian Society*, sup. vol. LXVI (1992), pp. 1–21; 'The Self and the Body: Alienation and Integration in Cartesian Ethics', in *Seventeenth-century French Studies*, vol. 17 (1995), pp. 1–13; 'Partiality and the Virtues', in R. Crisp (ed.), *How Should One Live?'* (Oxford: Clarendon Press, 1996), pp. 57–76; 'Cartesian Ethics: Reason and the Passions', in the *Revue Internationale de Philosophie*, no. 195 (1996), pp. 193–216; 'The Ethical Credentials of Partiality', *Proceedings of the Aristotelian Society* (1997–8), pp. 1–21; and '"The only sure sign": Descartes on Thought and Language', in J. Preston (ed.), *Thought and Language* (Cambridge: Cambridge University Press, 1998), pp. 29–50.

I am most grateful for helpful comments and questions which were put to me when I presented material from various sections of the book at a number of philosophy colloquia and reading groups in Britain and overseas, including those at the Ben Gurion University of the Negev at Beer-Sheva, the Instituto de Investigaçiones Filsosoficas of the Universidad Naçional Autonoma de Mexico, the Esprit Cartésien Congress at the University of Paris-Sorbonne, the University of Cape Town, the University of St Andrews, Birkbeck College and University College London, the University of Sheffield, the University of Warwick, St Anne's College Oxford and St John's College Oxford. My thanks are also due to many friends and colleagues including John Andrews, Stuart Brown, Max de Gaynesford, Hanjo Glock, Brad Hooker, John Hyman, Susan James, Andrew Mason, David Oderberg, John Preston, Michael Proudfoot, Howard Robinson and Tom Sorell, for stimulating discussions which helped me clarify my ideas. I have been saved from many errors by Brad Hooker and Rosemary Wright, who were kind enough to read earlier versions of Chapters One and Two respectively, and by Jim Stone who generously commented on the whole typescript. I am also very grateful to Judith Ayling and Hilary Gaskin of Cambridge University Press for their encouragement, and to no less than four anonymous readers for the Press who raised many searching questions and made a large number of constructive suggestions concerning various portions of the argument. Finally, I should like to thank Andrew Leggett for his invaluable help in preparing the index. My debts to a host of scholars and philosophers who have written on the topics covered in this book are manifold and heavy, and I have endeavoured to acknowledge the most important influences in the text and the notes (though this does not imply that those so credited would agree with all or any of my views). The many faults that remain are my own.

Note on references

Full details of the works cited in the notes by author and title only are to be found in the bibliography at the end of the volume. Dates in square brackets, both in the bibliography and elsewhere, indicate the date when the work in question first appeared.

To assist the reader I have often provided references to readily available translations of original Greek, Latin, French and German works. Passages quoted in the text sometimes follow the translations cited, but I have frequently modified the grammar and phrasing when it seemed appropriate to do so, and sometimes retranslated the material entirely.

In the case of works by Descartes, the following abbreviations are used:

AT   The standard Franco-Latin edition of Descartes by
           C. Adam, and P. Tannery, *Œuvres de Descartes* (12 vols.,
           revised edn, Paris: Vrin/CNRS, 1964–76)
CSM   The English translation by J. Cottingham, R.
           Stoothoff, and D. Murdoch, *The Philosophical Writings of*
           Descartes, vols. I and II (Cambridge: Cambridge
           University Press, 1985)
CSMK Vol. III, The Correspondence, by the same translators
           plus A. Kenny (Cambridge: Cambridge University
           Press, 1991)

Introduction

For non-human animals, life can be wretched or happy, but there is nothing much they can do about how it turns out. For human beings, by contrast, at least those who are fortunate enough to have the material resources to free them from the daily struggle for existence, there is the opportunity to reflect on how life should be lived. Among the educated citizens of the ancient Greek and Roman worlds, many found it natural to turn to philosophy for guidance; as for the philosophers themselves, though few were prepared to offer instant solutions, most saw it as a main part of the purpose of philosophizing to reach a view on how to achieve fulfilment in life. In the centuries that followed, philosophical systems became steadily more complex and elaborate, but their authors held fast to the old aspiration of philosophy to help humans lead happy and worthwhile lives.

Nowadays, things are very different. A good many academic philosophers, for much of our own century, have strenuously resisted the idea that philosophy can help us with how to live. And while others, particularly in more recent times, have addressed questions about happiness and well-being, for the most part they have shrunk from offering direct guidance on these matters to their fellow citizens. This generalization, like most, is subject to notable exceptions; but it remains true that the bulk of philosophical work on ethics is now addressed to those within the specialist confines of the academy. As far as the educated wider public is concerned, philosophy may, in the growing field of applied ethics, be perceived as making an increasingly important contribution on matters of public policy (problems concerned with such issues as the distribution of resources, the justification of punishment, the morality of abortion and so forth); but few probably now expect much help from philosophers in the task of trying to live fulfilled lives. If they are miserable, or find their lives in a mess, they are much more likely to turn to psychotherapy than to philosophy for guidance. It is an open question whether or not we should welcome this shift in the perception of what philosophy can do. But it is interesting to ask how the shift came about.

One way to do this is to examine older conceptions of philosophy, when it still held unashamedly and confidently to its traditional goal of helping us to live well. The centre of this book (Chapter Three) is a study of Cartesian ethics – a system which its author saw as an integral part of philosophy as a whole, an organic outgrowth from a fully worked out metaphysical and scientific understanding of the universe and man's place within it. Descartes is not generally regarded as much of a moral philosopher nowadays; but this perception is in part due to the collapse of the 'synoptic' conception of philosophy as a comprehensive system of thought encompassing all aspects of human understanding, including the ethical. The first chapter prepares the ground by saying something about this synoptic conception, and looking at some of the reasons for its eclipse in our own century. The second chapter goes back to the origins of the synoptic conception in Classical thought, and selectively examines some of the ideas of Plato, Aristotle and the Hellenistic philosophers about the role of philosophical reason in determining and moulding the conditions for the good life. The third chapter sets out Descartes' conception of ethics, his view of the relationship of morality to the rest of his philosophical system, and his conception of human nature (far richer and more complex than the idea of the incorporeal thinking self with which his name is so often associated); it is Cartesian 'anthropology' – the account of the human being as union of mind and body – that is the basis for Descartes' account of how we may use the resources of philosophy to help us achieve fulfilled lives.

The fourth and final chapter starts by exploring the characteristic modern loss of confidence in the power of 'ratiocentric' philosophical systems to cope with understanding the human predicament. The aspiration of philosophical reason to lay down a blueprint for how we should live tends to run aground when trying to deal with that side of our human nature which is largely opaque to the deliverances of reason – that affective side which has to do with the origins and operation of the emotions or passions. It is here that the contributions of psychoanalytic theory play a vital role. Though largely ignored by most specialists in moral philosophy, the concept of the unconscious turns out to have profound implications for the traditional task of ethics to seek out the conditions for human fulfilment. It will be argued that we neglect the insights of psychoanalytic theory at our peril if we aim to make progress in tackling the age-old problem of the relationship between reason and the passions – both inescapable ingredients in any plausible blueprint for human well-being.

Such results as emerge in the course of this study are obviously not meant to provide a set of firm solutions to the problems raised. The book will have achieved its modest objective if it succeeds in putting in a clearer perspective the task, which ultimately remains a philosophical one, of trying to see how human beings can best live, armed with the potent gift of reason, but unavoidably dependent on the intricate nexus of emotion, affection and passion which gives colour and meaning to their lives.

The story unfolded in these pages is at the same time both a schematic and a highly selective one. I am all too aware that some of the broad judgements about modern ethics made in the first chapter are likely to irritate specialists, and equally aware that by extracting one or two themes and arguments from the rich and complex philosophical corpus of ancient Greek philosophy I have risked certain distortions and oversimplifications. In the case of Descartes, I have perhaps run an opposite risk: by focusing in detail on his thought and largely ignoring the many other great thinkers of the early modern period, I could be charged with taking the part for the whole, and presenting a one-sided picture of the wide-ranging philosophical revolution of the seventeenth century that, in various and sometimes conflicting ways, has so profoundly influenced our contemporary outlook. Finally, in discussing the psychoanalytic outlook in the last chapter, I have been unashamedly eclectic, culling insights from a group of often divergent thinkers, where a more specialized treatment would have insisted on differences of nuance and emphasis.

Throughout the book I have indicated, in the notes, some of the qualifications that a fuller treatment would need to explore, and from time to time I have acknowledged at least some of the omissions that the demands of concision have made unavoidable; but these caveats will probably not be nearly enough to allay all the worries of specialists in the various fields. But since part of the book's aim is to bring ancient and modern ideas into a fruitful confrontation, and since it also invokes a broader conception of the enterprise of moral philosophy than is generally in favour nowadays, the strategy I have adopted, or something like it, seemed the only fruitful way to proceed. The sharp etching tool is required from time to time if philosophical argument is to be more than arbitrary assertion; but the broader brush is also needed to mark out some of the similarities and contrasts between different systems which need to be understood if philosophy is to discharge the task (which no other discipline is equipped to undertake) of placing specialized insights in their wider human context. The results offered here, such as they are, will have served their purpose if they manage to reveal something of the fascination of the age-old task of philosophy – to enable us to lead better lives through a reflective understanding of our human nature. Life might, in a certain sense, be easier for purely intellectual beings, on the one hand, or for unselfconscious life forms, on the other. But we are that strange hybrid, 'half beast, half angel',[1] and the resulting complexity, coloured by the vivid interplay of reason, emotion and bodily response, is what gives human life its special status – generating our fiercest challenges, but the source, too, of our greatest joys.

CHAPTER I

Philosophy and how to live

Toute philosophie est pratique, même celle qui paraît
d'abord la plus contemplative. ('Every philosophy is
practical, even that which at first appears to be the most
contemplative.')   Jean-Paul Sartre[1]

1. THE PROJECT

*Universae philosophiae finis est humana foelicitas ('The goal of a complete philosophy
is human happiness.')* Eustachius a Sancto Paulo[2]

This ambitious statement, from an early seventeenth-century textbook, the *Composite System of Philosophy in Four Parts*,[3] encapsulates a
view of philosophy that was widespread at the time, and had a long
ancestry. It has two aspects: the first, the notion of philosophy as a
complete system of thought encompassing all aspects of human
knowledge – metaphysical, physical and ethical – and, the second,
the idea that the ultimate raison d'être of such a system is its ability
to provide an authentic blueprint for human flourishing.

But can philosophy really show us how to live? The ancient
Greek philosophers certainly thought it could; Descartes, the 'father of modern philosophy' strongly maintained as much. But in
our own time, confused and conflicting answers have emerged,
mostly on the negative side. It is often said that we live in the
century of Freud; in the popular intellectual culture of our time,
reflected in literature and drama and the media, it is
psychoanalytical ideas, rather than philosophical theories, that
seem to play an increasingly important role in how we try to
understand ourselves and in our attempts to remove the obstacles
to fulfilled and happy living. Yet if philosophers have felt their
traditional function usurped by psychoanalytic theorists, few have

5

been prepared to acknowledge, let alone discuss, this encroach-
ment on their territory. For the most part academic philosophers
have dismissed or studiously ignored the ideas of Freud and his
successors; while some, it is true, have recognized they raise issues
of importance for philosophy of mind and philosophy of science,
hardly any have acknowledged that there might be any implications for ethics.[4] One of the motivating reasons for this book is the
belief that the resistance of professional moral philosophers to the
insights of psychoanalytic theory is a serious mistake.

The task of assessing the contribution of psychoanalytic
thought to the quest for human fulfilment, and evaluating its
philosophical implications, will be addressed in Chapter Four.
Before that, we shall be examining, in Chapters Two and Three
respectively, earlier and more traditional philosophical answers to
the age-old puzzle of how humans are to achieve fulfilled lives –
those provided first by ancient Greek and then by Cartesian
ethics. There is a linking thread that runs through the whole
project: the relationship between the rational side of our nature
and the darker and recalcitrant forces of the passions which so
often seem to threaten our psychic equilibrium. The problem of
mastering, or at least accommodating, the passions was seen both
in Greek and in early modern ethics as absolutely central to
philosophy's goal of teaching us how to live. But the solutions
offered by both these earlier systems were defective in important
respects, and it will be argued that the defects only begin to be
remedied with the development of the concept of the unconscious
– the notion that important parts of the self are not fully transparent to the deliberations of reason. Though today's philosophical
ethics has paid this idea scant attention, I shall suggest that philosophers ignore it at their peril if they wish to make a convincing
return to their traditional task of articulating the conditions for
human happiness.

The present chapter sets the scene, sketching some of the highly
ambitious ways in which earlier philosophical ethics conceived of
its task, and comparing the rather more modest aspirations of
ethical theory in contemporary academic philosophy. If this were
a purely historical study, one might, without preamble, have
proceeded in a straight chronological line. But philosophy, as has

often been observed, is never simply the 'history of ideas': the philosophical illumination we get from the ideas of the past is dependent on our placing them in the context of more recent developments; and conversely, any more than superficial understanding of our present predicament requires us to enter into a continuing dialogue with what has gone before.[5] Adapting an idea loosely derived from Freud, one might say that fruitful philosophizing operates at the locus of a dynamic interplay between *Nachträglichkeit*, the past that we struggle to recover and reinvent, and *Zukünftigkeit*, 'the futurality' towards which we strive, and which will bestow the 'meaning to come' on what we do now.[6]

2. SYNOPTIC ETHICS

Ces principes ... et la grande suite des vérités qu'on en peut déduire, leur fait connaître combien il est important de continuer en la recherche de ces vérités, et jusques à quel degré de sagesse, à quelle perfection de vie, à quelle félicité elles peuvent conduire.

('An examination of the principles of my philosophy, and the long chain of truths that can be deduced from them, will make people realize how important it is to continue the search for these truths, and to what a high degree of wisdom, and to what perfection and felicity of life these truths can bring us.') René Descartes [7]

Descartes' resounding statement of his ultimate goal as a philosopher has unmistakable affinities with the view of his scholastic predecessor Eustachius quoted at the start of the previous section: philosophy is conceived as a complete system, linking ethical and scientific understanding, and generating the recipe for a worthwhile human life. The conception was derived, in large part, from a much earlier Classical tradition. Elements of it are prominent in Plato and Aristotle, but it is perhaps in the Stoic philosophy of the Hellenistic age that it achieved its fullest expression in the ancient world. Philosophy, as conceived by the Stoics, was a universal and all-embracing system of thought – one which set out to investigate the nature of the cosmos, and man's place in it, and which, as a result of, or (to put it more aptly) as an integral part of, that investigation, aimed to uncover the key to a worthwhile and fulfilled human existence.[8] Zeno of Citium (335-263 BC), the founder of Stoicism, defined happiness as a 'good flow of life' – a life of harmonious attunement to the cosmos. Since the cosmos was a rationally intelligible order, governed by reason, philosophy could provide the wherewithal to understand the structure of that order, and to guide us towards the good life. The ultimate end was to obtain happiness through the cultivation of virtue, and the Stoic definition of virtue was none other than 'living in agreement with nature'.[9]

In many of the writers of the Middle Ages we can discern a kind of Christian analogue of the Stoic conception, where the harmony and rationality of the universe are linked to belief in the benevolent power of a supreme creator. The picture is vividly presented in the resonant lines of Dante's *Inferno*, composed at the start of the fourteenth century:

> Le cose tutte quante
> hanno l'ordine tra loro, e questo è forma
> che l'Universo a Dio fa simigliante.
> Quel veggion l'alte creature l'orma
> de l'eterno valore, il quale è fine
> al quale è fatta la toccata norma.

> All things that do exist
> have order deep within, which is the form
> that makes the Universe like unto God.
> The higher creatures see in them the stamp
> of value everlasting, the true end
> for which this rule and order was decreed.[10]

Higher creatures like man can discern the impress of eternal value (*l'orma de l'eterno valore*) stamped on all things. Value is here seen as deeply embedded in the cosmos, so that we can read off, from a study of the stars and planets, an intelligible plan which informs and gives worth to everything that happens. And so our own human values are to be grounded in a realization that everything that happens to us is a part of a rational, value-imbued universe. The broadly Stoic flavour of the underlying conception is elegantly encapsulated, much later, in a famous couplet by Alexander Pope: 'All are but parts of one stupendous whole / Whose body nature is, and God the soul.'[11]

Although, as we shall see, some of the central assumptions behind this kind of outlook began to be challenged in the scientific revolution of the early modern period, many philosophers nevertheless continued to be strongly drawn to the traditional conception of philosophy as an integrated system which could yield direct results for the attainment of human happiness. Descartes famously described philosophy as an organic unity – a tree of which metaphysics formed the roots, physics the trunk, and the specific sciences (medicine, mechanics and morals) the branches.[12] The metaphor has further implications: just as it is from the ends of the branches that one gathers the fruit, so, for Descartes, the fruits of the perfect wisdom he sought were to be expected in the practical applications of philosophy: man's power to control his environment (through mechanics),[13] to promote the health of the body and perhaps even prolong its life (through medicine),[14] and finally (through a system of ethics which was to be the crown of the whole enterprise) to secure our true happiness through the mastery of the passions and a proper understanding of the relation between mind and body.[15] 'Unshaken and balanced joy, peace and harmony of mind' – these had been laid down by the Stoics as the essence of the blessed life at which the philosopher aimed;[16] and for all his 'modernity' Descartes was in many respects attracted by the ancient conception of what ought to be achievable by a fully developed philosophy. And parallel hopes, sometimes less ambitiously expressed, sometimes elaborated with grandiose flourishes, can be found in many writers of the seventeenth and eighteenth centuries.[17] For want of a better term, I shall characterize the underlying grand conception of philosophy's role with respect to human fulfilment by using the label 'synoptic ethics'.

Though the echoes of this synoptic conception never completely died away, the evolving shape of philosophy from the seventeenth century down to our own time has made some of its aspirations seem highly problematic. Even as early as Descartes, we find signs of a growing tension between the implications of the new universe as revealed by science, and the ancient idea of the philosophical life as one of harmonious attunement to the cosmos. The chief source of the tension is the movement away from a teleological or goal-directed conception of the natural world towards a more impersonal and mechanistic physics. The physics of the classical and medieval world had been dominated by Aristotle's powerful advocacy of goal-directedness as the key to understanding nature and man's place within it. The very fabric of Aristotle's ethics, like that of his physics, is deeply imbued with a teleological conception of the world, in which each natural thing can be explained in terms of its final cause – the 'that for the sake of which'. Fact and value are inextricably intertwined here: the good for the acorn is to realize its potentialities, to grow into the healthy and flourishing oak-tree which represents the end-state towards which its nature tends. And so, *mutatis mutandis*, for human beings. In his *Physics*, Aristotle raises the question of whether nature might work 'not for the sake of something, nor because it is *better* so, but out of blind necessity'. It is impossible, he bluntly declares, that this could be the case. Teeth (the incisors for tearing, the molars for grinding) cannot be the result of coincidence, and so they must be for an end:

Action *for an end* is present in all things which come to be, and are, by nature. Further, where a series has a completion, all the previous steps are done for the sake of that. Now surely as in intelligent action, so in nature; and as in nature, so it is in each action . . . Now intelligent action is for the sake of an end; therefore the nature of things also is so . . . So each step in the series is for the sake of the next . . . It is absurd to suppose that the purpose is not present because we do not observe the agent deliberate. Art does not deliberate. If the shipbuilding art were present in the wood, it would produce the same result by nature. Hence if the purpose is present in art it is present in nature also. The best illustration is a doctor doctoring himself: nature is like that. It is plain, then, that nature is a cause, a cause that operates for a purpose.[18]

The most striking feature of the scientific revolution of the seventeenth century was its systematic rejection of teleology as the key to scientific understanding. The search for final causes, observed Francis Bacon in the early seventeenth century, 'is sterile, and like a virgin consecrated to God yields no fruit'; not long afterwards, Descartes firmly proclaimed that 'the customary search for final causes is utterly useless in physics'.[19] In place of purposive or goal-directed explanations, Descartes proposed an austere mathematical schema of explanation in which (as we shall see below, in Chapter three) all natural phenomena are to be subsumed under a set of general laws specifying the results of the blind collisions of matter in motion. It is true that the laws in question are described as being ordained by God, but Descartes insists that the divine nature is wholly beyond human grasp, and that his purposes are 'all hidden in the inscrutable abyss of his wisdom'.[20] Implied here is a conception of the universe in which the deliberative and purposive activities of mankind are separated off from the purely mechanistic operations of the physical world; so far from being part of the universe, we confront it as something whose nature is in crucial respects alien to our own.[21]

Coming down nearer to our own time, we see a further hammer blow to the traditional attempt to link a philosophical vision of the good life to a harmonious understanding of our place in the cosmos. With the Darwinian revolution of the nineteenth century, firm scientific credibility is at last given to the very idea Aristotle so adamantly rejected: that the origin of natural, seemingly 'purposive' processes is no more 'for the sake of' anything than the fall of rain on the threshing floor is 'for the sake of' spoiling the crops.[22] Random mutation and the blind forces of natural selection emerge as all that is needed to explain our origins. How can the philosopher find meaning, let alone the basis for serenity and harmonious attunement, in the face of the operations of a seemingly random and alien mechanical universe? The disturbing implications of the new outlook were tellingly articulated in the mid nineteenth century by the poet Alfred Tennyson, in his anguished attempt to cling to the old certainties:

> Oh yet we trust that somehow good
> Will be the final goal of ill,
> To pangs of nature, sins of will,
> Defects of doubt and taints of blood;
>
> That nothing walks with aimless feet;
> That not one life shall be destroy'd
> And cast as rubbish to the void,
> When God hath made the pile complete.[23]

The hopeless qualifier – 'somehow' – speaks volumes. The 'trust' in some final divine validation of every life falters in the face of the blind randomness of the new Darwinian cosmology ('nature red in tooth and claw') explored in the rest of the poem.

All this might seem to scupper the prospects for a viable 'synoptic' ethics in the bleaker cosmology of the emerging modern age. But here a distinction needs to be made. Our modern world-view seems to foreclose any attempt to articulate a blueprint for human happiness in terms of *harmonization* with the overarching natural order of the cosmos; but this need not preclude the use of philosophical reason to discover how best we should live *confronted with* a universe without inner meaning. To abandon Dante's providentially ordered universe in exchange for something more random, more mechanical, more distanced from human value and significance, need not mean abandoning the philosophical search for the conditions of human fulfilment. A world stripped of teleology need not be a world that is utterly opaque to human reason, nor does a random, mechanical universe necessarily have to be linked to an ethics of abandonment and despair. Indeed, there are examples long before the emergence of the modern age which suggest quite the reverse.

In the ancient system of Epicurus, we see a philosophical recipe for well-being that is in many respects as positive and optimistic as its contemporary Stoic counterpart, yet which stems from a vision of a world wholly void of the purposiveness and harmony that inspired the Stoics. Epicurus' universe is in many respects like the 'blind' post-Darwinian universe in which all comes about, ultimately, as the result of random particle collisions; yet for all that the philosopher can still aim at 'health of the body and calm of the soul'.[24] Freed from what might be called the 'pan-axial' fallacy – the vain attempt to locate value and worth (Greek, *axia*) within the structure of the universe as a whole – the philosopher, on the Epicurean model, is spurred on even more strongly to use the tools of reason to understand how humans should live worthwhile lives, delivered from false hope and empty superstition: 'To say that the time is not yet ripe for philosophizing, or that the time for philosophizing has gone by, is like saying the time for happiness has not arrived, or is no more.'[25] The result is what can still properly be called a 'synoptic' conception of ethics, since it still attempts to achieve an overview, to integrate its account of human well-being into its account of the nature of the universe as a whole; but such integration aims at showing how human reason can give us the courage necessary to resist false comfort by facing the real nature of the world in which we find ourselves, and by understanding both the limits of human life and what is nonetheless possible within those limits.

Another example of the way in which 'synoptic ethics' can be articulated without problematic teleological flourishes may be seen much later, in the system of Spinoza. Spinozistic ethics is clearly strongly influenced by parts of the Stoic model, but it manages to dispense with its 'pan-axial' solution.[26] Rather than searching for a holy grail (goodness is to be discovered in some general property present throughout the cosmos), it looks instead to a rational understanding of our human nature – the complex series of correspondences between our bodily states and our feelings, the relation between those feelings and our intellectual capacities and activities, and finally our position vis-à-vis our fellow human beings. It is not that the mysterious property 'value' is discovered inhabiting the universe all along (in the cosmic order, or in some providential plan); rather, an understanding of value emerges from a full and systematic understanding of the kinds of beings we are, and the kind of world we inhabit.

The ethical thinking of Descartes is rather more ambiguous in its relationship to the structures of traditional religion. The Cartesian vision of science, as already noted, rejects the old teleological model for physics; but as we shall see in Chapter Three, the picture with respect to our human nature as compound of mind and body is rather more complicated. Yet leaving these difficulties aside for the moment, it is clear from Descartes' general philosophical stance, symbolized by his metaphor of the unified tree of knowledge, that his aim is to achieve a synoptic vision of ethics as integrally linked to science; what is offered is a systematic account of the scope and limits of human nature that is pressed into the service of a fully articulated vision of the good life.

It should by now be clear that the 'synoptic approach' to ethics has many forms, some involving an explicitly teleological worldview, others avowedly mechanistic and anti-teleological; some providentialist, others wholly secularized. But the linking concept is that of ethics as an integral part of a comprehensive philosophical system including both a scientific account of the physical world and a theory of human fulfilment. Part of the aim of the next two chapters, dealing first with Greek and then with Cartesian ethics, is to explore the viability of the synoptic strategy for unfolding a coherent vision of human happiness using the full resources of philosophical reason.

3. TWENTIETH-CENTURY ETHICS AND THE PROFESSIONAL RETREAT

It can never be our job to reduce anything to anything, or to explain anything, Philosophy really is purely descriptive. Ludwig Wittgenstein[27]

Enough has perhaps been said in the previous section to indicate some of the possible attractions of the grand synoptic model of philosophical ethics, and to show how it need not necessarily be linked to the kind of teleological conception of the universe which is alien to our modern world view. Yet for all that, it is striking that the traditional conception appears to have lost much of its appeal for many modern philosophers. In order to see how this has come about, and to decide whether the synoptic conception should be consigned to the 'history of ideas' as possessing merely antiquarian interest, I want in the present section to provide a brief sketch of some of the key landmarks in the way moral philosophers in our own time have come to conceive of their role.

By the turn of the twentieth century, it started to be possible to discern a steady retreat from the traditional aspirations of 'synoptic' philosophy to provide firm guidance on how human beings could find fulfilment. Some of the important philosophical battles had in fact been fought much earlier (David Hume being a leading protagonist);[28] but there was also a series of broader influences which affected how philosophers now saw their role. In the first place, with the explosive growth of scientific knowledge, the very idea of philosophy as a fully unified system of knowledge began to seem hopelessly ambitious. As science itself became more specialized, and as each specialization became institutionalized into the fragmented structures of the modern university, the concept of an overarching *mathesis universalis*, a universal template for knowledge, began to look naive and simplistic.[29] And in the second place, philosophers themselves started to adapt their own subject to the new institutional models, and increasingly came to present themselves not as generalists but as specialists, defending their professional patch. The rise of the 'new' logic of Frege and Russell was but one manifestation of a rising conception of the subject as a special academic discipline which could boast as much rigour as any of the physical sciences; and in the application of new logical techniques to problems of meaning, truth and knowledge, there began to emerge a notion of philosophy as 'pure analysis',[30] aiming not at grand theories of the cosmos or of human welfare, but confining itself instead either to second order clarifications, or to puncturing the pretensions of earlier philosophizing. In the new academicized subject,[31] there was no room for overarching visions of the good life.[32]

Of the possible factors that may have influenced this retreat, the first one mentioned above, namely the explosive growth in science and the consequent difficulty of articulating a 'universal system' of knowledge, seems inadequate either to fully explain it or to justify it. It is, of course, true that no modern philosopher could hope to master the whole of current scientific knowledge in the way that was possible for an Epicurus, or even a Descartes. But 'philosophizing' in the sense in which its Hellenistic or even early modern practitioners conceived of it did not necessarily presuppose a complete mastery of the fine detail of each phenomenon and its explanation in every science from celestial astronomy down to human physiology. Descartes, to be sure, did take an acute interest in much of that fine detail; the Epicureans and the Stoics, we know, both had quite fully worked out systems of physics. But what they and other 'philosophizers' drew on in order to articulate their views on human well-being was something more schematic and more general: firstly, what we might call a cosmology (a broad, outline conception of the character and origin of the physical universe); secondly, a considered overview, stemming from that cosmology, about the kind of thing a human being is (for example, whether our essential nature is fundamentally continuous with, or fundamentally discontinuous with, the rest of the physical world); and thirdly, growing out of that overview, a set of systematic reflections on the capacities and dispositions of human beings, and how those capacities and dispositions can be utilized in the construction of a rationally articulated plan for the conduct of life. Characterized even in these very sketchy terms, the project appears a daunting and ambitious one; but it is not obviously open to the charge that it presupposes a level of scientific expertise beyond the scope of a single individual.

A deeper reason for the 'professional retreat' from synoptic ethics may have been linked to a certain cautiousness about the whole enterprise of moral philosophy as traditionally conceived – a cautiousness which, in one way or another was a fairly pervasive feature of the philosophical outlook during the rise of twentieth-century 'analytic modernism'.[33] In its most radical form, the cautiousness turned into a blank refusal to enter territory deemed to lie outside the bounds of sense. For the Wittgenstein of the *Tractatus*, for example, the realm of value lay outside the totality of sayable facts, and the proper behaviour for the enlightened philosopher was silence.[34] And in the later positivist phase of analytic modernism, the meaningful parts of ethical discourse were reduced to empirical observations about the psychological and sociological phenomena surrounding moral language (roughly, statements about people's preferences and practices), plus analytical comments of a 'meta-ethical' kind about grammar and meaning. From this catalogue of legitimate (empirical or analytic) propositions, ethical judgements themselves, actual value judgements, were excluded as nonsense.[35]

The theories of ethics constructed in the immediate aftermath of positivism were still strongly influenced by its ruling assumptions. Emotivist and prescriptivist accounts of ethical language, though they were increasingly prepared to allow significance to ethical pronouncements, still treated those pronouncements as essentially isolated from the propositional world of science and cognitive philosophizing. Terms like 'good' and 'ought' became, in Mary Midgley's apt phrase, 'exotic pink balloons',[36] capriciously tied on to our goals and desires, but unrelated to the empirical world in any way which would merit the accolade of rational justification for those goals and desires. And this in turn entailed that, while philosophers were no longer barred a priori from giving voice to such utterances as 'knowledge is good' or 'we ought to be honest and truthful', such utterances were perceived as embodying preferences which were ultimately arbitrary, or at any rate beyond the reach of full and systematic philosophical justification. The upshot was that there seemed to be nothing that a philosopher, *qua* philosopher, could contribute to the task of delineating the route to fulfilment.

The narrower and more cautious approach perhaps reached full tide in the philosophical climate of the nineteen-fifties and sixties. Though it would be an over-schematic distortion to suggest (as is sometimes done) that the moral philosophy of that period was entirely restricted to purely conceptual inquiries,[37] there was nevertheless a widespread tendency to insulate the subject from the wider conception of its role still held by the educated public at large, and a disinclination to risk any overarching normative pronouncements on the good life. Such protectionism still survives today in the kind of response sometimes heard from professional academic philosophers when faced by questions from 'lay' audiences such as: 'And what is *your* philosophy?' or 'And tell me, have your studies led you to your own *philosophy of life*?' The typical answer may be an embarrassed (or supercilious) smile, and a smooth explanation that *that* sense of 'philosophy' has nothing much to do with the modern academic subject. This was very much the stance taken with respect to ethics at the height of the so-called 'linguistic' phase in philosophy. For a philosopher to give forth pronouncements on the place of man in the universe, or the recipe for a worthwhile life, would have been seen, for the most part, as an improper excursion beyond the boundaries of the clear, precise and comfortably legitimized activity of linguistic mapping and conceptual clarification. The drive towards professionalism seems to have exerted a strong pressure here. The special expertise of the philosopher could carve out a professionally respected role when it came to carefully sifting the nuances of linguistic usage, but to pronounce on the meaning of life, or the route to human fulfilment, was seen as an imprudent voyage outside the harbour of safe professionalism. There was, in short, an unspoken premise restricting the claims which most philosophers felt themselves entitled to make during this period: we can help you clear up some conceptual confusions, the academic teachers of the subject seemed to be saying to their pupils, but if you hanker for actual guidance on how to live, you should (perhaps, if you are *really* that way inclined) go to the preacher, or the guru, or the psychoanalyst. Having at last achieved professional respectability by earning his harbour-master's ticket, the academic philosopher was disinclined to risk his specialized status by rash forays into the uncharted ocean.

Yet philosophy's self-conception is something that is inevitably revised with each new generation, and in the latter decades of the twentieth century the pendulum appears to have swung back to a richer and more ambitious conception of philosophical ethics: in the words of a recent commentator, philosophers began to be 'freed from an overly restrictive conception of their task' and to refocus their attention 'on the fundamental questions about how to live that have always given the subject its significance and appeal'.[38] If there is a prevailing mood nowadays, it is probably one of self-congratulation about just how exciting and wide-ranging today's moral philosophy has become. Some of the dominant assumptions of the earlier model of philosophy as 'pure analysis' may retain a strong hold in many quarters; certainly some of today's leading moral philosophers have taken an 'unashamedly' meta-ethical stance, insisting on the priority of conceptual and analytic questions for moral philosophy.[39] But for all that, there has clearly also been an enormous resurgence of interest in normative ethics, in questions about the standards of right action, how we should behave, and how society ought to be structured. We need to ask, therefore, whether this undoubted resurgence has changed the ground rules for moral philosophy, perhaps after all reopening the way for the kind of authoritative philosophizing about the good life that once characterized the synoptic ethics of the past.

4. MODERN NORMATIVE ETHICS

Certain principles of justice are justified because they would be agreed to in an initial situation of equality . . . this original position is purely hypothetical . . . It is natural to ask why, if this agreement is never actually entered into, we should take any interest in these principles ... The answer is that the conditions embodied in the description of the original position are ones that we do in fact accept. John Rawls[40]

The most obvious point of difference between normative ethics, as currently understood, and traditional systematic moral philosophy of the Hellenistic or Cartesian kind is that the modern approach implicitly rejects the notion of a unified system in which a conception of the human condition is intimately connected with a philosophical world-view – with an overall conception of reality, or (to use a term usefully explicated by Edward Craig)[41] a *Weltbild*. Even in its most sweeping mode, modern normative moral philosophy manifests a certain metaphysical austerity, tending as far as possible to avoid engagement with the grand structural questions tackled by earlier philosophers. Such austerity is clearly apparent, for example, in John Rawls's *Theory of Justice*, a work that in many ways launched the late twentieth-century revival of normative ethics, and has set much of the subsequent agenda.

Scrutiny of the Rawlsian project suggests that it is essentially a matter of axiomatizing our pre-philosophical intuitions about right conduct. The theory involves the devising of a generative apparatus, the 'original position', explicitly designed to produce acceptable decision procedures about the maxims to be adopted in society. The output of that apparatus is tested and adjusted, via the now famous search for 'reflective equilibrium': this prolonged exercise of fine tuning can involve, on the one hand, subtle changes being made in the original generative mechanism, and on the other hand a preparedness to modify or jettison pre-reflective conceptions of fairness or justice, until we arrive at an endpoint where philosophical theory and ground-floor intuitions are in some kind of balance. Rawls himself compared his enterprise with that of the linguistic theorist or grammarian[42] – a model which suggests that the groundwork for ethics is supplied by a fairly modest descriptive analysis involving a scrutiny of the relevant 'data', in this case our actual ethical concepts and considered beliefs. Another comparison he used was that of the geometer[43] – a model which allows the appeal of the resulting system to rest on a combination of factors: the economy and simplicity (or 'thinness') of the original position, its richness or generative power, and a final harmony between its results and at least some of our pre-reflective beliefs. But as early critics were quick to point out, the rationale for such a procedure seemed to rest ultimately (though in a complex and roundabout way) on a form of intuitionism: the appeal of Rawlsian justice-as-fairness rested, at the end of the day, on no stronger justification than that it chimed in with (some, all, or a substantial chunk) of the 'intuitively plausible' beliefs of Rawls himself and like-minded *'bien pensants'*.[44]

Whether this amounts to a decisive criticism of the Rawlsian project is not something that need be adjudicated here. The point being made for the present purpose is simply that the conception of moral philosophizing involved is very much less ambitious than that of traditional synoptic ethics. The Rawlsian is not proclaiming a vision of the good life, or articulating that vision against the backdrop of an overarching world view. Whether construed as moral grammarian or moral geometer, the Rawlsian ethicist is operating a much narrower and more specialized conception of moral philosophy. It is ethics without a supporting metaphysic – except of the slimmest kind that presupposes only a body of accepted 'data' (our ordinary pre-reflective beliefs).[45] Most significantly, the context of the 'original position' (the starting point for Rawlsian ethics) is characterized in a way that explicitly excludes any substantive vision of the good life. The Rawlsian contractors, deliberating about the arrangements for society, are not only prevented from knowing their particular circumstances in the actual world (whether they are rich or poor, intelligent or stupid, male or female), but are assumed 'not even to know their conceptions of the good, or their special psychological propensities'.[46] Ethical reasoning, in short, is conducted within an abstract zone where presuppositions about whatever it is that makes for human fulfilment are kept as 'thin' as possible. So far from making pronouncements on how we are to live, the moral philosopher's task is merely to set up a kind of 'committee ethics' – an ethics which specifies the most effective social arrangements for individuals to pursue their goals – whatever those goals eventually turn out to be. This in itself certainly need not undermine the value of the Rawlsian approach: it could be argued that since human beings differ in their substantive visions of the good life, it is quite appropriate to limit the role of normative ethics to the 'committee' function of trying to specify a social contract for the distribution of benefits and burdens that will be as far as possible acceptable to all. But what is clear is that this conception of the moral philosopher's task represents a substantial retrenchment from the traditionally conceived role of moral philosophy to provide substantive guidance on how human beings are to achieve harmonious and fulfilled lives.[47]

The general point is also applicable in many respects to the utilitarian approach, which, alongside the Rawlsian or contractarian model (derived mainly from Kant), represents the other principal framework within which most modern normative ethics is conducted. Questions of ultimate ends, observed the movement's most distinguished promoter, are not amenable to proof.[48] And that granted, it is a short step towards limiting the role of the utilitarian ethicist to an essentially instrumental one: that of determining the types of action or the kinds of institution which, as a matter of empirical fact, can be expected to conduce to the posited end. Again, this is morals largely divorced from a metaphysics, and again it reflects a clear retreat from the traditional project of synoptic ethics. The moral philosopher becomes a kind of specialist in decision theory, justifying his activity by the fact that he has devoted more than usual reflection to the instrumental question, but not pretending to be able to contribute anything, *qua* philosophizer, to the articulation of a contentful vision of the good life. It is striking, in this connection, that the successor theories to those of Mill and Bentham which are most in vogue nowadays are various kinds of 'preference utilitarianism', which may roughly be characterized as utilitarianism with its original hedonistic colouring bleached out.[49] The resulting conception is of an almost contentless, or at any rate markedly 'thin', ethics which defines right action in wholly instrumental terms, namely as that which maximizes whatever happens to be selected as a goal.

It would be misleading to suggest that all contemporary consequentialists are content with this purely instrumentalist stance. Following the lead of J. S. Mill, who insisted on a rich conception of utility grounded in what can give fulfilment to 'human beings with highly developed faculties',[50] many of his liberal successors have reflected long and hard about the kinds of opportunities for individual self-development which human beings require if they are to lead a life that goes beyond the 'puerile and insignificant' satisfaction of immediate desire.[51] But even among those who are prepared to nail their colours to the masthead of substantive values, the conception of the moral philosopher's role still emerges as a relatively narrowed one, in comparison to the systems of the past.

To be sure, some modern writers in the liberal tradition give pride of place to the value of autonomous rational choice, and to this extent at least seem to espouse an ethics grounded in a pure, non-instrumental value. Yet appearances may be deceptive. On one possible analysis, autonomy emerges not as an end in itself but as a second order value, or meta-value; that is, it lays down an essential precondition for human pursuit of the good, while leaving the content of the good itself entirely undetermined.[52] Against this, others have argued that the exercise of autonomous rationality is, for human beings, an integral part of the content of a worthwhile life, and, further, that the pursuit of 'neutrality' is incoherent (since a theory which allows maximum scope for autonomous choice is already committed to the special importance of certain kinds of value – those linked to the development of individuality). There are many complex issues arising from this contrast (connected with the distinction between 'neutral' and 'perfectionist' liberalism)[53] which I cannot pursue here. What is striking, nonetheless, about the actual philosophical output of modern liberalism (whether of a contractarian or a consequentialist stamp) is that it seems most at home, and least embarrassed, when it can operate safely within the domain of instrumental political theory. That is, it characteristically starts from an acknowledgement that individuals differ in respect of their conception of the good life in ways which it is probably beyond the professional competence of the philosopher, *qua* philosopher, to adjudicate.[54] Of course this concessive premise need not be merely a knee-jerk reaction stemming from what I have called professional caution: it may depend on well-articulated doubts about the objectivity and ontological status of substantive values; or it may derive from a pluralistic conception of value, coupled with worries about incommensurability.[55] But either way, the resulting philosophical activity is much closer to what I have called 'committee ethics' than it is to the traditional project of helping individuals to see how best to live. The grand issue of the recipe for the good life is typically left on one side, and attention becomes mainly focused on the next stage – the task of articulating the structure of an optimal political system in which maximum scope is given for the pursuit (within certain limits) of whatever values are in fact chosen by the citizens. In a certain sense, this still involves a narrowed conception of the role of philosophizing: it is, as it were, conceded from the outset that the blueprint for a worthwhile life is a matter for each of us to decide independently, without the resources of professional philosophy. There may of course, be perfectly sound philosophical reasons for such a retrenchment; that remains to be determined. But it is striking how far it takes us from the grand synoptic ethical systems of the past in which almost the whole focus is on the values themselves, and how they fit into a rationally determined blueprint for the good life.

5. THE REVIVAL OF VIRTUE ETHICS AND THE LIMITS OF REASON

Philosophical doctrines which profess neutrality, whether they are professedly analytic (against preaching) or scientific (against value) cannot help, by what they obliterate or what they emphasise, making moral judgements. Iris Murdoch[56]

Whatever the reasons for the 'professional retreat' that has marked much twentieth-century moral philosophy, Iris Murdoch's trenchant observation suggests that it is in a certain sense pointless: if they cannot avoid evaluative commitments, why should not philosophers become the kind of moral thinkers who, in Murdoch's words, are 'frankly and realistically high-minded . . . able to scan a wide vista of human life'? Why should they not set about overtly proclaiming the values they espouse? Given the scope and complexity of much post-war normative ethics (as indicated, if only schematically, in the previous section), it is clear that moral philosophy has long since begun to emerge from the self-constructed ghetto in which it was often confined earlier in the century;[57] but it remains true, as we have seen, that many normative ethicists have shrunk from an 'overt proclamation of values', at least as far as these relate to the ancient project of articulating a philosophical blueprint for the good life.

In the closing years of the twentieth century, however, we have seen a spectacular revival of philosophical interest in the question 'how should one live?' The resurgence of so-called 'virtue ethics' as an alternative to Kantian or contractarian approaches on the one hand, and consequentialism on the other, represents a powerful attempt by recent philosophers to leave behind a restrictive conception of their role, and to engage with the traditional philosophical project of articulating a vision of how human beings are to achieve fulfilled lives. Virtue ethics is a rapidly growing area of inquiry in contemporary philosophy, and it takes many forms, but its guiding light is the Aristotelian notion of *arete* or excellence. Human beings, part of the biological world, but endowed with the special characteristic of rationality, have the capacity to use their reason so as to maximize their potentialities for fulfilment. Guided by excellences of intellect, we can set about training ourselves so as to develop excellences of character – courage, generosity, magnanimity, and so on – the permanent dispositions of action and feeling that will constitute true virtue, the 'activity of the soul in accordance with reason'.[58] Strengthened by the instilling of the right habits, and guided by a rational vision of the good life, we shall be able to actualize the potentialities we are born with, and achieve an optimally successful and enriching life – the life of *eudaimonia* or happiness.[59]

The drive among contemporary ethicists to undertake a systematic re-exploration of the Aristotelian model certainly seems to mark a significant increase in the territorial claims of the moral philosopher. This need not, of course, imply a return to all the aspirations that have characterized the 'synoptic ethics' of the past. We saw earlier that some traditional versions of synopticism were deeply committed to a teleological vision of the universe; but not surprisingly this aspect, harshly out of tune as it is with our modern scientific world-picture, is carefully bypassed by contemporary virtue theorists. Thomas Hurka, for example, (one of the most interesting of Aristotle's contemporary successors) explicitly disowns the grand teleological framework of traditional virtue theory, offering instead a 'stripped down' version, which claims to be free of metaphysical and other 'accretions'. Divested of this supporting structure, the resulting theory is not supposed to enjoy any grand justification by reference to its place in a general system of thought, but rests instead on a far more modest framework of a kind closely similar to that developed by Rawls: the best that can be shown is that the theory 'matches our intuitions and gives them a satisfying rationale'.[60]

This may not, in fact, be as cautious as it sounds, since such revived versions of Aristotelian ethics still share Aristotle's central assumption: that the good for humankind can be identified by reference to *human nature*. In this sense the project does emerge as having close affinities with what we have called the 'synoptic strategy': it attempts to link ethics with systematic kinds of empirical, conceptual and structural inquiry into the human condition. In Martha Nussbaum's words, 'Aristotle's arguments ask us to recognise the depth and pervasiveness of certain human beliefs and practices, claiming that they are constitutive of humanness as we conceive it.'[61] But here a problem emerges for the neo-Aristotelian. An analysis of what it is to be human, how human beings can actualize their special potentialities, seems indispensable for any plausible blueprint for *eudaimonia*. But this 'human nature' is not some timeless given: to articulate what our human nature 'essentially' consists in is to invoke a whole backdrop of social and political (and other) assumptions; and where these assumptions have ceased to be tenable, the resulting ethic may have to be rebuilt. As Bernard Williams, one of the most searching critics of the neo-Aristotelian movement, has put it: 'the modern world has left behind elements necessary to making [Aristotle's] style of ethical theory as a whole plausible, however many useful thoughts we can, quite certainly, gain from it'.[62] Some defenders of the Aristotelian revival have frankly acknowledged that 'human nature' is a concept which cannot be free of evaluative presuppositions, and which may even need to be the subject of a continuing philosophical dialogue. Thus Nussbaum suggests that '[w]hat is proposed is a scrutiny that seeks out, among our evaluative judgments, the ones that are the deepest and the most indispensable, the ones that lie at the heart of the way in which human beings over time have defined themselves to themselves . . . '[63] The problem here, however, is that the more open-ended and subject to continuing dialogue the notion of 'human nature' turns out to be, the more indeterminate the resulting blueprint for *eudaimonia* risks becoming.

Despite these difficulties, one might still hope for some form of radically reconstructed virtue ethics – one which might have a distinctively different shape from Aristotle's, while still adhering to his broad aim of constructing a rational pattern for a worthwhile human life. Such a pattern might be far more responsive than Aristotle would have allowed to the historical and social contingencies which make our grasp of 'the human condition' such an elusive affair; but it might still seem that reason can attempt to do the job – not by uncovering universal truths about our supposed 'essential nature', but by working with the only available materials – the materials drawn from our continuously developing understanding of ourselves and the world we inhabit. Can we not (in the words of John Kekes, in a recent study written from within a broadly Aristotelian and eudaimonistic tradition) still aim at *moral wisdom* – at 'increasing our control by developing a reasonable conception of a good life, and bringing our actions in conformity with it'?[64]

The sobering answer is that the achievement of such an aim is fraught with difficulties.[65] In the first place, the contingency and precariousness of human existence, all the problems associated with what has so aptly been called 'the fragility of goodness',[66] mean that our most heroic efforts to adhere to a rational plan for good living may be insufficient to guarantee success. The tragic dimension here is one that it is hard to appreciate fully from the perspective of abstract philosophical debate, but which (as some philosophers have begun to see) is perhaps best grasped by reflection on the fine details unfolded in the work of the great dramatic poets – details which bring vividly home to us the complexity of the human condition, and the powerful internal and external obstacles to the achievement of human happiness.[67]

Yet true and important though this may be, it does not in itself seem fatally to undercut the traditional philosophical task of articulating the conditions for human fulfilment. For whoever supposed that discovering the good life was supposed to be easy?

Zhizn' prozhit', nye polye pyeryeiti, says the Russian proverb: there is more to getting through life than crossing a field. That the task facing us is such a formidable one, and so uncertain of success, may give us pause, but is no decisive ground for giving up in despair, nor for concluding that there is anything inherently suspect in the philosophical goal of striving for a life guided by a rationally informed vision of the good.

Here however we come up against a more formidable roadblock, one which is all the more daunting because so many philosophers in the analytic tradition have been unwilling to confront it explicitly. The obstacle is nothing less than a radical loss of confidence in the power of human reason itself. Paradoxically, in a century which has seen so many spectacular developments in the growth of our scientific understanding of the universe, we have progressively lost our faith in the ability of human reason to look within and discern the structure of our own human psyche, of the inner workings of the mind. Self-knowledge, for Socrates, was the spring of all sound philosophy. Yet for human beings in the twentieth century, the project of self-knowledge has become profoundly problematic. Achieving awareness of our inmost selves turns out to be a vastly more complex task than was acknowledged in the mainstream philosophical ethics of the past.

The old models of transparent rationality have been systematically eroded by the steady advance of psychoanalytic modes of understanding, to the point where the very idea of a rationally planned structure for the good life begins to look like a piece of naive self-deception. Since Freud and Jung, we have, in the words of a recent commentator, 'lost confidence in the ability of those rational accounts we give of our motivations and actions, our projects and understandings, to reveal what is really going on'.[68] For those who have begun to come to terms with the implications of this loss of confidence, it must be something of a mystery that so many moral philosophers continue to write as if the mind were a transparent goldfish bowl, populated by clearly identifiable items called our 'beliefs and desires', in such a way that we only have to focus carefully on the relevant items, presented unproblematically to consciousness, in order to set about drawing up a rational plan for action.[69]

The last illusion which Freud so vigorously exposed – the belief that the rational ego is master in its own house[70] – is one which twentieth-century analytic philosophy has been signally reluctant to abandon. And the damaging effects of that reluctance still lurk beneath the seemingly transparent surface of modern philosophical ethics. Of course philosophers have long understood that humans are not angelic creatures whose actions are determined by the deliverances of pure, unsullied rationality. One of the most ancient tasks in ethics, from Plato onwards, has been to try to come to terms with the phenomenon of *akrasia* – the fact that, owing to the influence of the passions, our rational perceptions of the best course to follow are not always translated into action. But the solutions offered in the past all involve a measure of denial – either an insistence that the passions which obstruct reason can be brought wholly within its control, or else the optimistic idea that the solution to the problem lies simply in the enlarging and educating of our understanding. Yet if it is the case that the very structure of the beliefs and desires on which we act can be subject to serious distortion of a kind which is often not accessible to us as we plan and deliberate, if our very grasp of what we truly want can be subject to a pervasive and potentially crippling opacity, then we need to rethink the optimistic vision of a rationally planned and organized life – the vision that informs so much of traditional synoptic ethics, and continues to underpin the work of its modern would-be revivers.

The ramifications of the Freudian challenge to rational self-knowledge, its implications for our view of ourselves and for the traditional strategies of moral philosophy, will be the subject of our final chapter. Our first task, however, will be to examine the flowering of the grand traditional project of synoptic ethics, first in the Classical and then in the Cartesian era, and to explore its vision of the power of philosophical reason to construct an overarching framework from which a theory of the good life emerges as the great prize of philosophical inquiry. Only by understanding the appeal of that grand project can we come to appreciate why it ultimately failed, and only in the light of such an appreciation can we grasp the shape of our modern predicament, and begin the search for new modes of self-awareness.

CHAPTER 2

Ratiocentric ethics

Plac'd on this isthmus of a middle state
A being darkly wise, and rudely great . . .
He hangs between; in doubt to act or rest,
In doubt to deem himself a God or Beast . . .
Chaos of Thought and Passion, all confused;
Still by himself abus'd or disabus'd;
Created half to rise and half to fall;
Great lord of all things, yet a prey to all,
Sole judge of Truth, in endless Error hurled:
The glory, jest and riddle of the world!

Alexander Pope[1]

I. THE FRUITS OF PHILOSOPHY

[Philosophia] animam format et fabricat, vitam disponit, actiones regit, agenda et omittenda demonstrat, sedet ad gubernaculum et per ancipitia fluctuantium derigit cursum.

('Philosophy shapes and constructs the soul, arranges life, governs conduct, shows what is to be done and what omitted, sits at the helm and directs our course as we waver amidst uncertainties.') Seneca[2]

It is central to the ancient Greek conception of philosophy that it provides human beings with the way to lead a better life. A significant part of the philosophy of both Plato and Aristotle is concerned with laying out the framework for human fulfilment. For Plato (in some of his writings) the good life turns out actually to consist in philosophical theorizing,[3] while Aristotle vacillates between this conception and a more down-to-earth vision of ordinary 'practical wisdom', in which, nonetheless, the achievement of the good life depends, at its deepest level, on the systematic

exercise of reason.[4] Both the two great founding fathers of the
subject conceive of philosophy as contributing to human happiness; and both of them see rationality and the good life as inextricably intertwined.

In the later ethics of the Hellenistic period, even more striking
connections emerge between the fruits of philosophizing and the
aim of living a worthwhile life. The Stoics dreamed of philosophy
as a fair and fertile field: τὸν μὲν περιβεβλημένον τὸ λογικόν, τὴν
δὲ γῆν τὸ φυσικόν, τὸν δὲ καρπὸν τὸ ἠθικόν – logic the fence,
physics the soil, and ethics the fruit.[5] Philosophy, in Stoic thought,
was a unified system, and within that system a place could be
found for human beings to understand how they should best live.
The Stoic cosmos is essentially animate – an organic whole permeated with rationality. It is not, in our sense, a 'spiritual' universe, if by that is meant a universe which should be understood by
reference to some transcendent creative Mind. On the contrary,
the Stoics were firmly physicalist in their outlook: matter, 'unqualified substance' is common to all things – a single, indestructible,
indefinitely modifiable substrate. But it is imbued throughout by
an active principle, called variously 'reason' (*logos*), 'god' or 'cause'.
The passive principle of matter and the active causal principle
together provide the metaphysical basis for an explanation of
everything that exists or occurs in the world.[6] Within the Stoic
system, the term 'soul' is often used to refer to the animating
functions of the active principle of the world, and an analogy is
drawn between the individual human soul and the universe as a
whole: 'that the world is ensouled is evident from our own soul's
being an offshoot of it'.[7] The comparison between macrocosm and
microcosm is taken very seriously: the rationality or intelligence of
the world soul is taken to ground the moral prescription for human
life – being parts of the whole, we should live in harmony with
universal nature by perfecting our rationality.[8] A belief in rational
providence as the governing principle of the universe provides a
clear link between philosophical understanding and living a happy
and fulfilled life, and this idea is particularly prominent in the
writings of the later Stoics. 'In the thought that I am part of the
whole', declared Marcus Aurelius, 'I shall be content with all that
comes to pass.'[9]

This is perhaps the strongest form of what we have earlier called 'synoptic ethics' – the idea of linking a vision of the good life with an overarching world-view.[10] For the Stoic sage, it is the nature of ultimate reality, and the fact that his life is lived in conformity with it, that is the key to the good life. This is how Diogenes Laertius sets out the Stoic vision, drawing together threads from Zeno (the founder of Stoicism) and his successors Cleanthes and Chrysippus:

The end is to live in harmony with nature, which amounts to living in accordance with virtue; for nature leads us towards virtue. Now living in accordance with virtue is the same as living in accord with our experience of what happens by nature; for our natures are parts of the nature of the whole. So the end comes down to this: to live in agreement with nature, that is, in accord with our own nature and that of the whole, engaging in no activity forbidden by the universal law. This law is right reason that pervades everything, and is identical to God who directs and disposes everything that exists. So virtue, and the smooth flow of life, which we see in those who are happy, arises when everything is done according to the harmony of each person's individual spirit with the rational will of the disposer of all things.[11]

In a different way, while denying providentialism and accepting a 'cosmology without teleology' (in Long and Sedley's apt phrase)[12] the Epicureans also grounded their ethics in a philosophical account of the nature of the universe. The universe described by Epicurus is remorselessly mechanistic, all phenomena being the result of continuous collisions of atoms in the void. The great Epicurean apologist Lucretius compares the endless interactions of atoms to the ceaseless interplay of sunbeams:

> Many the tiny bodies you will see
> in rays of light, weaving through empty space,
> and battling as in everlasting fight,
> advancing and retreating without end;
> thus, you may guess, are the primordial specks
> tossed round forever in the mighty void.[13]

It is this world of ceaseless mechanical interactions that gives rise to all existing things, including human beings. So far from being a microcosm of the whole, mankind is the result of a kind of accident, the product of a blind and directionless evolutionary process.[14] But this very fact provides the basis for an acceptance of our place in the scheme of things. Freed from the illusion that the universe is here for our benefit, or is moving towards some predetermined good, we can calmly contemplate the inevitability of death (and the ultimate end of the world itself) with dignity and self-assurance. True piety consists in freedom from superstitious awe and false hope, a state of tranquil acceptance in which the enlightened philosopher will, in Lucretius' phrase, *pacata posse omnia mente tueri*, be able to view all things with a mind at peace.[15] The end-product of philosophy for the Epicureans thus turns out to be remarkably similar to that envisaged by the Stoics – a rational understanding of the nature of the universe, and a resulting state of tranquillity in the conduct of our lives.[16] The famous Epicurean goal of calmness and freedom from inner disturbance (*ataraxia*) stems from a true understanding of the way things are, just as does that tranquillity and 'concord of mind' (*animi concordia*) which is the highest good in Stoic philosophy.[17]

In broad outline, then, the picture which emerges from the classical world is one where there are strong connections – much stronger than our contemporary culture tends to make – between the use of philosophical reason and the achievement of a good life. The 'rationalistic' colour of Greek ethics is perhaps all the more striking when set against the backdrop of a culture, revealed in the tradition of poetry and drama from the Homeric epics down to the great classical tragedians, which had powerfully exposed the extent to which human life is subject to the irrational forces of the passions.[18] Reflecting on the importance of this darker side in Greek culture, the nineteenth-century philosopher Friedrich Nietzsche famously analysed the creative power of Greek art as arising out of a tension between two elements corresponding to the separate domains of the two ancient Greek art deities, Apollo and Dionysus. Apollonian art maintains a 'measured restraint', a 'freedom from the wilder emotions': the more frightening, more impersonal forces of the unconscious mind are kept in check.[19] Only in Dionysian art – typified in the frenzied singing and dancing of orgiastic festivals – do these wilder forces break through. Nietzsche describes the Dionysian state as one of ecstasy, in which the self is submerged, and the Apollonian 'principle of individuation' gives

way to a sense of 'primordial unity' between man and man, and
man and nature:

The curious blending and duality in the emotions of the Dionysian
revellers reminds us – as medicines remind us of deadly poisons – of the
phenomenon that pain begets joy, that ecstasy may wring sounds of
agony from us . . . The Dionysian music in particular excited awe and
terror . . . The music of Apollo was Doric architectonics in tones, but in
tones that were merely suggestive, such as those of the cithara . . . In the
Dionysian dithyramb man is incited to the greatest exaltation of all his
symbolic faculties; something never before experienced struggles for
utterance – the annihilation of the veil of *maya*, oneness as the soul of the
race and of nature itself . . . To grasp this collective release of all the
symbolic powers, man must have already attained that height of self-
abnegation which seeks to express itself symbolically through all these
powers – and so the dithyrambic votary of Dionysus is understood only
by his peers. With what astonishment must the Apollonian Greek have
beheld him! With an astonishment that was all the greater the more it was
mingled with the shuddering suspicion that all this was actually not so
very alien to him after all, in fact, that it was only his Apollonian
consciousness which, like a veil, hid this Dionysian world from his
vision.[20]

The details of Nietzsche's highly speculative view of the development of Greek music need not concern us here. His contrast
between the Apollonian and the Dionysian is nevertheless valuable because it gives us a vivid sense of the precariousness of the
rationalistic vision of the Greek philosophers, in which human life
is harmoniously ordered by the calm prescriptions of reason. The
defining myths of Greek culture, so brilliantly explored by Aeschylus in the *Oresteia*, by Sophocles in the *Oedipus* trilogy, by
Euripides in the *Medea* and the *Bacchae*, presented a world of terror
and anguish, a world in which ordered rational planning was
always in danger of being overwhelmed by the forces of unreason,
either externalized in the inexorable power of fate and the implac-
able anger and fury of the Gods, or internalized in the blind
passions, driving the tragic protagonists to irrevocable horrors of
arrogance, cruelty and lust. To those reared on such a cultural
diet, the confidence of Platonic, Aristotelian and Hellenistic ethics
in the powers of human rationality may well have appeared quite
extraordinary.

The current revival of interest in ancient Greek ethics, and its recipes for virtue,[21] may be construed as indicating the undimmed appeal of the old aim of providing a blueprint for the good life informed by philosophical reason. But we need to resist the temptation to sanitize the past so that its theories become part of a comfortable agenda suitable for handling within the cautious, compartmentalized categories of contemporary academic scholarship. Much of today's academic moral philosophy has become a fairly self-contained enterprise, brilliant, to be sure, in the subtle dissection of arguments, but one whose direct recommendations on how we should live (if offered at all) often tend to be cautiously hypothetical or provisional in character.[22] It is important, even if it is sometimes disturbing, to confront the authoritative tone which we find in the grand ethical systems of the Classical world. 'Since the ultimate end is to live in conformity and harmony with nature, it necessarily follows that those possessed of philosophical wisdom live their lives in a state of happiness, perfection and good fortune, without any restriction, hindrance or need.'[23] This type of majestic pronouncement could not be made by a philosopher who considered his role to be merely the analysis of meanings, or the systematizing of pre-reflective intuitions. Its tone makes sense only given the conviction that philosophical wisdom can reveal something about the universe and the nature of humankind that makes the relevant ethical model compelling. And the optimism of its philosophical programme can only be seen in its full colouring when set against the darkness and disorder of the non-rational part of our nature, of which the cultural heritage of its proponents must have made them all too well aware.

In our 'postmodern' culture, which has come to be so sceptical of many of the aspirations of philosophy to construct a rationally informed overview of the human predicament,[24] the optimistic aims of ancient Greek philosophical ethics may well strike many as bizarre. Yet part of the point of a philosophical study of the history of thought is that it should generate what Nietzsche called an 'untimely perspective' on the past, making the familiar seem strange and vice versa.[25] To confront the grand classical systems is to realize how far they diverge from most modern philosophy in their assumption of the magisterial authority to lay out the conditions for the good life. From our contemporary perspective, such ambitions may now seem overweening, and the implied conception of the scope of philosophical reason appear to verge on the grandiose. But unless we keep clearly in view just how ambitious were the claims made in these ancient ethical systems, we will miss that enriching sense of strangeness that has the power to reinvigorate our grasp of how our modern world-view diverges from what has gone before. In order to appreciate our present situation, we need to understand how and why the traditional authority of philosophy to pronounce on the good life has been lost. Part of the answer (as I shall be suggesting in Chapter Three) lies in the Cartesian divorce (to some extent prefigured in the ideas of the Epicureans) which isolated the nature of man from that of the rest of creation, and thus put increasing pressure on the idea of a systematic synoptic vision linking together scientific and ethical understanding. Another part of the answer (which will be the theme of Chapter Four) lies in a progressive loss of confidence in the powers of reason itself, both to understand our nature and to direct the course of our lives. The effects of both processes have been long and gradual, and we should beware of overdoing the relevant contrasts, or seeing them in terms of an abrupt discontinuity between ancient and modern thought; we could not enter into a constructive dialogue with the systems of the past unless there were some points of contact. But keeping the differences clearly in view helps to preserve the sense of distance which is needed if a study of the past is to play a philosophical role in giving us a sharpened perspective on our own predicament. To advance that process, let us now take a closer look at how the ancient Greek ethical theorists developed their vision of the controlling power of reason to determine the structure of the good life.

2. THE ETHICS OF REASON IN PLATO AND ARISTOTLE

In homine quid est optimum? ratio: hac antecedit animalia, deos sequitur. ratio ergo perfecta proprium bonum est . . . haec recta et consummata felicitatem hominis implevit . . . haec ratio perfecta virtus vocatur eademque honestum est.

('What is best in man? Reason: with this he precedes the animals and follows the gods. Therefore perfect reason is man's peculiar good . . . Reason, when right and perfect,

makes the full sum of human happiness . . . This perfect reason is called virtue, and it is identical to rectitude.') Seneca[26]

Seneca's resounding advocacy of the credentials of reason is compatible with several possible accounts of its precise function in the good life. We have drawn attention, in the previous section, to some general features which suggest a 'ratiocentric' orientation in the ethical systems of the ancient Greeks. But 'ratiocentrism', like many of the schematic (though nonetheless often useful) labels employed in the historiography of philosophy, should not be understood as denoting a simple, monolithic idea; it is rather a 'cluster concept', indicating a number of distinct though often crisscrossing and overlapping strands.[27] Our broad classification now needs to be broken down into at least three possible conceptions of reason's supposed role. The first might be called *rational exclusivism*: the idea that the good for man consists precisely in an exclusive, or near exclusive, concentration on rational activity in its narrowest intellectual sense. The best life, on this view, would be a life of specifically 'philosophical' activity in the restricted scope of that term: critical analysis of the logical structure of arguments; the construction and evaluation of abstract theories about meaning, truth, and value; to put it rather more grandly and generally, the pursuit of intellectual enlightenment. A second and much broader conception is what could be termed *rational hegemonism*: a view of the good life as one in which no supreme predominance is assigned to intellectual activity as such, but where the development of a full range of human capacities and dispositions, emotional as well as ratiocinative, enters into the blueprint for fulfilment – subject nonetheless to their being appropriately channelled and guided by reason. Yet a third possibility is what can be labelled *rational instrumentalism* – the kind of view perhaps most closely associated with the ethics of David Hume in the eighteenth century, according to which rationality plays no leading role in the determination of the goals for the good life (since these are set by sentiment, not reason),[28] but where reason is nevertheless needed as a kind of instrumental organizer and deliberator, to establish the most appropriate means for reaching our desired destination.

Looking first at the ethical thought of Plato, it needs at once to be said that this has several diverse aspects, many of them subject to competing interpretations by commentators, so that any summary pronouncement on 'Platonic ethics', as if it were a single, simple system, risks imposing a straitjacket. For the present purpose, I shall do no more than claim to isolate one strand from the complex web – a strand which perhaps emerges most strongly in many parts of the *Republic*. Here Plato argues that 'it is fitting for the reasoning part of the soul (*to logistikon*) to rule, since it is wise and takes thought for the whole soul'.[29] It is certainly clear that this conception is very far removed from the Humean approach to reason's role that we have called 'rational instrumentalism': for reason to pimp for the passions would, in Plato's eyes, be the ultimate abdication of responsibility, as if the guardians were to abandon their high philosophical calling to serve the fickle and irrational whims of the people.[30] To classify Plato as a 'rational hegemonist', on the other hand, is not out of the question: such an interpretation is suggested by some of the things Plato says about the well-being of individuals and states,[31] and it to some extent fits Plato's model of justice as an internal 'harmony', with the philosopher-rulers overseeing things for the good of all, and the other parts acquiescing in that rule.[32] But it is the first, narrowly intellectualist, picture, that of 'rational exclusivism', that seems closest to Plato's heart.

The philosopher-guardians of the *Republic* are promised 'the greatest possible happiness';[33] their life achieves the utmost fulfil-ment of which man is capable, and that fulfilment derives from the fact that they are in touch with the ultimate truth about the nature of reality. Emerging from the darkness of the cave, they move upwards to contemplate, ultimately, 'the Form of the Good, the cause of all that is right and fair, the source of light in the visible world, and the sovereign cause of truth and reason in the intelli-gible world'; it is the philosophical understanding of the nature of things that makes it appropriate to call the lives of those who achieve it 'happy' or 'blessed'.[34] The life of philosophical wisdom, of detachment from the senses, a life of abstract reasoning and intellectual contemplation – this is the highest good for man (or at any rate for those men who are genetically capable of such a life);[35] other types of life are systematically denigrated as 'lower', both in

terms of intrinsic worth and in terms of the fulfilment they accord
to the subject.[36] To the Platonic way of thinking, the passions are
always potentially dangerous, always threatening the health and
stability of the individual (and the state). The good life is the life of
reason – a life whose ultimate worth depends on the systematic
pursuit of rational inquiry:

> When the guardians have come safely through, and excelled everywhere
> and in everything, both in action and in knowledge, they must now be
> brought to their final goal. They must be made to raise up the bright
> glance of their soul to contemplation of that which gives light to all; and
> when their vision is fixed on the good itself, they will use it as a model,
> bringing adornment not just to the city but to the private individuals –
> their very selves, for the rest of their lives . . . [37]

The life so described is (Plato goes on to say) the life of philosophy
itself – a life consisting of the individual pursuit of wisdom and the
contemplation of the good. And while the good order of the state
requires that the guardians go back down to the 'cave' from time to
time to take their turn at the chores of civic administration, it is
made abundantly clear that this is an unwelcome necessity; the
arena of public life is, as the simile of the cave itself indicates, a
shadowy and inferior world, inherently unsuited to the fullest
flowering of the soul.[38]

It is hard, though, not to have serious qualms about such
advocacy of the exclusive concentration on reason as the key to the
good life for human beings. Plato's ethical intellectualism is
achieved at a considerable cost – that of systematically denigrating
a whole range of emotional and sensory satisfactions which give
colour and richness to our lives.[39] Many centuries later, John
Stuart Mill attempted to show that the pleasures of the intellect are
intrinsically more worthwhile than those of the senses, but was
notoriously reduced to a circular argument: intellectual activity
brings satisfactions which are 'nobler' and 'higher', as shown by
the fact that those competent to judge would always 'knowingly
and calmly' prefer them to anything else on offer; but the 'competent judges' are then picked out precisely by the fact that they
accord preference to the relevant intellectual activities.[40] In Plato,
there is a whole metaphysics to back up the advocacy of narrow

intellectualism: since ultimate reality, the source of all truth and goodness, consists in what can be apprehended only by the intellect, the senses, the appetites, indeed anything whatever connected with the body, are obstacles to those higher activities of the soul which will bring it into contact with this ultimate reality. At its most stark, the dualistic separation between higher intellect and base carnality is so extreme that it leads Plato to argue (in the *Phaedo*) that only death, a complete separation from the body, will open the way to supreme fulfilment.[41] Here, surely, we have the ultimate paradox. We begin with a sharply alienating thesis – that the best kind of life for humans is one in which they are separated, root and branch, from ordinary society, from the day to day joys and sorrows which make up the very fabric of our human existence;[42] and we move to an even more outlandish conclusion in which the ultimate goal for humankind is supposed to lie beyond death, in a state where we cease to be human altogether.

The influence of Plato's alienating intellectualism is strong in Aristotle, who ends the *Nicomachean Ethics* by proclaiming that intellectual contemplation (*theoria*) is the 'highest form of activity', the objects which it apprehends being the 'highest things that can be known'. Echoing Plato's point that philosophizing adorns the lives of the 'private individuals' (*idiotai*) who practise it, Aristotle observes that the philosopher is the 'most self-sufficient of men' since he 'can practise contemplation by himself, and the wiser he is, the more he can do it'.[43] But there are severe reservations underlying this apparent support for Plato. Throughout most of his ethics, Aristotle is at pains to stress not self-sufficiency but, by contrast, the cultivation of those virtues which presuppose that I am closely interacting with, and dependent on, my fellow men; man, indeed, is defined as a social being,[44] and most of the fulfilment of which he is capable requires the cultivation of harmonious patterns of thought and feeling which enable him to enter into rewarding civic and personal relationships. This is part of the reason why, in his account of happiness or fulfilment (*eudaimonia*), Aristotle links it to our specifically human function defined as 'some sort of *practical* life of the part of the soul that has reason'.[45] Reason is crucially involved here but very much *not* in the Platonic sense of a purely theoretical or contemplative activity.

The focus for these tensions between the theoretical ideal and the requirements of a more practical ethics, adapted to the actual human condition, is a principle which Plato himself had canvassed, namely that the good for man lies in the performance of his proper 'job' or 'function' (*ergon*). The function of each thing, as Plato had defined it, was 'what it alone could do, or do best', and there are strong analytic connections between the identification of this function and the determination of the good for each class of things (the good of a knife resides in its ability to cut).[46] Now since the rational exercise of the soul is the function of man (that which is peculiar to the species), it will follow that the good for man lies in the activity of reason.[47] But even if we are impressed with the notion that the good for a species must lie in what is 'proper' to it, it does not seem to follow that the correct recipe for human good must lie in an *exclusive* concentration on that of which man alone is capable. What makes an automobile good involves, to be sure, excellence in respect of the functions peculiar to cars (for example the utilization of a certain sort of internal combustion engine), but also requires a host of other functions (such as safe brakes and comfortable seating) which it shares with other vehicular conveyances.[48] Even the briefest sketch of what makes human life worth living will sound impossibly abstract unless it includes at least some of the satisfactions which arise from our inescapably biological nature. Aristotle is from first to last determined to accommodate this more humane and down-to-earth conception of our human good; for even when, in the final book of the *Nicomachean Ethics*, he extols the supremacy of Platonic-style contemplation, he pointedly observes that 'such a life will be above the human level, for anyone who lives it will do so not as a human being but in virtue of something divine within him'.[49] The good life should involve the full flowering of our humanity in all its dimensions, rather than the exclusive concentration on something ideal and trans-human.

The predominant Aristotelian conception of the good life, then, involves the harmonious flourishing of all our human capacities, under the broad guidance of reason. Like Plato, Aristotle makes a division within the soul between rational and non-rational elements, but the relationship between them is interestingly different from what is found in Plato. The prevailing Platonic assumption (at any rate in the picture found in many parts of the *Republic* and the *Phaedo*) is that feeling and emotion are inherently disruptive to the good life. Raw appetite, where it is present, needs to be curbed and controlled (corresponding, in the political sphere, to the ideal constitution where the guardians ordain every aspect of the city's government, and the 'many-headed beast' that is the mass of the people is prohibited, at all costs, from having any say in the running of the state).[30] In Aristotle, by contrast, the 'part of the soul that has reason', and whose exercise is the key to the good life, turns out to have two aspects – one actually involved in rational thought, while the other is 'obedient to reason'.[31] It is subsequently suggested that the appetitive part of us 'in a sense shares in reason in so far as it listens to and obeys it; this is the sense in which we speak of paying heed to one's father or one's friends'.[32] In this context, Aristotle develops a quite complex account of the role of reason in various categories of human conduct. On the one hand, he acknowledges the disturbing but all too common predicament in which what is 'by nature irrational' 'strains' and 'fights' against reason.[33] This can give rise to the situation where bodily appetites sway us to take a course which is contrary to our best perceptions of the good, so that we end up acting badly (the phenomenon of 'lack of control' or *akrasia*). But the fact that there is something in our appetitive nature that is 'receptive to reason' can allow us to act in a less damaging way, so that despite the presence of bad and irrational desires, the outcome is one where the resulting behaviour is 'obedient to reason'; such is the behaviour of someone who has what Aristotle calls 'self-control' (*enkrateia*). Best of all, however, is the case of someone who has acquired the right habits of true 'virtue' (*arete*); here it is not a matter of reason having to 'prevail' over recalcitrant appetite; rather, the structure of our appetites is 'responsive to reason' in a deeper, more stable and more balanced manner, which will lead to our acting in a way which 'is in complete harmony with the rational principle'.[34]

To get a clearer idea of the ethical psychology involved here, it may be helpful to indicate how appetite and reason are related for Aristotle in various possible cases involving the appraisal of action. This is shown in Table 1.

Table i.

	Character	Goal	Appetite	Conduct
1	Virtuous	good	good	good
2	Self-controlled	good	bad	good
3	Uncontrolled	good	bad	bad
4	Vicious	bad	bad	bad

The best situation (row 1) is the one where our rational perception of the good leads us to identify a worthwhile goal, our appetites are harmoniously and gracefully trained so as to accord with that good, and our resulting action is good. We act in accordance with 'right reason', and there is no conflict in the soul; all is as it should be – this is the paradigm of Aristotelian ethical virtue. Very different is the situation of conflict where appetites pull against our rational perception of the best. In such a situation Aristotle allows for two possibilities. The first (row 2 in our table), is where the agent is sufficiently 'self-controlled' (*enkrates*) to ensure that the recalcitrant desires are kept in check, so that the resulting action is in accordance with reason.[55] The second (row 3) is where the agent is 'weak' or 'uncontrolled' (*akrates*), and the bad appetites lead to action which is not in accordance with the rationally determined goals of virtue. And finally (row 4), there is the case of vice, where the goals are themselves bad, so that the possibility of right conduct is foreclosed from the outset.[56]

Before we look in more detail at how the conflict between reason and desire are handled in Aristotle (and later Greek thinkers), it will be useful to draw some threads together. The faculty of reason is, indisputably, mankind's great glory – what separates us from the other animals who are wholly controlled by the forces of instinct and appetite,[57] and what gives rise to the very possibility of ethics – of the attempt to step back from the immediate urgencies of our quotidian existence and systematically direct our living towards what is fulfilling and worthwhile. This alone suggests that there must inevitably be at least something of a 'ratiocentric' dimension to any ethics that is worth the name. But alongside this result is the indubitable fact that we are not pure disembodied spirits located in a noumenal world of timeless forms; we are biological creatures whose lives are immersed in a complex soup of physiological, emotional and cultural ingredients, many of which we cannot alter, and many of which we can only imperfectly understand. The 'Platonic' response to this is a certain kind of escapism – a retreat from the complexities of real life to a narrow intellectualism which finds salvation in attempting to surmount everything about the human condition that is messy and recalcitrant to reason.[58] The Aristotelian response is more nuanced and more complex. Man is still seen as an essentially rational animal, and the recipe for ethics still lies in the exercise of reason: 'not to have one's life planned with a view to some end is a sign of great folly'.[59] But the conception of reason invoked is one which allows a distinctive role for the emotional side to our nature. Intellectual virtue, to be sure, consists in the right exercise of reason in its often purely theoretical role (and, as indicated above, Aristotle is sometimes in spite of himself attracted to the Platonic thought that this alone is sufficient for the good life). But the main subject-matter for ethics is 'excellence of character',[60] and this consists not exclusively in the right use of reason, but in the systematic nurturing of those parts of ourselves that are 'responsive to reason' – habits of feeling and emotion which, though not themselves strictly 'rational', are nonetheless capable of being brought into conformity with the perceptions of reason.[61]

To revert to the threefold classification introduced at the start of this section, it should by now be quite clear that this conception of the role of reason in ethics is far removed from the narrowly intellectualistic conception that we labelled 'rational exclusivism'. Equally (as becomes clear in Aristotle's account of rational deliberation concerning the constituents of the good life), it is worlds away from a neutral Humean instrumentalism: reason does not merely work out the means to achieve whatever happens to be the object of desire; on the contrary its task is to set the goals and rules for action by deliberating 'about living well in a general way': this is a process that concerns not just means, but the rational evaluation of ends.[62] From these results it might seem most appropriate, as suggested above, to classify Aristotle's ethics as a species of 'rational hegemonism'. In important respects this is right: reason is, for Aristotle, in control of the good life, and the legitimacy of the other, emotional, ingredients in the recipe for fulfilment hinges on their conformity to what 'right reason' (*orthos logos*) prescribes.[63] But there is an interesting ambiguity in talking of reason being the 'leader', or 'in charge'. It might suggest dominance or suppression – the kind of supremacy which Plato's guardians exercise over the state, ever suspicious that their power may be usurped by the unruly elements, ever insistent that those elements be kept strictly in their (subordinate) place. Or it might (more in line with the original Greek meaning of the verb *hegemoneuein*) suggest a kind of 'guidance' or 'leading the way' – not so much the suppression of the emotions as their channelling into fruitful paths. From our late twentieth-century perspective, we have (rightly) become suspicious of normative models which encourage the dangerous delusion that man can, with impunity, dominate and suppress the world around him – whether the external world of nature, or the complex inner world of the human psyche. If Greek ethics is to speak to us with a persuasive voice, it is thus important that it be cleared of the accusation (voiced by a recent commentator) of 'constructing a normative model of human identity as reason, excluding or in-feriorising the whole rich range of other human characteristics or construing them as inessential'.[64] To see whether an acquittal from this type of charge is in the end possible, it is time to take a closer look at the deeply troublesome phenomenon of *akrasia*, or lack of control. This is a phenomenon whose complexities Plato, Aristotle and the Hellenistic philosophers all struggled in differing ways to come to terms with, and one which provides a crucial test case for the viability of any form of ratiocentric ethics.

3. REASON AND SELF MASTERY

σκοπῶ . . . ἐμαυτόν, εἴτε τί θηρίον ὂν τυγχάνω Τυφῶνος πολυπλοκ-ώτερον καὶ μᾶλλον ἐπιτεθυμμένον, εἴτε ἡμερώτερόν τε καὶ ἁπλούστερον ξῷον, θείας τινὸς καὶ ἀτύφου μοίρας φύσει μετέχον.

(*'I shall examine myself, to see whether I am really a wild, many-headed monster, full of lusts and appetites, or instead a milder, humbler and more unitary creature, whose nature shares something with the divine.'*) Plato[65]

In a number of celebrated passages Plato outlines a model of human action which does not merely presuppose the dominance of reason in determining right action, but which invokes an ethical psychology in which no course of action is logically or psychologically possible other than one in which reason prevails. When Hume, many centuries later, provocatively declared that 'reason is and ought only to be the slave of the passions, and can never pretend to any other office but to serve and obey them',[66] he was self-consciously proposing a radical reversal of the hallowed Platonic model. In Plato (or at least in some of his writings), the passions not only ought to be, but inescapably are the slaves of reason: the idea that reason might be 'dragged around like a slave' by the passions is not just unwelcome but actually absurd.[67] This is the structure of the argument as presented by Socrates in the *Protagoras*:

> No one who either knows or believes that there is another possible course of action, better than the one he is following, will ever continue on his present course when he might choose the better. To 'act beneath yourself' is the result of pure ignorance; to 'be your own master' is wisdom... No one willingly pursues the bad, or what he thinks bad. To go for what one believes to be bad, instead of going for the good, is not in human nature; when faced with the choice of two evils, no one will choose the greater when he might choose the less.[68]

If, as I move along the cafeteria counter, I rationally perceive that enjoying the nice taste of a sticky chocolate bun is a lesser good than keeping to a healthy diet (say, having a glass of nutritious carrot juice instead), then it is inconceivable, for Plato, that I could knowingly select the bun. Choosing the bun could only be due to some mistake – for example an ignorant underestimate of the long-term costs of obesity in comparison to the gains of immediate gratification. Pure weakness or lack of control (*akrasia*) – knowingly and deliberately selecting the option which is all things considered worse – simply cannot happen.[69]

We might well be inclined to say here that Socrates' enthusiasm for the life of reason has got the better of his common sense; for the plain fact, unfortunate though it may be, is surely that we do often 'backslide' and choose the lesser good when the greater is staring us in the face. As Aristotle dryly observed, Socrates' reasoning in the *Protagoras* seems 'glaringly inconsistent with the evidence'.[70] But what does Aristotle offer us instead? His discussion is complex and subtle, and it would take us too far round to examine all the details here (they have been the subject of endless analysis by commentators);[71] but at the end of his tortuous manoeuvrings he shows himself curiously unwilling to break fully free from the dominant Platonic model. When 'akratic' behaviour does occur, there is always, for Aristotle, some kind of cognitive defect in the agent. One of the rationally accessible premises which determine our action is either not grasped, or grasped only in a dim and 'clouded' fashion that does not amount to full knowledge but merely to the sort of awareness a drunken man has when he 'babbles' a piece of verse.[72] Knowledge in the full and strict sense is not present; if it were, it could not possibly be 'dragged around by the emotions'; and so 'the conclusion Socrates tried to establish seems after all correct'.[73]

Akrasia is a label that covers many possible cases, and one can certainly conceive of instances that fall under Aristotle's explanation. Perhaps I am so strongly under the influence of a passionate desire for chocolate cake that my cognitive grasp of the situation is impaired – I just cease to be vividly aware that the object in front of me is an unhealthy mass of cholesterol, or somehow fail to draw the conclusion that it is something I should avoid.[74] But this is not the typical or interesting case. The greedy backslider, at the moment he bites into the chocolate, will typically be all too aware of its damaging properties, well conscious that this delicious feast will violate the healthy diet he has rationally determined to adopt. The speeding driver on the freeway has, at the moment he puts his foot down, not suddenly lost sight of the salient fact that he is breaking the law and endangering the personal safety which his reason judges to be a greater good than that afforded by the temporary thrill of going fast.[75] The adulterer driven by the immediate urgency of passion to risk his marriage is often all too clear, at the moment of action, of just what he is doing. What is true is that something – the passion – 'knocks out' or 'renders inoperative' the reasoning process that would otherwise have led to a more prudent, more rational course of action.[76] But Aristotle's stubborn insistence that the 'knocking out' must somehow involve a 'clouding' of cognitive awareness seems to indicate that he cannot free himself from Plato's ratiocentric model of human conduct. The presupposition throughout is the Platonic one that rational cognition must always 'wear the trousers';[77] its power and authority can only be undermined when cognition itself is somehow weakened. Passions are allowed to play a role in the dynamics of human action only in so far as they can interfere with the knowledge which would otherwise inevitably lead to right conduct.

Despite the difficulties in which Aristotle's residual Platonic assumptions land him, there is, I believe, something important and illuminating to be extricated from the suggestion that *akrasia* arises through a 'clouding' of our cognitive faculties, though Aristotle does not have the resources at his disposal to unpack the suggestion in a convincing way. As I shall argue more fully later on (in Chapter Four), there is a sense in which ignorance of a certain kind is central to the way in which we often lack rational control over our lives. Roughly, the influence exerted by unconscious phantasies and desires is such that the full significance of the materials over which reason solemnly deliberates is often not fully transparent to the agent herself. It is not so much that the sway of the passions drives out knowledge of the premises or conclusions of a rational argument; rather, what is lacking is the right sort of *understanding* of our innermost motivations and their (often imperfectly perceived) relationship to our overt actions. But Aristotle, lacking the modern concept of the unconscious, does not have a philosophy of mind sophisticated enough to explain the kind of clouding involved, or the associated difference between a surface grasp of the facts surrounding our decisions, and a deeper understanding of their emotional and symbolic significance.

As a first shot at making this suggestion more vivid, consider one of the more potent sources of akratic conduct, the influence of erotic passion. It is striking that Aristotle says very little in his ethics about sexual desire and its associated emotions. He has a great deal to say about love, but, as befits a treatise devoted to the cultivation of lifelong habits of harmonious and balanced emotion, this is love in the sense of *philia* – mutually respectful affection. Sexual passion, or *eros* is something very different, much more 'vehement and intransigent' (in J. B. Leishman's apt phrase)[78] – a force which, as the Greeks knew when they deified it, always retains some aspect of the alien and the terrible. It is the recalcitrance of erotic passion to being guided along the ordered paths decreed by reason which makes it grist for the tragedians mill, from the Greeks down to Shakespeare and beyond. Against this backdrop, Aristotle's calm prescriptions for virtue, the injunction to lay down habits which make us feel the right amount of passion at the right time and for the right objects, start to look at best naive, and at worst like *hubris* – the self-assertive arrogance of puny reason in the face of an awesome power that it cannot hope fully to encompass or control.[79] This is not to say that we simply have to accept the power of erotic passion as non-evaluable from the ethical point of view. 'These violent delights have violent ends', says Friar Laurence in *Romeo and Juliet*,[80] aptly making the point that the desperate vehemence and intensity of sexual love can bring potent dangers to those in its grip. Equally, on other occasions, its influence may be benign, bringing together those who are destined to enjoy a long and fruitful relationship. But whether any given episode of passionate love will or will not derail the prospects for the achievement of a worthwhile life often hinges on factors which are not fully amenable to rational planning.

Part of the problem here is that we are dealing with an area where the very determination of whether a desire accords with, or runs counter to, the best interests of the agent will itself depend on information which is often simply not available at the time of action. This is a point which has been aptly highlighted by Bernard Williams:

The relevant descriptions of what happened are available, in many cases, only retrospectively, as part of an interpretation that establishes or re-establishes one's identifications of the importance of one reason rather than another. Consequently, whether an episode was an episode of *akrasia* at all may depend crucially on later understandings. A married man having an affair with another woman and trying to bring it to an end may find himself wavering in that attempt and seeing his lover when they had decided not to meet. If he ends up with his wife, he may well see those episodes as *akratic*. But if in the end he and his wife separate and he goes to live with his lover, it may be that those episodes will not count as *akratic*, but rather as intimations of what were going to prove his truly stronger reasons.[81]

Several insights emerge from this. Firstly, what validates or justifies a decision from the perspective of rational evaluation may often depend on how things subsequently turn out, which can often be in important respects a matter of luck. This has come to be known as the 'Gauguin problem', after the painter Paul Gauguin, who abandoned his wife and family to pursue an artist's life in Tahiti. In his widely discussed use of this example, Bernard Williams argues that whether such an action can be justified depends partly on whether Gauguin was in fact going to succeed in becoming a great painter – something that could not be foreseen at the time of the original decision.[82] The point here is not just that our plans may or may not work out because of pure luck in the sense of unforeseen accident; this is no doubt troubling enough, but we all have to live with the fact that 'the best laid schemes o' mice an' men / gang aft a-gley'.[83] The deeper issue is that the justifiability of Gauguin's action hinges on whether he is a genuinely gifted painter who can succeed in producing genuinely creative art – and this is something that, at the time of the original decision, was still in doubt.

But even this dimension of uncertainty does not quite exhaust the problem. To recapitulate a point canvassed at the start of Chapter One, modern psychoanalytic theory suggests that our attempts to understand ourselves must operate at the locus of a dynamic interplay between the past that we struggle to recover, and the future towards which we strive, and which will bestow the meaning to come on what we do now.[84] In attempting to understand who we are, and what we might best become, we engage in a kind of perpetual interrogation of the future, reaching out in a way that is not subject to any firm logical methodology, but is always conjectural and tentative. A powerful analogy can be drawn here with the conception of the methodology of natural science famously advanced by Karl Popper. For Popper, there is no definitive 'logic of science', in the sense of a rational procedure for arriving at new theories; rather, the scientist perpetually 'sticks his neck out', groping for hypotheses whose acceptability will always remain tentative, always subject to subsequent experimental refutation.[85] Something very similar seems to characterize the human ethical predicament. If the very *meaning* of events is often only apparent with hindsight, it is hard to see how even the most precise and accurate deliberations will be enough: even when our rational and cognitive faculties are working at optimum efficiency, they will necessarily be hampered by the inherent sparsity of the surface information which they have to go on when measured against what may later be grasped as its deeper significance. To adapt a celebrated observation of Kierkegaard, it is all too unfortunate that life has to be lived forwards, since its meaning is to be understood only retrospectively.[86]

The difficulties so far raised evidently have some general implications of a worrying kind for Aristotle's conception of the role of deliberative rationality in the good life. But they become especially pressing in connection with the problem of *akrasia*. The cultivation of virtue, as defined by Aristotle, presupposes that right habits of feeling and action have been laid down, in such a way that if things go wrong because of bad luck, or because a given course of action turns out with hindsight to have been mistaken, or its significance misinterpreted, at least the general patterns of conduct and emotion we aim to cultivate are ones which reason has determined as authentic ingredients for a fulfilled life. But the disturbing problem about conflicts between reason and the passions is that those cross-currents which threaten to drive us off course are ones which by their very nature often operate largely beneath the surface. The forces at work are ones whose significance for our psychological equilibrium we often only imperfectly understand at the time, and whose ultimate role in our pursuit of the good we are therefore often unable to evaluate until much later, if at all.

The phenomenon of erotic passion again serves as a cardinal illustration of the problem. As a recent commentator has observed, 'when it comes to the roots of sexuality in the human psyche, self-knowledge often fails and we are pretty much in the dark'.[87] To begin with, when we are in the grip of sexual passion, the predominant phenomenology (as suggested by the etymology of the term 'passion') is a sense that we are not so much 'acting' as having something happen to us. The modern metaphor of 'falling' in love conveys something of this potentially dangerous passivity, and the same notion is expressed by more vivid and exotic classical metaphors like being 'hit' with Cupid's darts. In the face of this passivity, the hope that reason can lay adequate plans in advance, that we can train ourselves to feel the right kind of passion at the right time and towards the right objects, looks, to say the least, bizarre.[88] As for the second best Aristotelian solution, that when passions arise which are not in harmony with what reason requires, we should aim to exercise 'control' (*enkrateia*) over recalcitrant desires so as to bring our action into line with our perception of the good, this also appears curiously inappropriate to the case in hand. For, in the first place, as tragedies like that of Pentheus in Euripides' *Bacchae* powerfully demonstrate, and as the more systematic investigations of Freud and his successors make compellingly plain, the psychic pressures generated by such attempts at control often threaten to burst the dam of rationality with catastrophic results for our lives. But the difficulties run deeper still. The extent to which we are in the dark with respect to the operation and significance of our erotic emotions and passions means that even if we were able in such matters to exercise rigid control, or to rely on carefully devised patterns of previous self-habituation, it would not be at all obvious that the outcome would bring us an ethically better life.

Here there is an especial piquancy to Williams' suggestion that episodes which from one perspective may seem akratic may later count as 'intimations of what may prove truly stronger reasons'. Though Williams does not put it this way,[89] our relationship to our erotic passions is such that the possible link between their operation and our achievement of a good life is not wholly within the scope of unaided reason to determine at the time when we are required to deliberate. Sexual desire can, on the one hand, be the source of some of the most rewarding and fulfilling goods that human life can offer; for us systematically to attempt to train it within the bounds of Aristotelian 'moderation', or failing that to exercise rational 'control' over it, may threaten to cut us off from the roots of what makes us most endearingly vulnerable and most fully human. But we also know that such desire can often have elements of the pathological or the neurotic; it can be linked with childhood traumas we only imperfectly, if at all, understand or recall; it can be bound up with phantasies of power and domination, obscure subconscious desires to redeem or reclaim the past, powerful yet only dimly apprehended drives to re-establish as adults an integrity and autonomy that we failed to enjoy as

children, when our emotional responses were laid down in the
context of abject dependence on parental affection that we were
helpless to evaluate or control. Given these complexities, the
fourfold Aristotelian schema of psychological-cum-ethical classification – virtue, control, lack of control, vice – begins to seem
simplistic; for the recipe for right conduct presupposes a transparency in our relationship to the passions that very often just does not
obtain. This is not to say that the operation of the passions, and
their role in the good life, is subject to a perpetual and ineradicable
opacity. But what it does suggest is the need for a comprehensive
programme of 'therapeutic' self-examination, one which holds out
the hope that we can lift the veil on the inner structure of our
irrational desires and passions, and begin the process of coming to
terms with their deeper significance for our emotional equilibrium.
It is only with the advent of psychoanalytic theory that the prospects for such a programme have begun to be canvassed in
anything like a systematic way (though as I shall indicate shortly,
there may be glimmerings of it in some of the ideas of the
Epicureans). What the argument of this section has suggested is
that the Aristotelian model for ethics, for all its virtues, lacks the
resources to cope with the ethical and psychological significance of
those parts of our nature whose operation resists direct rational
understanding and evaluation.

4. STOIC DETACHMENT AND EPICUREAN TRANQUILLITY

Κενὸς ἐκείνου φιλοσόφου λόγος ὑφ' οὗ μηδὲν πάθος ἀνθρώπου
θεραπεύεται.

*('Empty are the words of the philosopher who offers no cure for the passions of
mankind.')* Epicurus[90]

Aristotle's idea of virtue, centred around the doctrine of the
'mean', holds out the hope that we can systematically train our
emotions so as to achieve permanent dispositions of character
enabling us to feel the right amount of emotion, 'at the right times,
about the right things, towards the right people, for the right end,
and in the right way'.[91] There is clearly something laudable about
this ideal, but the difficulties canvassed in the previous section

suggest that it is an unstable one: at least with respect to certain key areas of human feeling, there are serious worries about the viability and appropriateness of any such rationally predetermined programme of training. In the aftermath of Aristotle, the Stoic philosophers mounted a comprehensive critique of the Aristotelian ideal of *metriopatheia* (the cultivation of moderation in our feelings and emotions), and proposed instead that the wise and happy philosopher should aspire to *apatheia*, the condition of being entirely free from the passions.[92] The Stoics defined a passion as an 'impulse which is excessive and disobedient to reason' or as a 'movement of the soul which is contrary to nature'. The result of such going against nature and reason will always be damaging, as the account given by Stobaeus makes clear:

Every passion is overpowering, since people in states of passion, though they frequently see that it is not suitable to do something, are carried away by the intensity, as though by a disobedient horse, and induced to do it . . . In states of passion, even if people realize . . . that one should not feel distress, or fear or be in any state of passion, they still do not give these up, but are brought into a position of being controlled by their tyranny.[93]

Although this passage may suggest an 'inner conflict' model of the mind (between rational and irrational parts), the early Stoics (notably Chrysippus) were keen to stress the unitary nature of the human soul. Emotional behaviour (as a recent commentator has pointed out) is typically seen 'not as internal conduct of breakdown, but as the whole unified person being out of control'.[94] What is at the root of such conduct is not so much a quasi-'external' force dragging me against my will (as the Platonic model of the divided soul sometimes implies), but rather that my rational grasp of what the situation requires is faulty. If I am distressed at failure to seduce someone to whom I am passionately attracted, or my inability to avenge myself on an assailant, this arises from a false belief (that satisfying erotic passion, or anger, is good, and that failure to do so is bad). Indeed, the fundamental cause of all the passions is 'a set of mistaken beliefs about what is good and what is bad'.[95] For the Stoics, only moral virtue, action in accordance with what reason demands, is truly good in itself;

the emotions are damaging because they 'get in the way of our accepting and living by the moral point of view which reason reveals'.[96]

The Stoic account of the passions is highly complicated (and the difficulties are compounded by differing emphases and strategies within the school),[97] but however interpreted it gives rise to major problems. In the first place, the Stoic commitment to a unitary account of the soul led them to give a tortuous and (at least to many critics) unconvincing account of the phenomenon of weakness or *akrasia*; instead of seeing weak action as the result of a conflict between reason and the passions, the Stoics offered the picture of weakness as arising from a very rapid 'fluttering' between inconsistent opinions and impulses: 'one and the same reason turns to both sides, but we do not notice this because of the suddenness and speed of the change'.[98] Many commentators have condemned this attempt to 'resolve simultaneous conflict into [an imperceptibly rapid] temporal succession' as wildly counter-intuitive;[99] others have thought that the Stoics are on to something important: that weakness can arise through a failure to 'think things through more fully', or because of a gap between 'a person as he is [at the moment of choice] and as he might be if he exercised his full potentiality for human reason'.[100] Interpreted this way, the Stoic account accommodates the undeniable fact that we do hold ourselves responsible for our weak conduct, and offers an explanation of a kind: what is blameworthy is our failure to 'think things through' – to pursue the rational analysis of the facts which would dissolve the false beliefs responsible for our weak impulses. What it does not fully explain, however, is the (seeming) fact that we often continue to have weak and irrational impulses (desires to select the lesser good) even when we grasp all the relevant information. The chocolate binger's problem (as noted in the previous section) just does not typically seem to be a cognitive one, a failure to exercise reason in thinking things through. For the normal picture of the typical backslider is of one who is all too clearly aware, at the moment of choice, of all the relevant information – one who says regretfully, but with clear eyes, 'The good that I would, I do not, and the evil that I would not, that I do.'[101] It *may* be, despite all this, that a sufficiently radical cognitive transformation, a deep enough shift in our awareness of the significance of what we are doing when we give in to passion, would somehow eliminate the most important causes of weak action; but (as I shall suggest in Chapter Four) to make this convincing we need a far richer account of the nature and sources of human emotion than can be provided by the monistic ethical psychology of the Stoics.

As for their general aim of completely eliminating the passions from the good life, here the Stoics have been charged by their critics with attempting to escape from the pitfalls of Aristotelian 'moderation theory' at the cost of retreating to a narrow Platonic intellectualism, where the value of the emotions is denied altogether, and all that is required for the good life is the austere pursuit of right reason, in a state where what makes us most human – the 'sensible warm motions' of the human heart[102] – are robbed of value and significance. Defenders of the Stoics have been at pains to protest that such criticism involves a distortion: it is wrong to accuse the Stoics of 'extreme intellectualism', since 'nothing demands that the virtuous Stoic would or should be affectless'.[103] What is certainly true, however, is that the Stoics consistently condemned all the main types of ordinary emotion as destructive of the good life. Everything that is subsumable under the four Stoic categories of *pathos* is outlawed, and the list is a pretty comprehensive one: 'Appetite (including anger, sexual desire, love of riches and honours); pleasure (including self-gratification, rejoicing at the misfortunes of others); fear (including hesitancy, anguish, astonishment, shame, superstition, confusion); distress (including pity, grief, worry, sorrow)'.[104]

Some of the items in this list (for example rejoicing at the misfortunes of others) are of course pretty nasty. But the fact remains – and it is an alarming one – that a person who fully followed the Stoic recipe would be devoid not just of nasty feelings but of emotional *commitments*, in the sense which leads ordinary humans to be deeply moved by the successes and failures which attend their endeavours, and those of their loved ones. Serenity, for the Stoics, is the hallmark of the good life,[105] and this involves, in the famous recipe of Epictetus, 'not seeking to have everything that happens as you wish, but wishing for everything to happen as it actually does happen'.[106] The prescription may sound noble enough, but a little reflection is enough to reveal just how strangely different one who followed it would be from those who participate in the intensely personal interplay of emotions that characterize ordinary human life. When it is combined with the Stoic insistence on the 'widening circle' – the idea that moral duty extends beyond family and friends to all mankind, [107] it begins to be clear that the Stoic sage would have to be nothing less that an austerely motivated moral saint, calmly pursuing the rationally perceived good in detachment from almost everything that gives vividness and colour to our human existence. Such a character is, in the end, hard to regard as someone we would really want to have around us – a point which has been nicely made (though in a rather different connection) by Susan Wolf:

[We might reasonably] begin to regard the absence of moral saints in [our] lives as a blessing. For there comes a point in the listing of virtues that a moral saint is likely to have where one might naturally begin to wonder whether the moral saint isn't, after all, *too* good – if not too good for his own good, at least too good for his own well-being. For the moral virtues, given that they are by hypothesis all present in the same individual and to an extreme degree, are apt to crowd out the nonmoral virtues, as well as many of the interests and personal characteristics that we generally think contribute to a healthy, wellrounded, richly developed character.[108]

The damaging implications of this for Stoicism are given added piquancy when we remember that for the Stoics what Wolf calls 'nonmoral virtues' are not allowed to be virtues at all. To the Stoic way of thinking, *nothing* is virtuous save rationally determined allegiance to the morally good; everything else is classified as 'indifferent'.[109]

It is true (and much underlined by those defenders who insist that the Stoic sage is not wholly 'affectless') that Stoicism allows for some *eupatheiai*, or 'good feelings'. These are listed by Diogenes as 'joy' (a 'well-reasoned elation'), 'watchfulness' or 'caution' (a 'well-reasoned shrinking') and wishing (which in contrast to non-rational appetite is a 'well-reasoned wishing').[110] These are (as Julia Annas has elegantly put it) the 'rational analogues' to the four (condemned) passions of fear, desire and pleasure (the list of 'good feelings' is limited to three, there being no rational analogue to pain).[111] But it is hard to see how they make the Stoic sage more recognizably human. Given that there is no authorized rational analogue to pain, any emotion whatever that is felt in the face of, for example, a bereavement, is condemned as irrational and inappropriate. Yet eliminating the possibility of such pain carries, paradoxically, a terrible cost: one who has reached a state in which any such feeling does not arise will necessarily also be without the sort of deeply committed, positive yet never wholly unanxious joy which a parent takes in the achievements of a child, or the kind of vulnerable, overwhelming and never entirely secure joy which a lover finds in the presence of the beloved – not to mention a host of other similarly precious emotions.[112] Joy would not be *human* joy without the possible yield of pain of which Keats spoke so elegantly – the pain of potential loss which dwells in the 'very temple of delight'.[113] Without that special human dimension, all that can remain as positive 'joy' for the Stoics is simply a calm 'expansion of the soul' signalling the presence of what reason perceives as worthy of pursuit, namely a purely moral value. It is, if not exactly a chilling picture, at least a strangely colourless one which takes us to the very edges of recognizable human emotion. Even its defenders admit that we have 'no very intuitive idea' of what it might be like to experience things in this way.[114]

The Epicurean view of the emotions was less negative than that of the Stoics; indeed, those familiar with the famous Epicurean doctrine that pleasure is the final end for mankind might expect that it would lead to enthusiastic advocacy of the passions as helping to gratify the relevant appetites (think of the sharp pleasure the angry man feels when punching the rival who has insulted him, or the ecstasy of the lover enfolding the beloved). But two crucial elements in Epicureanism foreclose such a conclusion. The first is the empirical observation, heavily underlined by Epicurus, that many of the passions are in the long run (and even in the short run) destructive, not productive, of pleasure. Lucretius' famous description of the agonies of erotic passion tells the story eloquently enough:

The wound grows raw and ugly from the salve;
Daily the madness grows, the ache gets worse,
Unless by new cuts you distract the pain
Moving on restlessly in search of cure . . .
For at the very moment of possession
Love's ardour fluctuates, a prey to doubt
Uncertainty and error . . .
Of all things, sex alone has this strange power,
The more we get, the hotter burns our blood
With ever stronger, never slaked desire.[115]

Linked to the failure of passions like lust and anger to satisfy us is another important Epicurean theme – that such emotions are inextricably bound up with mistaken beliefs. The Epicurean philosophical agenda, an essentially 'curative' programme, aims to 'reveal to the lover (and the same would apply to those involved in many other passions) the futility of his projects and the falseness of the beliefs on which they are based'.[116] But despite the emphasis by recent commentators on the 'therapeutic' aspects of Epicureanism, it is important not to lose sight of the fact that the programme for the achievement of tranquillity is in the main a ratiocentric one.[117] The 'therapy' is not characterized in terms which prefigure in any substantial way the insights of modern psychoanalytic theory.[118] What is envisaged is not a rediscovery of our psychological past, or a reinterpretation of the significance of our feelings in the light of previous patterns of emotional dependency. Rather, the project is one of eliminating the false beliefs to which passion is often linked, and these are to be cast aside by *rationis potestas* – by the power of philosophical reason uncovering the true nature of the cosmos, and exposing the groundlessness of superstition and the futility and misguidedness of human desire (for ambition, for power, for domination).[119] The right use of reason will enable us to see the truth of the famous Epicurean *tetrapharmakon* – the fourfold remedy for the ills of mankind: 'Nothing to fear in God; Nothing to feel in death; Good can be achieved; Evil can be endured.'[120] The programme here is largely an intellectual one, to do with the systematic exercise of reason; and it shares with other intellectualist visions of ethics (such as Plato's) an ambition not so much to reintegrate the passions into our lives, as to purge ourselves of them entirely.

The reading just offered would seem to some commentators to underrate the flexibility and subtlety of Epicurean ethics. Martha Nussbaum, an eloquent advocate of a 'therapeutic' reading of Epicureanism (and one of the most insightful writers on Greek ethics in general) casts the Epicurean fight against anger and fear in far less ratiocentric terms. Lucretius 'believes that confronting one's desires is a long step in the direction of making them more healthy'; when the emotions are cleansed of their accompanying false beliefs, the way will be clear 'for more fruitful relationships with one's lover and family in which vulnerability is not completely removed, and in which the other's separateness can be a source of pleasure'. But attractive though this vision may be, we need to recognize that the kind of 'confrontation' envisaged is taken to operate largely at the level of relatively transparent cognitive and emotional self-awareness; there is (not surprisingly, given the historical context) no clear sense of the need, underlined by later psychoanalytic theory, for a prolonged and painful struggle to rediscover and reinterpret the dark roots our emotional lives, buried in the half-forgotten patterns of response laid down in early childhood. Typically, the actual Epicurean confrontation with the desires seems aimed not so much at making them more 'healthy' (in the modern psychotherapeutic sense, involving a rediscovery of their past genesis, and the lifting of damaging projections and distortions), but rather at exposing them to the intellect as inherently confused and confusing, as dangerous disturbers of our peace. And the ultimate goal is to be above the tumult of passion and desire: 'sweetest to reach the temple, safe on high / walled by the tranquil teachings of the wise'.[121] The underlying conception of the good life is one which is wedded to the ratiocentrism which characterizes so much of Greek ethical thinking (creating an impasse which, as I shall argue in Chapter Four, can only be circumvented using the more sophisticated resources of modern psychoanalytic theory). Always on the horizon in Epicurean thinking is the destination of 'godlike self sufficiency', allowing the sage to achieve invulnerability by complete detachment from normal passion.[122] The resulting state of tranquillity is one in which the pains of commitment and dependency are transcended,[123] a life of rationality and calm philosophical wisdom, where (not unlike what happens with the Stoics) philosophy's claim to provide the good life for humankind is made good at the risk of jettisoning that very emotional dimension which makes us most richly and most intensely human.

Ancient Greek culture, in the triumphant work of its poets and dramatists, produced an understanding of the workings of human emotion so rich and vivid as perhaps never to have been equalled since. But in all the distinctively *philosophical* recipes for living which that culture produced, what seems sooner or later to happen is a retreat from the dark and tangled forests of feeling to the brighter and safer plateau of reason. The Greek philosophers were deeply committed to trying to show us how best to live, but the ratiocentric ethical systems which they came up with all tended (though to very different degrees) to shy away from the fullest acceptance of our humanity.[124] Although the need for it was perhaps faintly glimpsed by the Epicureans, a programme for the therapeutic reintegration of the human psyche, allowing us to come to terms with the darker forces of the emotions, without the need for rationalization, suppression or elimination, was never successfully realized within the conceptual resources of Greek culture.[125] This is perhaps a paradoxical result, given the feature stressed at the outset of this chapter – the drive in Greek thinking towards a holistic vision of ethics as something to be integrated in the fullest way with understanding of the world around us and our own human nature. But the classical failure fully to carry through that integrative project pales into insignificance when set against what was to happen to ethics many centuries later, in the Cartesian revolution of the early modern period. For the effect of that revolution, whose reverberations are still with us, was to threaten a divorce between ourselves as conscious subjects and the nature not just of the physical world, but of our own biological makeup as human beings. The result, as we shall see in the next chapter, was a growing challenge to the age-old ambition of philosophy to provide the key that could open the door to a fulfilled and worthwhile life for humankind.

CHAPTER 3

The ethics of science and power

Meta autem scientiarum vera et legitima non alia est quam
ut dotetur vita humana novis inventis et copiis.
('The true and lawful goal of the sciences is none other than
this: that human life should be endowed with new
discoveries and powers.')   Francis Bacon[1]

1. THE CARTESIAN REVOLUTION: MATHEMATICAL TRANSPARENCY AND ARBITRARY LAW

Le silence éternel de ces espaces infinis m'effraie.

('The eternal silence of these infinite spaces terrifies me.') Blaise Pascal[2]

It is a familiar fact that the seventeenth-century revolution in
philosophy profoundly altered our conception not just of the
physical universe but of the very nature of scientific understanding. But although that revolution is often presented by historiogra-
phers as a purely epistemological and scientific affair, it also subtly
and irreversibly altered philosophy's relationship to its age-old task
of providing an account of how humans can live fulfilled lives. In
order to understand how that shift came about, it will be necessary
first to lay out the principal respects in which the new seventeenth-
century world-view differed from what had gone before.

The old picture, dominant in the Middle Ages, and broadly
based on Platonic and Aristotelian elements incorporated within a
Judaeo-Christian metaphysic,[3] was of a benign and intelligible
cosmos, with the earth at its centre – a universe made up of
substances whose nature could be understood in terms of readily

graspable forms and essences (what Aristotle had called 'formal causes'),[4] and whose behaviour could be understood teleologically, in terms of a progression towards a series of specifically ordered goals or end-states. This last notion (corresponding to the Aristotelian idea of 'final causation') implied that we can understand natural phenomena by reference to the functions and purposes of things: plants have roots for the sake of taking up nutrients from the soil; cats have sharp claws for the sake of catching their prey.[5] It is arguable that such teleological explanations still have a central (and perhaps ineliminable) place in the modern biological sciences;[6] but as developed in medieval and scholastic philosophy the idea of teleology became inextricably linked with belief in the plans and purposes of a benevolent creator specially concerned for the welfare of mankind: 'It is God's will', as Paracelsus put it in the sixteenth century, 'that nothing remain unknown to man as he walks in the light of nature, for all things belonging to nature exist for the sake of man'.[7]

The resulting world-view was in many ways a cosy and consoling one. Though humankind had little power to control the environment, and was a prey to insecurity through constant fear of the ravages of disease and natural disasters, people could at least take comfort from the thought that they were the noblest of God's earthly creatures, inhabiting a privileged home at the centre of a rationally ordered cosmos in which all things, ultimately, served the benevolent design of a loving creator. The 'revolution' which heralded the emergence of the bleaker modern age was a long and gradual process, but it is probably fair to say that within a hundred years of the death of Paracelsus (in 1541), almost every aspect of the traditional picture had been systematically challenged. In the realm of cosmology, Copernicus' hypothesis, dethroning the Earth from its fixed and central seat, had been experimentally confirmed by Galileo, beginning with his discovery of the moons of Jupiter in 1610 (the following year, the scholars at the Jesuit College of La Flèche in Anjou, including the schoolboy Descartes, put on an entertainment celebrating the achievement).[8] Descartes himself was later to become a convinced, if cautious, advocate of the new cosmology;[9] and alongside his rejection of a privileged place for the Earth went a radical hostility (shared by other modernistically inclined thinkers of the period, notably Francis Bacon) to the whole notion of teleological explanation in science: 'the customary search for final causes', Descartes wrote in his *Meditations* (1641) 'is . utterly useless in physics'.[10] Hand in hand with the mistrust of purposive explanations, there came a vigorous advocacy of a new model for the sciences, which avoided reference to the 'substantial forms' and 'real qualities' of traditional scholastic physics in favour of a quantitative approach based on mathematical equations.[11] 'The great book of the universe', Galileo observed in 1623, 'is written in the language of mathematics';[12] Descartes, that great champion of the 'mathematicization of physics', proudly declared in his *Principles of Philosophy* (1644) that he acknowledged 'no matter in corporeal things apart from what the geometers call quantity and take as the object of their demonstrations, i.e. that to which every kind of division, shape and motion is applicable'.[13]

Part of the appeal of the new model was that it offered the hope of a genuine advance in our explanatory knowledge. The previous qualitative models of explanation had been largely classificatory, formally tabulating observed phenomena under groups of standard 'genera' and 'species', and attempting to explain the behaviour of any given item in terms of definitions specifying the essential properties of the supposed 'natural kind' of which it was composed;[14] unfortunately, the type of explanation which this schema yielded was often circuitous and ultimately uninformative (thus, heavy bodies were said to move downwards because it was 'of the nature' of terrestrial matter to seek a place below the airy and fiery elements).[15] In place of this static and largely vacuous explanatory apparatus (which often boiled down to little more than the naive observations of 'common sense', dressed up in a plethora of technical terms),[16] the new science could claim to discern underlying structural patterns, whereby a host of seemingly diverse phenomena could be explained in terms of the mechanical interactions of the micro-particles involved.[17] And because the underlying laws could be expressed in simple mathematical terms, there was for the first time a real prospect of a physics with genuine predictive power: the simple, mathematically expressible laws of mechanics, Descartes wrote in his *Le Monde* (1633), have such marvellous scope that the eventual behaviour of all the particles in the entire universe can in principle be derived from a sparse set of initial conditions specifying the shape, size and quantity of motion that obtained in the original configuration of matter when the universe began.[18]

Although the new model for science was mathematical and mechanistic, rather than qualitative and teleological,[19] it might seem at first that it is just as wedded as its predecessors to the idea of a rationally intelligible universe. Descartes, the 'father of modern philosophy', was famous for his commitment to a physics based on 'clear and distinct ideas': the key to the system was the paradigmatically simple notion of geometrical extension, yielding a universe precisely describable in terms of the shapes and divisions of moving particles. The old universe of 'real qualities' had dealt largely in terms whose application depended on the often vague and confused deliverances of the senses: 'when we say that we perceive colours in objects, this is really just the same as saying that we perceive something whose nature we do not know, but which produces in us a vivid sensation'.[20] The new quantitative laws of physics, by contrast, yielded a science which could boast the kind of exactness and clarity which had hitherto been reserved for 'pure' subjects like geometry.[21] In short, Descartes and his fellow innovators could claim it as a signal benefit of the language of the new science that it possessed just as much – indeed, properly understood, far greater – transparency and intelligibility than anything that had gone before. As if to underline this claim to transparency, the innovators often stressed that the traditional conception of a rational creative power sustaining the universe remained firmly in place in the new science. The God of physics, to be sure, was no longer a comfortably anthropomorphic designer of the 'commonsense' world as perceived by the five senses, but was now seen as operating in terms of austere and abstract mathematical principles; yet, for all that, the universe could still be seen as the product of a supreme ordering intelligence. Presenting his new mathematical conception of physics in the *Discourse on the Method* (1637), Descartes describes it in terms which suggest a fully transparent science underpinned and underwritten by the decrees of a rational creator: 'I noticed certain laws which God has so established in nature, and of which he has implanted such notions in our minds, that after adequate reflection we cannot doubt that they are observed in everything that exists or occurs in the world.'[22]

The implied picture here might seem to be that of a physical universe wholly and transparently accessible to human reason – and indeed this is part of what is behind labels like 'the age of reason', so often used to describe the era inaugurated by the Cartesian revolution in philosophy. But the picture, though supported by much of the language which the new philosophers of the seventeenth century themselves employed, is in various crucial respects a seriously misleading one, though it will take a few moments to see why. The starting point is the fact that Cartesian physics makes a clean break from the ontology of medieval and scholastic philosophy. Descartes' rejection of occult powers, and his abandonment of 'substantial forms' and 'real qualities', is well documented.[23] More important for the present purpose is the way in which the traditional framework for causal explanation is systematically replaced. As we have noted, Descartes forcefully and repeatedly declared that final causes, or purposive explanations, had no place in the new scheme of things. But the change goes much deeper than this: in effect, almost the entire ontological structure of the traditional world-view is ruthlessly discarded. Terms like 'substance' and 'essence' do, to be sure, make a residual appearance, particularly, for example, in the first part of Descartes' *Principles of Philosophy* (1644), which was largely designed to make Cartesian science palatable to the university traditionalists by employing terminology with which they were comfortable. But the terminology does no real *work* when Descartes comes to unfold his scientific system. In place of the Aristotelian plurality of substances, each with its defining nature or essence, there is simply *res extensa* – extended stuff.[24] And this last (though Descartes does not advertise the fact) is not in effect a substance at all, as traditionally conceived, since its structure and functioning is established not by the unfolding of definitions, or the analysis of essential properties, but by the formulation of universal mathematical covering laws, the values for whose variables are purely quantitative representations of dimension and motion.[25]

What becomes of causality, in this new conception of physics? In one sense, as traditionally conceived, it drops out of the picture altogether. For there is no question of following the traditional explanatory pattern (with which Descartes himself had flirted, with dubious success, in his *Meditations*) – that is, of isolating a given effect or type of effect, specifying its essential qualities or properties, and then reasoning that these qualities must have been inherited or passed on by a prior cause itself possessing (actually or in some higher form) the relevant properties, or the appropriate degree of perfection.[26] In the first place, it turns out that there are, in Cartesian physics, no true individual substances or properties; there is only a universal plenum of homogenous matter.[27] In the second place, the characterization of that matter makes little or no reference to its supposed 'real essential nature'; there is simply the abstract geometrical notion of extension and divisibility, plus the assumption of an initial quantity of motion in the system as a whole, which is subsequently conserved.[28] There is, of course, what Descartes calls a 'primary cause', namely God himself, who creates the extended universe with a determinate quantity of motion ('in the beginning he created matter along with its motion and rest, and now, merely by his ordinary concurrence, he preserves the same amount of motion and rest as he put there in the beginning').[29] But no special forces, no divine interventions, no real essences or powers are needed in order to explain the occurrence of any given event. Even if the initial state of the universe is wholly chaotic, Descartes asserts, 'the laws of nature [the mathematical covering laws of motion] are sufficient to cause the parts to disentangle themselves and arrange themselves in such good order that they will have the form of a quite perfect world'.[30]

It is in many respects plausible to interpret Descartes' stance here as prefiguring the mathematical operationalism that is characteristic of much of our modern scientific outlook. In place of the traditional attempt to discern the ontological structure of the universe, to uncover the real essences of things, the job of the scientist seems to be conceived simply as the formulation of general abstract principles to describe the uniform regularities that in fact obtain. Such an interpretation, to be sure, runs afoul of the conventional classification of Descartes as a philosophical and scientific 'rationalist', but this should not bother us very much in the light of recent work showing just how problematic and unsatisfactory that glib historiographical label can be.[31] It must be admitted that some of the things Descartes says about science are suggestive of a strongly realist and rationalistic approach: mathematics is sometimes described as if it were a kind of hot-line to God himself, a human cognitive mirror of the ultimate structure of reality.[32] But against this we have to set the important, and still too often overlooked, Cartesian insistence on the doctrine of the divine creation of the eternal verities. Traditional theology maintained that divine omnipotence does not entail the power to do absolutely anything, if 'anything' is taken to include even what is logically impossible. God cannot, on pain of absurdity do what is self-contradictory (for example make something which is both three-sided and a square); his supreme power operates, as it were, only within the sphere of the logically possible. One might suppose that it is hardly an objectionable limitation on the power of God that he cannot do nonsensical and incoherent things like creating three-sided squares; but Descartes' conception of the deity is of a being of absolutely infinite power – a being who is immune to any limitation which the human mind can conceive. Thus, not only is he the creator of all actually existing things, but he is the author of necessity and possibility; he was 'just as free to make it not true that the radii of a circle were equal as he was free not to create the world'.[33] What this doctrine entails is that God is not in any way constrained by the laws of logic and mathematics; rather he himself creates them by a sovereign act of will. And this in turn entails (as Stephen Gaukroger has pointed out in a perceptive recent study)[34] that there is no graspable sense in which the laws of logic and mathematics can be said to be 'true for God'; for they are not objects of understanding in the divine intellect but fiats of divine volition – the products of God's inscrutable will, which Descartes frequently declares to be utterly beyond the power of human reason to comprehend.[35]

Seen against this perspective, Descartes emerges as a strikingly 'modern' thinker, prefiguring, in his conception of the scientific enterprise, the work of Hume.[36] True, in his programme for science, Descartes insists constantly on the immutability and coherence of the fundamental laws which govern the universe: by appealing to these laws, we are able, asserts Descartes, to derive a whole structure of necessary connections which operate in the world, and unravel a complex series of results which describe the behaviour of matter in motion in accordance with the laws of mathematics.[37] But now, given that the rationale behind these 'necessities' is ultimately opaque to us, it seems to follow that the 'rationally ordered' universe revealed by the new science rests, in the end, merely on a series of arbitrary divine fiats; and against this background it is hard to see how the laws of nature could ultimately be construed as anything more than brute regularities. In short, the doctrine of the divine creation of the eternal truths generates, from our perspective at least, an ineradicable element of contingency in the system. The standard picture of 'Cartesian rationalism', with its alleged project of uncovering a universe whose structure is supposed to be in principle transparent to the human intellect, now emerges as radically distorted. At the heart of the actual Cartesian system is an element of arbitrariness which prefigures, if only faintly and in outline, the post-Humean world in which the working of the universe is in the end opaque to human reason.[38] The fact that Hume describes the ultimate laws of causation as mere natural regularities, while Descartes characterizes them as divinely decreed correlations emanating from the inscrutable will of God, seems ultimately to matter much less that at first appears. What both agree on is that the job of the scientist is not to investigate powers, forces and influxes, not to unfold a world of supposedly necessary connections between interacting substances, but instead to subsume all the diverse phenomena we encounter under abstract covering laws of maximum simplicity and generality. And this is the methodologically ambitious but ontologically modest programme which defines in large part what we think of as the scientific outlook of the modern age.[39]

2. ETHICS FOR MAN IN AN ALIEN UNIVERSE

Terram, totumque hunc mundum aspectabilem, instar machinae descripsi.

('I have described the earth, and indeed the whole visible universe, as just like a machine.') René Descartes[40]

How do our reflections so far bear on the status of ethics in the early modern period? To see the seventeenth-century revolution as confined to the isolated domains of 'epistemology' and 'philosophy of science' (as some commentators are still inclined to) is to risk a serious distortion; for we cannot fully understand the motivations and concerns of the early modern philosophers if we constrain their thought within the rigid confines of today's compartmentalized academicism. As has emerged in the previous two chapters, if we reach back beyond our modern specialized world, we find a recurring conception of philosophy as searching for an all-embracing 'synoptic' schema of thought – one which could locate a programme for human fulfilment within a broad understanding of the nature of the universe and man's place within it. Within this perspective, it would have been quite unnatural to isolate the domain of ethics from the results of the newly emerging science, and the implications of its underlying model of the natural world. It should thus be no surprise to find that the great thinkers of the seventeenth century saw it as a crucial part of their philosophical task to try to come to terms with the ethical implications of the new cosmology.[41]

Descartes, as we have seen, banished teleology from his new physics, and this in itself implied a conception of the universe in which the deliberative and purposive activities of mankind were in a sense separated off from the purely mechanistic operations of the physical world. As far as divine purposes went, Descartes sometimes tentatively suggested that an appeal to God's benevolence might be appropriate in the ethical sphere: adoring God for his 'marvellous works' could lead to the pious response of 'giving Him thanks and burning with love for Him'.[42] But he coupled this suggestion with a reminder of the vastly expanded size of the post-Copernican universe: the likely existence of innumerable other worlds, and the puny status of our planet in comparison with the vastness of the cosmos made it impossible to regard man as 'the dearest of God's creatures';[43] it was 'wholly improbable that all things were created for our benefit'.[44] Even with respect to phenomena nearer home, Descartes was adamant that appeals to divine benevolence were absurdly off-target: to say that God's purpose in creating the sun was to give light to the Earth is to fall into a naive anthropocentrism.[45] The general conception of the deity in Descartes is an austerely impersonal one (prefiguring the 'deistic' outlook of the following century): God's nature is beyond anything we can grasp, and what purposes he may have are forever locked up 'in the inscrutable abyss of his wisdom'.[46] There is a clear link here between physics and ethics. Just as in physics there is no useful mileage to be gained by speculating about the supposed purposes of God, so in ethics we have to come to terms with a universe in which we are in important respects 'on our own'. We should aim for human fulfilment 'without external assistance';[47] to believe that God is disposed to make special providential interventions in his creation is mere superstition, for it is vain to suppose that the eternal and immutable decrees of the creator can be altered in the light of some special human relationship with God.[48]

None of this is to suggest that Descartes went so far as to abandon the traditional picture of a perfect and benign creator. As is well known, the idea of God provides an epistemological escape route for the Cartesian meditator, trapped within the private prison of isolated subjective awareness that allows him to be certain only of his own thoughts. It is because God is 'supremely perfect and cannot be a deceiver on pain of contradiction' that human beings have the possibility of escaping from their inherent proneness to error, and of developing a reliable route to science.[49] And in Cartesian ethics too, as will appear later, the divinely ordained regularities, on which the preservation of human life and health depends, play a key role in enabling us to develop a happy and worthwhile life. But for all that, Descartes' model for ethics within the new cosmology is crucially different from what is typically found in earlier systems. As we have seen, one dominant idea in classical ethical theories, most notably those of the Stoics and their later Christianized successors, had been the notion of a life lived 'in accordance with nature' – a life of harmonious attunement to the rhythm of a providentially ordered cosmos.[50] Mankind had a rationally determined place in the harmony of the whole, and his life could realize significance and the possibility of fulfilment precisely by being conducted in accord with the natural order of things. But the position of man in the new Cartesian universe is profoundly altered.[51] The physical world which Cartesian man confronts is very far from an ordered organic whole of which man is a natural part. Instead, it is in crucial respects a strangely alien world, from which all the 'colouring' dependent upon our human sensory faculties has been 'bleached out'.[52] It is a world not of colours, tastes, smells, sounds and textures, but an impersonal and abstract world of mechanical particle interactions. No vital rhythm, no colour, no meaning or purpose, imbues the universe; everything that occurs comes about purely in virtue of the geometrical structure of inert, extended matter, plus the immutable, mathematically determined principle of the conservation of rectilinear motion.[53] True, the resulting world is one whose structure and workings we can map out, using the abstract principles of mathematical physics. But it is a universe which, from the human point of view, is 'poker faced' – a universe which operates autonomously and largely without reference to our human concerns, governed by abstract and immutable laws whose ultimate rationale, resting on the unconstrained and inscrutable will of its creator, is finally opaque to human reason.

The blankness, in a certain sense the deadness, of the new mechanical universe was something which Descartes himself was quite prepared to underline, and he pointedly criticized those of his contemporaries, like the English philosopher Henry More, who wanted to revert to an earlier (and in Descartes's eyes naively anthropomorphic) picture. More, inspired by a Neoplatonic model, had argued in correspondence with Descartes that 'what we call a "body" is in every case alive – albeit dimly and as it were in drunken stupor; for though it lacks any sense or awareness, it is nonetheless, at the lowest and most remote grade, a shadow and image of that divine essence which I hold to be life in its most perfect form.'[54] Descartes sharply replied that talk of matter being 'alive', was just a 'pretty phrase'; the Neoplatonic notion of the universe as a 'shadow of the divine essence' was one of those imaginative 'fabrications' which 'bar the road to the truth'.[55] The new physics had no room for anything beyond geometrical descriptions of matter operating in accordance with the mathematical laws of motion.[56] Adopting this picture of an essentially 'dead' or inanimate mechanical universe clearly ruled out in advance the type of traditional ethic which saw man's fulfilment in terms of harmonious adjustment to the natural world of which he was a part. For to put it crudely, man is *not* part of the new universe:[57] he can describe it, and map its workings using mathematical models, but the physical world remains an alien substance with which he has no natural affinity.

From this crucial shift in outlook there emerges a momentous change in man's attitude to nature. Instead of searching for a proper place within the natural order of which he is an integral part, man finds himself set over against an alien physical world, and as a corollary of this, his destiny from now on lies not in attunement with the natural order, but in the ability he now has, fortified with the new mechanical science, to manipulate and control it. In the new age, technological power replaces harmonious submission as the guiding vision for human life. The new manifesto is set out quite uncompromisingly by Descartes in a celebrated passage from the *Discourse on the Method* where he announces his technological vision to a waiting public:

[The principles of my new physics] opened my eyes to the possibility of gaining knowledge which would be very useful in life, and of discovering a practical philosophy which might replace the speculative philosophy taught in the schools. Through this philosophy we could know the power and action of fire, water, air, the stars, the heavens and all the other bodies in our environment, as distinctly as we know the various crafts of our artisans; and we could use this knowledge as the artisans use theirs, for all the purposes for which it is appropriate, and thus make ourselves the masters and possessors of nature.[58]

The idea of the 'alienation' of man from nature, which has surfaced several times in our discussion, requires some further examination before we conclude this section. We have already seen how the transition from a teleological and qualitative to a mechanistic and mathematical science serves, in a certain way, to separate the physical world which is the subject of science from the ordinary 'common-sense' world of the five senses, and to distance our conception of the workings of nature from the old anthropocentric models invoking design and purpose. But there is a deeper schism than this involved in the Cartesian revolution, one which goes beyond the adoption of new explanatory models, and takes us into the heart of a new metaphysics of man and his relation to the physical world. In developing the metaphysical foundations of his new system, Descartes, as is well known, articulated a fundamental distinction between physical or 'extended' substance (*res extensa*) and 'thinking substance' (*res cogitans*). Examining his own nature or essence, the Cartesian meditator comes to the conclusion that he can form a complete conception of himself as a pure 'thinking thing', wholly separated from matter:

I saw that while I could pretend that I had no body, and that there was no world and no place for me to be in, I could not for all that pretend that I did not exist . . . From this I knew that I was a substance whose whole essence or nature is solely to think, and which does not require any place, or depend on any material thing, in order to exist. Accordingly this 'I' [*ce moi*] – that is, the soul by which I am what I am – is entirely distinct from the body . . . and would not fail to be whatever it is, even if the body did not exist.[59]

The resulting thesis of the essential incorporeality of the thinking self – what has come to be known as 'Cartesian dualism' – was certainly not accepted in unqualified (or even qualified) form by all the philosophical promoters of the 'new science',[60] but it exerted a profound and pervasive influence on the philosophical thought of the early modern age; indeed, Descartes' metaphysics of incorporeal consciousness continued to command a remarkably wide allegiance in the philosophy of mind until the counter-Cartesian revolution of our own century systematically dismantled its ruling assumptions.[61]

The result of Descartes' dualistic separation of mind and matter led, in effect, to a twofold alienation of man from the natural world. In the first place, our essence as thinking creatures, as construed by Descartes, is understood in terms which do not merely make us separate and different from the physical world, but which define us as the kind of beings whose essential nature is utterly incompatible with anything material. Matter consists of extension – whatever can be defined in the language of three-dimensional geometry and described by particle physics in terms of indefinite modifications of size and shape. The mind, by contrast, is simple, unextended, indivisible, and hence inexplicable via any of the quantitative categories employed by physical science. 'I have a clear and distinct idea of myself, in so far as I am simply a thinking, non-extended thing; and on the other hand I have a distinct idea of body, in so far as this is simply an extended, non-thinking thing.'[62] As a result, the place of the thinking subject within the natural physical world is not merely problematic or difficult to understand; rather, I am in virtue of my very nature, what makes me *me*, necessarily and permanently alienated from the world around me. From the perspective of 'this "I" by which I am what I am', the natural world has to be confronted as 'alien' in the strict etymological sense: it is 'the other'.

But the alienation involved goes deeper still. For the *res extensa* which constitutes the physical universe includes not merely the stars and planets, and the whole terrestrial environment, but the human body itself. I am distinct not merely from 'body' in the general sense of corporeal matter, but from the physiological structures of my own body.[63] The result is that the 'alien' world which we confront, and over which we aim to gain technological control via the new science, includes our entire bodily makeup. No longer straightforwardly biological creatures of flesh and blood, we become incorporeal inhabitors of a bodily machine;[64] and the 'machine of the body' (as Descartes frequently calls it) is there to be scientifically manipulated and brought for the first time under mechanical control, just as artisans control the operation of their tools.[65] There is a striking analogy here between Descartes' conception of the relation of God to his creation, and man's relation to the natural world. The Cartesian God, as we have seen, is a mechanical controller who lays down the conditions for the operation of the universe by the pure exercise of his sovereign will. Man, of course, is infinitely less perfect and powerful, but at least in respect of his unrestricted will Descartes insists, he enjoys quasi-divine powers.[66] And just as the authoritative will of God controls the workings of the machine that is the physical universe, so we, exercising our own infinite will, and armed with the new science, have the power to put that machine to use, not only by modifying the environment around us, but also, more intimately, by direct manipulation of the machine of the body. The stage is set for a new kind of ethics – one in which cognition and understanding (corresponding to the old 'ratiocentric' ideal examined in the previous chapter) still play a crucial part, but where, as we shall see, there is a new and striking emphasis on our ability to achieve the right kind of control over the bodily mechanism we inhabit.

3. MORALITY AND THE NEW METHOD

[Par la morale] j'entends la plus haute et la plus parfaite morale, qui présupposant une entière connaissance des autres sciences, est le dernier degré de la sagesse. Or, comme ce n'est pas des racines ni du tronc des arbres qu'on cueille les fruits, mais seulement des extrémités de leurs branches, ainsi la principale utilité de la philosophie dépend de celles de ses parties qu'on ne peut apprendre que les dernières.

('By "morals" I understand the highest and most perfect moral system, which presupposes a complete knowledge of the other sciences and is the ultimate level of wisdom. Now just as it is not the roots or the trunk of a tree from which one gathers the fruit, but only the ends of the branches, so the principal benefit of philosophy depends of those parts of it which can only be learned last of all.') René Descartes[67]

This resounding declaration, from the 1647 preface to the French edition of Descartes' magnum opus, the *Principles of Philosophy*, makes it quite clear that the construction of a perfect moral system – *la plus parfaite morale* – was to be the crowning aim of Cartesian philosophy. Nowadays Descartes is not widely regarded as a moral philosopher; indeed, in the anglophone philosophical tradition he is still widely seen as an almost exclusively 'epistemological' theorist, preoccupied with the conquest of scepticism and establishing the foundations for reliable knowledge. This narrow view of Descartes' philosophical concerns – owing much to the specialized concerns of the our modern academic curriculum, and the demands of the 'theory of knowledge' courses on which most philosophy undergraduates cut their teeth – cannot (as we shall see) survive scrutiny of the voluminous writings on ethics and psychology which occupied Descartes' later years. But it turns out to be seriously misleading even with respect to his first published work, the *Discourse on the Method* (1637) in which he announced his philosophical aims to the public.

A principal theme of the *Discourse* was the practical thrust of Descartes' scientific work: the new science, as we have seen, was not to be merely speculative, but was designed to yield real benefits for mankind. But the remarks Descartes ventured to include on morality were mostly of a fairly cautious and tentative nature, devoted in the main to the articulation of a 'provisional moral code' designed to keep the meditator out of trouble while he withdraws from the world in order to establish the metaphysical foundations for the new science. The first of the four maxims which constitute the *code provisoire* is timidly conservative in tone: the author records his resolution to 'obey the laws and customs of my country, holding constantly to the religion in which by God's grace I had been instructed from my childhood, and governing myself in all other matters according to the most moderate and least extreme opinions – the opinions commonly accepted in practice by the most sensible of those I should have to live with'.[68] The implied reluctance to enter the arena of public controversy certainly corresponds to an enduring element in Descartes' outlook. He aimed throughout his career to be 'a spectator rather than an actor in the comedy of life',[69] and seems to have been quite sincere when he later wrote to a correspondent who had asked about his 'views on morals' that he was reluctant to publish his opinions, since 'it is the proper function of sovereigns and those authorised by them, to concern themselves with regulating the behaviour of others'.[70] One main objective of Descartes' moralizing in the *Discourse* seems to have been to foreclose the possibility of malicious attacks on his method of doubt by critics who might have presented the Cartesian 'truth rule' ('Accept only what cannot possibly be doubted') as subversive of public order. Hence he proceeds, in the second rule of his 'provisional moral code', to make a clear distinction between intellectual judgement (where the suspension of belief is recommended wherever there is the mere possibility of doubt), and the sphere of ordinary practical life, where it is appropriate to follow prevailing opinion. In a letter written soon after the publication of the *Discourse,* Descartes showed himself sensitive to the criticism that 'universal doubt may produce great indecision and even moral chaos';[71] and he later commented in an interview that he had inserted the *code provisoire* in the *Discourse* specifically to avoid the charge that his new philosophy was such as to 'undermine religion and the faith'.[72]

Despite this caution, Descartes allows us, when he reaches the penultimate maxim of his provisional code, a glimpse of the wider ethical concerns that were to form an integral part of his eventual project of constructing a complete moral system. 'My third maxim was always to try to master myself rather than fortune, and to change my desires rather than the order of the world.'[73] The scope of this third maxim (with the remarks that follow it) seems to go well beyond the need to devise a temporary set of rules for living while metaphysical speculation is in progress. Though still avoiding issues of public and social morality,[74] Descartes now launches into the question of determining the conditions for individual happiness. The discussion takes us, in other words, to the central aspiration of philosophy, as traditionally conceived – that of articulating a plan for the good life; and it becomes clear that Descartes wishes to make his own philosophy as enlightening in this respect as anything that the classical authors had to offer. That Descartes sees himself as inheriting the traditional mantle of the moral philosopher is underlined both in the tone and the content of this part of the *Discourse*, where we find the argument couched in terms which would have been readily accessible to the thinkers of the ancient Hellenistic world. 'In general, I would [by following the third maxim] become accustomed to believing that nothing lies entirely within our power except our thoughts, so that after doing our best in dealing with things external to us, whatever we fail to achieve is absolutely impossible so far as we are concerned . . . In this, I believe, lay the secret of those philosophers who in earlier times were able to escape from the dominion of fortune and, despite suffering and poverty, rival the gods in happiness.'[75] The allusion here is unmistakably to the Stoics, who had diagnosed one of the root causes of unhappiness as a tension between the inner world of our aspirations and the outer world of external circumstances.[76] To live well, on the Stoic account, is to live 'in accordance with nature' (see preceding chapter); and since the external world is, for the inhabitants of the Classical age, largely something unalterable which one has to accept as it is, the Stoics reasoned that fulfilment must consist in a state of inner detachment, and acceptance of what cannot be changed. Descartes returned to discuss this ancient theme in his correspondence with Princess Elizabeth of Bohemia in the mid sixteen-forties, when he proposed as a text

for discussion the *De Vita Beata* ('The Blessed Life') of the celebrated Roman Stoic, Lucius Seneca. Expounding Seneca's ideas
to the Princess, Descartes commented that 'the things which can
give us supreme contentment can be divided into two classes:
those which depend on us, like virtue and wisdom, and those
which do not, like honours and riches . . . Everyone can make
himself content without any external circumstance provided . . .
he bears in mind that . . . all the good things one does not possess
are equally outside one's power, and hence becomes accustomed
not to desire them'.[77]

The initial impression which emerges from these texts might
suggest that Cartesian ethics consists merely in a kind of Stoic
addendum which Descartes tacked on as an afterthought to the
main body of his philosophy. But Descartes' conception of philosophy as an organic and unified system starkly precludes any
such interpretation.[78] If the 'perfect moral system' envisaged by
Descartes is, as he insists it is, an organic outgrowth from the new
physics, then its structure can be expected to differ in crucial
respects from that of ethical systems which rested on wholly
different foundations. That this is indeed so begins to come out
in the fourth and final maxim of Descartes' *code provisoire*, where
he touches on the question of which occupation is the most
worthy of choice, and resolves to 'devote the whole of [his] life to
the cultivation of reason'.[79] For the Stoics, as we saw in the last
chapter, the exercise of reason is the key to living in accordance
with nature, and the calm acceptance of our place in the cosmos
is one of the signal fruits of properly conducted philosophy.[80] But
for Descartes, the right use of reason is intimately linked with his
new method for 'reaching the truth in the sciences' – a connection explicitly made in the very title of the *Discourse*.[81] The projec-
ted results of this method go far beyond the passive and accepting contemplation of an unalterable providential order of nature.
For in the first place physical nature (as we have seen in the
preceding section) is, in Descartes' conception, crucially different
from the accessible pattern of providential design which had
impressed the Stoics; Cartesian science reveals the world as an
austere configuration of mechanical particle interactions, whose
essential structure man confronts as something alien to his own

nature as a thinking being. And in the second place, the new scientific understanding of that mechanical universe is of a kind which promises far more than mere submissive acceptance. The list of the fruits of the new science which Descartes himself sketches out in the later sections of the *Discourse* opens the door to the possibility of wide-ranging technical manipulation and control: armed with Cartesian physics, man can learn how to produce new compounds (such as glass);[82] how to understand the physiological processes in the human body such as the circulation of the blood;[83] how to use the results of this knowledge in the development of a new medical science capable of 'freeing us from innumerable diseases and perhaps even from the infirmity of old age';[84] how, in short, to develop a systematic experimental technology enabling us to become 'lords and masters of nature'.[85] Descartes, no less than his Stoic predecessors, has a 'synoptic' conception of philosophy in which the recipe for the good life is integrally linked to an underlying cosmology, a theory of knowledge, and a characteristic vision of mankind's place in the world; but precisely because all the ingredients are now worked out differently, the resulting conception of how we should live turns out to be crucially different.

This is not to deny that Descartes retains the Stoic prescription for a calm acceptance of what cannot be altered. But because his new conception of science is progress-driven (the word 'progress' makes a conspicuous appearance in the very first sentence of the *Discourse*),[86] the extension class of what can be altered has undergone a momentous and irreversible expansion. It may be true that it is 'only our thoughts which are *entirely* within our power',[87] but nevertheless the indirect power humans can now aspire to have over the mechanical world and the mechanisms of the body is vastly increased. And the effects of this expansion make themselves felt not just in the areas of physics and physiology, but in the very subject-matter of ethics itself. No less than the Stoics, Descartes sees it as his task to help us in the project of living a rationally ordered life, and coming to terms with the often problematic relation between reason and the passions. But he will now bring to bear on that project a different analysis of the nature of mankind, a different notion of the role of the body in that nature, and a different account of the structure of the passions, and how they can be controlled.

The starting point for all this is the Cartesian conception of man. It is now time to notice that despite his frequently advertised programme for control of the environment and of the machine of the body, and despite his official dualistic metaphysics, Descartes became increasing preoccupied, when he came to develop the details of his ethical system, with the need for a genuine 'anthropology' – one which would do justice to the inescapable fact that we are not *merely* incorporeal creatures inhabiting an alien mechanism, but creatures whose welfare is, in a special and intimate way, bound up with the operations of the body, and with the feelings, sensations and passions that arise from our embodied state. The subject-matter of Cartesian ethics becomes inescapably embroiled with what came to be the major task of Descartes' closing years, the task of coming to terms with – and trying to mitigate the harsher effects of – that alienation of man from nature which his own new model of philosophical understanding had generated.

4. CARTESIAN ANTHROPOLOGY

Si Angelus corpori humano inesset, non sentiret ut nos, sed tantum perciperet motus qui causarentur ab objectis externis, et per hoc a vero homine distingueretur.

('If an angel were in a human body, it would not have sensations as we do, but would simply perceive the motions which are caused by external objects, and in this way would differ from a real human being.') René Descartes[88]

An apt motto for the age of the enlightenment that flourished in the century after Descartes is Alexander Pope's famous dictum, 'the proper study of mankind is man'.[89] What may broadly be called an 'anthropological' orientation in philosophy is strikingly apparent in the thought of Kant and Hume, and this orientation is prefigured in different ways in the earlier writings of Spinoza, Locke and Leibniz.[90] In the case of Descartes, most of the philosophy of his early career was occupied not with the human sphere, but with mathematics and mechanics,[91] and then with applying the principles of the resulting scientific method so as to develop a comprehensive physics. In his compendious four-part textbook, the *Principles of Philosophy* (published in 1641), he fully expounded his results to date, dealing first with the metaphysical foundations of his system, second with the general principles of his theory of matter and motion, third with his account of the nature and origins of the universe, and fourth with his explanation of the origins of the earth, and of a wide variety of terrestrial phenomena. But he ended the book with an indication that there was more work to be done: the project would not be complete unless it could include the results of his 'proposed [but never to be completed] treatises on animals and on man'.[92]

In the old Aristotelian world-view, the concept of man was relatively straightforward. Living things formed a clear hierarchy, and what distinguished man from other animals (possessed of nutritive, sensory and locomotive faculties) was the additional faculty of reason: man, in the famous definition, was of the *genus* 'animal', with the special differentiating characteristic (*differentia*) of rationality.[93] In Descartes' scheme of things, by contrast, the behaviour of animals (and indeed of the entire biological realm) is to be explained purely mechanically, in terms of the interactions of the extended particles of matter (*res extensa*) of which the bodily machine is composed. A radical mechanistic reductionism pervades his physiological writings,[94] and a whole range of familiar phenomena in living things (including respiration, digestion, growth, physical movements and behavioural responses) are ascribed to the operations of a self-moving machine which, like a 'clock or an artificial fountain or mill' has the power to operate purely in accordance with its own internal principles, depending solely on the 'disposition of the relevant organs'.[95] Descartes emphatically declares that it is not necessary to posit any special faculties or other biological principles apart from the 'combustion' occurring within the heart – a phenomenon which has the same basic nature as the fires to be found elsewhere in inanimate objects.[96] When it came to rationality, language and thought, however, Descartes' reductionistic programme ground to a spectacular halt. Thinking beings, as we saw in section 2, are set over against the physical order, and belong to an entirely distinct ontological category, that of 'thinking substance' (*res cogitans*). Each individual thinking creature, so defined, is understood as a 'complete thing' without reference to any biological or physical characteristics whatsoever.[97] But now a crucial question arises: how does this dualistic schema cope with the ordinary common-sense conception of a *human being*? Whatever one makes of Descartes' theory of the incorporeal thinking self or mind, it is at any rate clear that this notion of a pure *res cogitans* cannot be straightforwardly identified with the concept of a human being; for the latter refers to an inescapably biological creature – the familiar featherless biped, known in Latin as *homo*, or in French *l'homme*.[98]

Even in his relatively early writings, Descartes strove to make it clear that his official dualistic ontology, comprising on the one hand the machine of the body and on the other the incorporeal 'rational soul', had somehow to be supplemented, or at least adapted, so as to allow for the existence of a genuine human being:

> Next [after describing the machine of the body] I described the rational soul, and showed that, unlike the other things of which I had spoken, it cannot be derived in any way from the potentiality of matter, but must be specially created. And I showed how it is not sufficient for it to be lodged in the human body like a helmsman in his ship, except perhaps to move its limbs, but that it must be more closely joined and united with the body in order to have, besides this power of movement, feelings and appetites like ours, and so to constitute *a genuine human being (un vrai homme)*.[99]

Un vrai homme: the phrase (like its Latin counterpart *verus homo,* quoted at the opening of the present section) is a striking one, especially when it is set against the more familiar Cartesian notion of a specially created rational soul, annexed to the machine of the body. The latter notion has become all too notorious today, partly as a result of Gilbert Ryle's famous label 'the ghost in the machine', so often used to characterize Descartes' dualistic ontology. But while the label draws attention to the stark and awkward separation of mind from matter that does indeed mark out Descartes' official position, it fails to do justice to what Descartes goes on to say about the special nature of the connection, or, to use his own term 'union', between soul and body. In the second half of the passage just quoted, and in many other places in his later writings, Descartes is at pains to stress that there is more to a human being than a bodily machine moved around by an incorporeal soul. He emphatically dissociated his position from Platonic-style 'angelism' – the reduction of human beings to the status of immaterial souls temporarily making use of bodies. This latter picture suggests that a human being is not a genuine entity in its own right, but a mere accidental unity – in the scholastic jargon, an *ens per accidens*. Some of Descartes' critics considered that this was indeed what his dualistic arguments implied: 'it seems', wrote Antoine Arnauld in 1641 in his incisive comments on Descartes' metaphysics, 'that your view takes us back to the Platonic view that nothing corporeal belongs to our essence, so that man is merely a rational soul and body merely a vehicle for the soul – a view which gives rise to the definition of man as *a soul which makes use of a body*'.[100] Writing to a correspondent the following year, Descartes insisted that a human being was indeed a genuine unified entity, an *ens per se*, not merely an *ens per accidens*: mind and body are united 'in a real and substantial manner' by a 'true mode of union'. For 'we perceive that sensations such as pain are not pure thoughts of a mind distinct from a body, but confused perceptions of a mind really united to a body'. A *pure* thinking being, like an angel, would have thoughts, but would not have sensations.[101]

But what, in this context, is so special about *sensations*? The typical modern philosophical distinction between the 'mental' and the 'physical' ascribes to the former category *any conscious state or process whatever*; the mental, in other words, becomes a portmanteau term which includes not just cognitive and volitional items like beliefs and desires but also sensations such as pain.[102] But though this conception is often casually retrojected on to Descartes, the Cartesian approach is subtly and interestingly different. Descartes does *not* classify sensations as mental events *tout court*; on the contrary, he says quite explicitly that 'I could clearly and distinctly understand the complete "me" without the faculty of sensation.'[103] Now sensations, though not part of the defining essence of a 'thinking being', are an inescapable part of our daily experience *as human beings*. Sensation, as Descartes puts it in the *Meditations*, is a 'confused' mode of awareness that arises from the union and as it were intermingling of the mind with the body.[104]

We have now reached the heart of Descartes' anthropology.

Reflection on the passages just referred to reveals the inadequacy of the official interpretation of Descartes which has him classifying all phenomena into two exhaustive and exclusive categories, the mental and the physical. For it turns out that not two, but three categories are needed in order to accommodate our human sensory experience. The official dualistic model recognizes only two types of notion: the soul (the pilot, as it were) and the body (the ship). But our human sensory awareness, our having of experiences like those of 'pain, hunger, thirst and so on' reveals, says Descartes, that we are not merely 'lodged' in the body as a pilot in a ship, but are intimately united with the body. A pure *res cogitans* would be endowed only with intellection and volition, the two 'modes of thinking'.[105] A purely material creature, on the other hand, would not have any experiences at all, but would operate purely as a mechanical automaton.[106] But when a thinking thing is 'really and substantially' joined with a body so as to form a true unit, then there arises a distinct kind of phenomenon, sensory experience, which cannot be attributed to mind simpliciter, nor to the body, but which belongs to a third kind of being, a *human*.[107]

The classification here is not dualistic but irreducibly 'trialistic': a complete list of the essential attributes of thinking things and of extended things would not include sensory experiences; and conversely, human sensory experiences are not wholly reducible to, or fully analysable in terms of, the properties of thinking and extended things.[108] So entrenched has the label 'Cartesian dualism' become that many readers of Descartes are still reluctant to see the trialistic elements in his thought. But in his correspondence with Elizabeth, who had questioned him about the 'substantial union' of mind and body, Descartes makes it quite clear and explicit that his account of human experience requires a threefold distinction which cannot be reduced to a simple duality. There are not two but three 'primitive notions' which are 'the patterns on the basis of which we form all our other conceptions':

As regards body, we have only the notion of extension, which entails the notions of shape and motion; as regards the soul on its own, we have only the notion of thought, which includes the perceptions of the intellect and the inclinations of the will; lastly, as regards the soul and the body together, we have only the notion of their union, on which depends our notions of the soul's power to move the body, and the body's power to act on the soul and cause its sensations and passions.[109]

The upshot is that in virtue of our embodied state, as creatures of flesh and blood, human beings enjoy modes of awareness which (to use Descartes' own language) 'must not be referred either to the mind alone or to the body alone'.[110] The list of items comprised in this category includes 'first, appetites like hunger and thirst; second, emotions or passions which do not consist of thought alone, such as the emotions of anger, joy, sadness and love; and finally all sensations, such as those of pain, pleasure [and the other manifold kinds of sensory awareness arising from the stimulation of the sense organs]'.[111]

Descartes' understanding of the special nature of human beings has obvious and immediate implications for ethics. As we have seen, previous ethical systems developed by the Greeks tended to take on a 'ratiocentric' bias, which led to problems about applying a rationally devised life-plan to the awkwardly recalcitrant realm of human feeling and emotion.[112] The Cartesian model for science seems at first to be even more ratiocentric, viewing the world as an abstract, mathematically ordered system of 'extended matter in motion', and construing the human contemplators of that system as pure thinking things, detached from the world of extension, and alienated even from the physical mechanisms of their own bodies. But Descartes' attempt to develop a distinctive 'anthropology' puts all this in a rather different focus. Although the deliverances of reason reveal a rigidly dualistic world of extended matter plus incorporeal consciousness, our own daily experience as human beings provides a very different kind of awareness – one coloured by intimate and urgent feeling and emotion, one which projects us into the very centre of a 'substantial union' of mind and body; here, so far from operating as the cognitive pilot of an alien bodily machine, each one of us finds the operations of the body that is in a special and intimate sense his or her own giving rise to a rich and vivid sensory and emotional life. This is not to say that the Cartesian doctrine of man as 'substantial union' is free from problems; as Descartes himself had to admit, the way in which soul is united to body was beyond the power of philosophical reason to explicate fully, and has to be grasped on the level of our inner experience.[113] But what does emerge is a new account of the subject-matter of ethics. The 'most perfect moral system' which Descartes envisaged as the crown of his philosophical enterprise would, to be sure, presuppose a fully developed physics of matter in motion, an understanding of the mechanical operations of extended matter. And it would also require an understanding that our own nature as thinking beings is distinct from, and irreducible to, the operations of the material world. The picture so far, as we saw earlier, is of a predatory Cartesian ego, manipulating the alien material environment to its own purposes. But for all that, ethics will have its own distinct subject-matter – a subject-matter which is irreducible in the sense that it cannot be fully understood either in terms of the mathematical descriptions of physics, or of the purely intellectual and volitional operations of the mind. To understand what makes us most fully and distinctively human, we have to lay aside the categories of thought and extension, and focus on the affective dimension of which we are vividly and immediately aware in our daily experience as creatures of flesh and blood.

In his last work, *The Passions of the Soul*, written shortly before his ill fated visit to Sweden in the Winter of 1649–50, Descartes remarks that life's greatest pleasures are reserved for 'those whom the passions can move most deeply'.[114] Descartes himself was not destined to enjoy those pleasures for very much longer. Within a few months of his arrival in Stockholm, he succumbed to the rigours of the northern climate and died of pneumonia, just short of his fifty-fourth birthday. The *Passions of the Soul* is largely concerned with a detailed examination of the physiological basis for the occurrence of human emotions. But Descartes also insists on the subjective dimension – the way in which the passions affect the conscious subject who, as he had earlier put it, is 'not merely lodged in the body like a sailor in a ship, but closely intermingled with it'.[115] Descartes saw the passions as crucial for the ethical quality of our lives. And what matters from the ethical point of view is not just the physiological events (vital though these are for understanding how we work), but the way in which such events are presented to consciousness as fear, hope, anxiety, confidence, despair, jealousy, pity, anger, pride, shame, cheerfulness and love. Here Descartes offers the hope that by careful training we can achieve a genuine human fulfilment– a fulfilment that does not deny our biological inheritance. At the end of his survey of the passions, Descartes confidently declares that 'now we are acquainted with them, we have much less reason for anxiety about them; for we see that they are all by nature good (*elles sont toutes bonnes de leur nature*), and we have nothing to avoid but their misuse or their excess'.[116] The pleasures which belong to us as human beings, the pleasures which do not belong to 'the soul apart' but are 'common to soul and body', depend 'entirely on the passions', and enable us to taste the 'greatest sweetness that life has to offer (*le plus de douceur en cette vie*)'.[117]

For all his enthusiasm for reductionistic science, Descartes clearly saw that a complete philosophical system must find space for the affective dimension of our existence, for the significance of sensation, emotion and feeling in the way in which we understand ourselves, and conduct our lives. The 'perfect moral system', in short, would be an organic outgrowth from Descartes' 'anthropology',[118] and would rest on the fullest possible understanding of the workings of the passions in human life. It is to the Cartesian account of the passions that we must now turn.

5. THE ROLE OF THE PASSIONS

La philosophie que je cultive n'est pas si barbare ni si farouche qu'elle rejette l'usage des passions; au contraire, c'est en lui seul que je mets toute la douceur et la félicité de cette vie.

('The philosophy I cultivate is not so savage or grim as to outlaw the operation of the passions; on the contrary, it is here, in my view, that the entire sweetness and joy of life is to be found.') René Descartes[119]

In accord with his 'synoptic' conception of philosophy, Descartes aimed to make his work on ethics an outgrowth from the scientific understanding achieved through his theories of the physical universe in general, and of human physiology in particular. He wrote to a correspondent in 1646 that his results in physics had been 'a great help in establishing sure foundations in moral philosophy';[120] and when he finally published his treatise on the *Passions of the Soul*, in 1649, he distinguished his approach from that of many of his predecessors by stressing his goal of explaining the passions *en physicien* – from the point of view of a physical scientist.[121]

The etymology of the term 'passion' (derived from the Latin verb for 'to suffer'),[122] suggests something contrasted with an action – something that *happens* to a person, as opposed to that which he initiates. Hence Descartes observes that in the broadest sense anything which is not an active volition of the soul may be called a passion; but he reserves the term in its more restricted sense for those mental happenings which are the result of the soul's *union with the body*: 'those perceptions, sensations or emotions of the soul which . . . are caused, maintained and strengthened by some movement of the [animal] spirits'.[123] The 'animal spirits', in Descartes' physiology, are a very fine gas or vapour transmitted to the brain via the nerves from the internal and external sense-organs; in other words, they fill something of the functional role which is today filled by neuro-electrical impulses. The passions, for Descartes, are but one group of a class of phenomena whose operation depends on the transmission of neural impulses. According to Descartes, what we are aware of as sensations (such as those of heat or cold), feelings (such as those of hunger and thirst), and emotions or passions (like joy and sadness) are all caused, on the material level, by various physiological disturbances (for example in the heart, the blood, and the surface of the skin); these disturbances excite movements of the 'animal spirits' which are in turn transmitted, via the nervous system, to the brain.[124]

What mediates the resulting brain events and the ensuing awareness in the soul is the tiny organ in the centre of the brain called the *conarion* or pineal gland. Notoriously, Descartes identified this gland as the 'principal seat of the soul':[125] it is here that the minute fluctuations in the animal spirits produce a distinctive pattern of movement which causes the soul to have a particular mode of sensory or emotional awareness (and conversely, it is in the gland that the volitions of the soul are translated into movements that subsequently generate, via the nerves, appropriate muscle contractions for the performance of bodily movements like walking or speaking).[126] The positing of a kind of cerebral 'fax machine to the soul' (in Daniel Dennett's scathing phrase)[127] has not impressed subsequent critics; those exercised with the problem of psycho-physical causation (how an immaterial soul can be stimulated by, and cause movements in, the machine of the body) are unlikely to have their worries allayed by being told that the soul interacts, not with the body as a whole, but with a particular gland in the brain. But it is important not to be sidetracked by Descartes' bizarre choice of a specific organ to be the 'seat of the soul'. For all its awkwardness, Descartes' theory does succeed in pointing up a crucial feature about the nature of human sensory and emotional awareness, namely that the various modes of such awareness are intimately linked with physiologically determined processes– processes of which, in our ordinary lives, we are for the most part quite ignorant. This central point is quite independent of the truth or falsity of Descartes' official dualistic theory of an incorporeal mind. And it is also unaffected by the fine detail of the physiological story involved: Descartes's 'pneumatic' theory of the nervous system supposes the brain is stimulated by the rapid movements of a fine gas along the hollow pipes of the nerves; nowadays, we have at our disposal a vastly more sophisticated electro-chemical explanatory apparatus. But in our ordinary lives, unless we are neuroanatomists or biochemists, we are more or less ignorant of what is going on at this level. And even if we do happen to know about it, such knowledge plays no role in the immediate and direct awareness we generally have of our sensory and emotional states. What is crucial for ethics, and it is this which Descartes is about to explore with illuminating effect, is that the operation and functioning of those affective modes (such as joy, excitement, and distress), despite the direct awareness we have of them, is nonetheless not under direct conscious control. For the causal genesis of those states, at the physiological level, is largely opaque to the conscious subject.

It is here that Cartesian anthropology, Descartes' insistence on our essentially embodied nature as human beings, yields a rich harvest. The traditional project of Greek ethics (as we saw in the previous chapter) involved the goal of achieving the kind of rational mastery, or at least guidance, of the emotions and passions which would enable humans to lead a good and fulfilling life. And Descartes subscribes to this ancient aspiration: herein, he declares, lies the 'chief use' of philosophical wisdom.[128] But because of our embodied nature we cannot, by the mere exercise of our will, generate the desired patterns of emotional response, since we cannot directly control the relevant physiological changes in our bodies – any more than we can directly control any other events in the physical universe. The 'natural' or (as Descartes sometimes says, 'divinely decreed')[129] correlations between physiological events and psychological states are not within our power to set up from scratch; they were laid down, as part of our human nature, long before we came on the scene, so to speak – long before we emerged, either evolutionarily, as a species, or in our individual journey to adult life, as thinking beings.[130] But although human beings are not self-creating, although they are, as it were, 'lumbered' with genetically and environmentally laid down patterns of psycho-physical response, they are nonetheless in the unique position of being able to investigate, reflect on, and to a considerable effect modify, the relevant responses. It is here that Descartes makes a crucial contribution to the age-old debate over the relation between reason and the passions, by pioneering what we now know as the theory of the conditioned response.

Descartes' starting point is that even animals, who lack rational awareness, can be trained in such a way as to modify pre-existing patterns of physiological and behavioural response. As early as 1630 he had reflected on the possibility that 'if you whipped a dog five or six times to the sound of a violin, it would begin to howl and run away as soon as it heard that music again'.[131] A more detailed canine example is given in the *Passions*:

When a dog sees a partridge it is naturally disposed to run towards it; and when it hears a gun fired, the noise naturally impels it to run away. Nevertheless, setters are commonly trained so that the sight of partridge makes them stop, and the noise they hear afterwards, when someone fires at the bird, makes them run towards it. These things are worth noting in order to encourage each of us to make a point of controlling our passions. For since we are able, with a little effort, to change the movements of the brain in animals devoid of reason, it is evident that we can do so still more effectively in the case of human beings. Even those who have the weakest souls could acquire absolute mastery over all their passions, if we employed sufficient ingenuity in training and guiding them.[132]

In adapting the example of animal training to the human sphere, Descartes retains the central idea of the conditioned response as the key to how the innately predetermined mechanisms of the body can be modified to our advantage. The idea that the good life requires training and habituation had, of course, been explored by Aristotle: virtue depends, in the Aristotelian account, on our having acquired the right habits of feeling and action, on our possession not just of 'right reason', but of the appropriate kinds of ingrained dispositions to feel and behave in the right ways.[133] What Descartes now adds to this story is the perspective of the behavioural and physiological scientist who is able to investigate the physical causes of our emotional patterns of response, and in time learn to manipulate and 'reprogram' them.

A memorable example which Descartes provides from his own personal experience has direct implications for ethics:

The objects which strike our senses by mean of the nerves move certain parts of our brain and there make certain folds . . . [and] the place where the folds were made has a tendency to be folded again in the same manner by another object resembling even incompletely the original. When I was a child, I loved a girl of my own age who had a slight squint (*une fille de mon âge qui était un peu louche*). The impression made by sight in my brain when I looked at her cross-eyes became so closely connected to the simultaneous impression which aroused in me the passion of love that for a long time afterwards when I saw persons with a squint I felt a special inclination to love them simply because they had that defect; yet I had no idea myself that this was why it was. However, as soon as I reflected on it, and recognized that it was a defect, I ceased to be affected by it. So when we are inclined to love someone without knowing the reason, we may believe that this is because they have some similarity to something in an earlier object of our love, though we may not be able to identify it.[134]

There are two points of immediate importance here. The first is the notion of a physiological genesis for the passions: as a result of sensory stimulation, a 'fold' (or neural pathway, as we might now say) is set up in the brain which predisposes us to react in similar ways to future stimuli of a like kind. Second, there is the idea that an investigation of the circumstances of the original stimulus, (backed up by an informed physiological theory) can enable us to 'stand back' as it were from the causal nexus (in a way animals are unable to do), and consider the possibility of modifying our future responses. But there is a third, underlying, insight which has special significance for the role of the passions in the good life. Traditional 'logocentric' models had assumed a kind of transparency about the operation of the passions: we are aware of what we ought rationally to do, and we are also aware of emotions which often pull us in the opposite direction. Ethically correct conduct consists, on this model, in devising some way to bring the passions into line with reason, but we are offered precious little guidance as to how this desired outcome is to be achieved; more striking still, on the traditional model, it is something of a mystery that the 'greater good', once perceived by reason is not automatically chosen. This, as we saw in the previous chapter, left the classical moral philosophers signally ill-equipped to understand the phenomenon of weakness, or *akrasia* – the plain fact that, as a result of the passions, human beings often just fail to select what is clearly perceived as the better of two options. To tackle this problem, Descartes now offers a strikingly original insight: *the causal genesis and subsequent occurrence of the passions is intimately linked to corporeal events in ways which often make the force of the resultant emotion opaque to reason.*

What so often threatens to overwhelm us when we are in the grip of a potentially damaging passion is precisely the fact that something is happening to us whose basis, in our physiological makeup, and our past psychological history, we only dimly, if at all, understand. And realizing this in turn offers for the first time the hope that humans may be able to achieve successful 'management' of the passions. 'As soon as I reflected on [the causes]', says Descartes about his infatuation with cross-eyed women, I ceased to be affected by it.' Here there emerges the idea of a genuine 'therapy' for the passions which offers a completely new route from the old Stoic and Epicurean ideas of suppression and avoidance, on the one hand, and the purely cognitive exercise of eliminating false beliefs on the other.[135] Examining the passions *en physicien*, from the point of view of a natural scientist, reveals the full extent to which their influence depends on factors below the threshold of consciousness. We now have a striking paradox: Descartes, the very thinker who is so often glibly accused of having a naive theory of the 'perfect transparency of the mind',[136] is actually telling us that our emotional life as embodied creatures, as human beings, is subject to a serious and pervasive opacity. A proper understanding of our human nature involves recognition of the extent to which we are not just angelic minds inhabiting bodily mechanisms, but creatures whose deepest and strongest feelings are intimately tied up with structures and events which are concealed from us as 'thinking beings'. Coming to terms with the essential opacity to the conscious mind of the operation of the passions now becomes the chief task of what might be called Descartes' 'anthropologically informed' ethics.

In what is, in some respects at least, a striking anticipation of the Freudian line, Descartes links his new approach to the passions with an analysis of the way in which the structure of our emotional lives is influenced by the forgotten events and pre-rational experiences of early childhood. In 1647, Queen Christina of Sweden, with blandly regal authority, had commanded the French resident in Stockholm to obtain Descartes' answer to the momentous question 'What is love?'[137] In his reply, Descartes made an important distinction between 'purely intellectual or rational love' and 'the love which is a passion'. The former consists simply in the calm volition of the soul to 'join itself' to some rationally perceived good. This is the kind of love, presumably, that a pure intellectual being such as an angel might enjoy, and which human beings experience when they pursue, rationally and without disturbance, those goods which their reason adjudges worthy to be obtained. But things are very different when, as so often happens, we desire something in an emotionally charged way, when, as we say, we feel 'churned up' about someone or something. What complicates the picture here is, on the physiological level, the powerful patterns of bodily response which have been laid down in the past, and, on the psychological level, the compelling, though often obscure and confused, emotions which we experience without fully understanding their causes. In such cases, 'the rational thoughts involved are accompanied by the confused feelings of our childhood which remain joined to them'. A full explanation of the passions, in short, involves a detailed examination of the history of our early lives, going back, says Descartes, to our experiences at the breast at infancy, 'when we first came into the world'; 'it is this which makes the nature of love hard for us to understand'.[138] Recovering and re-evaluating the significance of the past for the present structure of our emotions thus becomes a crucial step towards achieving the self-awareness on which any sound ethics must be based.[139]

Descartes' theory of the passions offers us the hope that by an informed understanding of the psycho-physiological causes of the passions we may be able to lead enriched lives, free from the feeling that we are dominated by forces outside our control. It might seem at first that this would lead his ethics back in a broadly Platonic or Stoic direction, towards the thought that the source of our human problems is an essentially cognitive one, and that a purified understanding would leave us free to pursue the goods which are revealed by reason to be most worthy of attainment. There are certainly places where Descartes appears attracted by the Platonic idea that all weakness is due to ignorance. In the *Discourse on the Method* he remarks that 'to act well it is sufficient to judge well' (*il suffit de bien juger pour bien faire*); defending this claim to a correspondent he quotes with apparent approval the maxim *omnis peccans est ignorans* ('whoever sins does so in ignorance'), an echo of the Platonic doctrine that no one intentionally chooses the lesser good.[140] A residual allegiance to the old intellectualist approach to the ethics of reason and the passions also surfaces in a letter to Elizabeth written in 1645:

Often passion makes us believe certain things to be much better and more desirable than they are; then, when we have taken much trouble to acquire them, and in the process lost the chance of possessing other more genuine goods, possession of them brings home to us their defects; and thence arise dissatisfaction, regret and remorse. And so the true function of reason is to examine the just value of all the goods whose acquisition seems to depend in some way on our conduct, so that we never fail to devote all our efforts to trying to secure those which are in fact the more desirable.[141]

But although Descartes clearly shares with Plato and the Stoics a firm belief in the importance of an informed rational evaluation of the options open to us, he nonetheless goes on to resist the kind of austere intellectualism which rejects the operation of the passions as harmful to the good life. The Stoic ideal of *apatheia*, the transcendence of the normal human passions, is one which he implicitly condemned as early as the *Discourse* (1637): the supposed virtues of the Stoic heroes, Cato and Brutus, are in his eyes, examples of insensitivity, pride and despair.[142] Taking up the theme with a correspondent ten years later, he insisted not only that the passions were not to be suppressed, but also that some of them were a positive good, indeed the sole source of our greatest human joys.[143]

Here once more Cartesian 'anthropology' exerts its influence; for the 'substantial union' of soul and body that constitutes a human being requires, for its survival and well-being, not just intellection and volition, but the whole range of sensory and affective states. All sensory states, as we have seen, are attributable to us not *qua* pure 'thinking things', but *qua* embodied creatures – human beings. And it is clear that many of the psycho-physical correlations involved are crucial for our survival, both as individuals and as a species: that we feel a characteristic kind of discomfort when the stomach is empty and the blood sugar low has obvious survival value in impelling us to eat (and thus relieving the feeling of hunger); that I feel pain when I tread on a thorn has evident utility in encouraging me to avoid such noxious stimuli in future. Nowadays, Darwinian explanations are available to account for the origin of this kind of beneficial sensory monitoring of our bodily states; Descartes, in more metaphysical terms, but with the same implicit functional thesis in mind, invokes the benevolence of God in providing human beings with 'information of what is beneficial or harmful for the [human] mind-body composite'.[144] The upshot, in the case of the passions, is that we are dealing with a psycho-physical system whose operation has a signal utility for our life and health as human beings; thus, 'the principal effect of all the human passions is that they move and dispose the soul to want the things for which they prepare the body – for example, the feeling of fear moves the soul to want to flee, and that of courage to want to fight, and similarly with the other passions'.[145]

If the good life is to be a life for human beings, the passions are to be embraced, since their operation is intimately related to our human welfare. This is not to say that they are always and uncontroversially good. Because of the relatively rigid way innate physiological mechanisms and environmentally conditioned responses operate, we may become locked into behaviour that can lead to distress, misery or harm. The dropsical man feels a strong desire to drink, even when fluid is the last thing his health requires;[146] the young Descartes feels strongly attracted to cross-eyed women irrespective of how far they are worthy of his affection. But the appropriate way to cope with such irrational impulses is not to retreat to an austere intellectualism, nor to suppress the passions, but rather to use the resources of science and experience to try to understand what has caused things to go awry, and then to attempt to reprogram our responses so that the direction in which we are led by the passions corresponds to what our reason perceives as the best option. Despite the alienation of man from nature which Cartesian science often threatens to bring about, Descartes' underlying vision of the human condition is pervaded by a deep optimism. Awkwardly hybrid creatures of pure mind compounded with mechanical body, we are nonetheless, at the level of our ordinary daily experience, intimately aware of a whole range of sensory and emotional responses whose operation, in general and in the long run, is designed to conduce to human fulfilment.[147] This is why Descartes insists that 'the pleasures of the body should not be despised, nor should one free oneself altogether from the passions.'[148] The Christianized Platonist in Descartes acknowledges that 'the soul can have pleasures of its own'; but, that said, he immediately moves to a ringing endorsement of the affective dimension which arises from the inescapably corporeal side to our humanity:

The pleasures common to soul and body depend entirely on the passions, so that persons whom the passions can move most deeply are capable of enjoying the sweetest pleasures of this life. It is true that they may also experience the most bitterness when they do not know how to put these passions to good use, and when fortune works against them. But the chief use of wisdom lies in teaching us to be masters of our passions and to control them with such skill that the evils which they cause are quite bearable, and even become a source of joy.[149]

6. FORTUNE, EXTERNALS AND THE WILL

Au lieu de trouver les moyens de conserver la vie, j'en ai trouvé une autre, bien plus aisé et plus sûr, qui est de ne pas craindre la mort.

('Instead of finding ways to preserve life, I have found another, much easier and surer way, which is not to fear death.') René Descartes[150]

Acknowledging all that is involved in the affective dimension of our nature as human beings takes a certain courage. The Cartesian vision, though it offers some hope of progress in the traditional ethical task of coping with the passions, comes up against the inescapable vulnerability of the human condition in at least two respects. The first of these arises directly from the results of Cartesian anthropology. For Descartes, as we have seen, the underlying patterns of psycho-physical response which give rise to the passions are not of our own making, since they depend on pre-existing structural features of the mind-body union; and this makes us, as rational planners of the good life, more dependent, less in control, than we might ideally wish to be. Moreover, though we have limited power to modify the psycho-physical responses associated with the passions, we are working with materials that are often opaque to conscious reflection. Furthermore (to recall the point made at the end of the previous section) understanding the genesis of the passions takes us back to a time of abject dependence: what makes us what we now are stems in part from the ultimate vulnerability of early infancy.

A second source of anxiety is that even were we to achieve an ideal 'reprogramming' of all our emotions and affective states so that the passions operated in a way that was always in accord with our rationally perceived good, humans would still face the age-old problem of vulnerability to external fortune. Descartes himself had known only too well the agony that can arise from the uncontrollable blows of fate; in his early forties, he lost his only child, Francine, who died tragically of scarlet fever at the age of five.[151] In several letters that have survived to friends who had suffered similarly tragic bereavements, he reveals, albeit in the dignified guise of the philosophical 'consoler', a deep understanding of the horrifying way in which human happiness is always hostage to external circumstances.[152] Perhaps as a result of these experiences, we find that towards the end of his life, Descartes increasingly came to see some of the limitations of his optimistic dream of mastering the passions and controlling the external world. In place of the outgoing, technocratic vision of man as taking full charge of his destiny, Descartes increasingly felt the pull of an older, more resigned recipe for how to live – a strategy that looks not outwards, to the mechanisms of the body and the external environment, but inwards, to the supposedly secure domain of the individual will.

In this respect, Descartes' thinking was the very opposite of revolutionary. The 'inward turn' had been the stock in trade of Hellenistic ethics: as summarized by Seneca, the key doctrine was *nullum bonum malumque nisi bonus malusque animus* – it is one's state of mind alone that can truly be called good or bad.[153] The same theme is expounded in more detail by the Stoic philosopher Epictetus, who argues that adopting the right mental attitude is the key to escaping the dependency of human life on externals:

> Fittingly enough, the one thing which the gods have placed in our power is the one of supreme importance . . . What does Zeus say? Epictetus, if it had been possible, I would have made your wretched body and trappings free and unhindered. But as it is, please note, this body is not your own, but a subtle mixture of clay. Since however I was not able to [provide you with these free and unhindered goods], I have given you a portion of myself, the power of impulse and repulsion, desire and aversion. If you take care of this, and consider that here belongs everything that is truly yours, no one will ever compel you or obstruct you.[154]

This stress on the supreme importance for the good life of the inner domain was to some extent a reaction against earlier classical models of virtue which had confidently extolled the value of lives enriched by outward prosperity. It is clear in Aristotle, for example, that the successful cultivation of such excellences as liberality, magnificence, magnanimity, proper ambition, and social fluency or wittiness, presupposes the enjoyment of favourable external circumstances.[155] Indeed, Aristotle's underlying blueprint for civic and individual excellence assigns value in a way which is heavily dependent on a decent upbringing, a tolerably secure position in society, solid endowments of wealth and income, a modicum of health and personal charm – in short, the requirements not just for a worthy (in the inner Kantian sense) life, but for outward success and flourishing. Reflection on what we now call 'moral luck' brings this aspect of traditional virtue ethics into particularly sharp relief. To take the central Aristotelian virtue of μεγαλοψυχία (*megalopsychia*), for example, (magnanimity or 'great-souledness'), there seems no escaping the fact that this excellence presupposes a life which depends in large part on the propitious-

ness of fortune. Aristotle's noble or 'great-souled' man is born into
a high culture, healthy, intelligent, affluent and calmly confident of
his entitlement to honour and esteem. From a post-Christian
perspective on morality (as John Casey has pointed out) the pre-
sumptions behind this paradigm of excellence may seem simply
'odious'.[156] How can we stomach the thought that Pericles, in
building the Acropolis, is more to be admired than the poor widow
who casts her two mites into the Temple treasury? ('Verily I say
unto you that this poor widow hath cast in more than all they, for
she of her want hath cast in all that she had').[157]

'Odious' or not, the central vision of classical virtue theory was
still vividly alive in the ethical thinking of renaissance writers like
Montaigne, who often take for granted the presuppositions of
Aristotle's aristocratic conception of excellence:

Man in his highest estate is one of that small number of excellent and
select men who, having been endowed with fine and particular natural
ability, have further strengthened and sharpened it by care, study and
art, and raised it to the highest pitch of wisdom. They have fashioned
their soul to all directions and angles, supported it with all the outside
assistance that was fit for it, and enriched and adorned it with all they
could borrow, for its advantage, from the inside and outside of the world;
it is in them that the utmost height of human nature is to be found.[158]

Though he was undoubtedly familiar with such classical models of
virtue,[159] in Descartes' treatment of the good life, as developed in
the *Passions of the Soul*, the traditional catalogue of cardinal virtues is
boiled down to just one, which he calls *la générosité*. This is the
crowning virtue – the 'key to all the other virtues and a general
remedy for every disorder of the passions'.[160] The translation of
the French term is a difficult matter. The English transliteration
'generosity' is almost unavoidable, and is not entirely misleading (it
would have been perfectly natural, even in seventeenth-century
French, to apply the term *générosité* to acts which we should nowadays call acts of generosity); but for Descartes the term had
powerful resonances which are largely absent in our modern
usage. As a fluent Latinist, Descartes was of course acutely aware
of the connotations of the cognate Latin adjective *generosus*, of
which the primary sense is 'noble' or 'well born' (being derived
from the Latin noun *genus*, whose basic meaning is 'race' or

'family'). By a simple shift, *generosus* then came to mean 'noble-minded' or 'magnanimous' (and was used by some Latin writers to indicate the possession of Aristotle's overarching virtue of 'great-souledness'). Descartes himself compares his own notion of generosity to the scholastic concept of magnanimity in article 161 of the *Passions*.[161]

At first sight, then, the Cartesian virtue of *générosité*, or nobility of spirit, plugs straight into the aristocratic or excellence-centred presuppositions of traditional virtue theory. The connection Descartes makes is that the virtue of noble-mindedness, as traditionally conceived, implied a certain dignity and legitimate self-esteem, and this will precisely be true of the person of *générosité*: it 'causes a person's self-esteem to be as high as it legitimately may be'.[162] But on closer inspection, a decisive shift from the *arete* tradition can be discerned.[163] Descartes' moral education, at the hands of the Jesuits at La Flèche, had been dominated by the presuppositions not just of pagan humanism (though these did play a large role) but also, inevitably, of Christian morality. And what this meant, above all, was a commitment to the central notion of the kingdom of heaven as open to all. 'Le chemin au ciel', Descartes writes in the *Discourse*, 'n'est pas moins ouvert au plus ignorants qu'au plus doctes'; the road to heaven does not depend on the vicissitudes of birth or education.[164] There is, incidentally, a strong epistemic analogue of this universalism in the Cartesian account of knowledge. Good sense, the innate natural light of reason, is equally present in all men, and as Descartes explains in his dramatic dialogue the *Search for Truth*, the untutored Polyander ('Everyman') has as good, if not a better, chance of achieving enlightenment than Epistemon ('Mr Knowledgeable'), whose inner intuitions are clouded by the sophistications of technical philosophy.[165] In the ethical sphere, this comes out as an insistence that the good life, like the achievement of reliable knowledge, should in principle be available to all who set about the task of achieving it in the right way. Now clearly *générosité*, in the traditional genetic sense of 'nobility' depends very largely on accidents of birth and natural endowment. 'It is easy to believe', Descartes observes, 'that the souls which God puts into our bodies are not equally noble and strong'; and while 'good upbringing is of great help in correcting defects of birth', this too, will presumably depend largely on factors outside the agent's control.[166] But Descartes' Christianized understanding of ethics leads him to construe the crowning virtue of *générosité* in a radically different way from Aristotelian nobility – as a virtue whose achievement must at all costs be immune to the vicissitudes of fortune, and (in a striking anticipation of Kant) will depend on inner rectitude alone.

True generosity, Descartes proclaims (and the epithet should warn us that some spectacular high redefinition is going on) is a matter not of outward achievement but of the inner exercise of our will. 'Nothing truly belongs to us but the freedom to dispose our volitions, and we ought to be praised or blamed for no other reason than for using this freedom well or badly.'[167] We now have a striking turn around; for the calm self-esteem of the Aristotelian *megalopsychos* is retained, but not as the satisfaction of one whose outward achievements match his natural endowments and civic status, but rather as the *'feeling within ourselves* that we have a firm and constant resolution to use our freedom well, that is, never to lack the will to undertake and carry out what we judge to be best'.[168] True *générosité*, then, involves, like its pagan original, justified self-esteem, but, quite unlike the pagan model, it is self-esteem for the resolute and well-directed use of free will, which is (allegedly) within the power of all.[169] The resulting conception is of an ethical domain largely sealed off from the effects of moral luck. Those possessed of *générosité*, says Descartes:

will not consider themselves much inferior to those who have greater wealth or honour, or even to those who have more intelligence, knowledge or beauty, or generally to those who surpass them in some other perfections; but equally they will not have much more esteem for themselves than for those they surpass. For all these things seem to them to be very unimportant by contrast with *the virtuous will for which they alone esteem themselves,* and which they suppose also to be present, or at least capable of being present, in every other person.[170]

Descartes' earlier, highly ambitious, goals – scientific mastery of the environment and technical control of the mechanisms of the body – would evidently require, for their effective realization, a considerable degree of outward success and prosperity. In his theory of *générosité*, by contrast, he offers fewer hostages to fortune, hankering for a life which is, in Stoic terms, 'safe, impregnable, fenced and fortified'.[171] The primacy which his account gives to the autonomous power of the will, as the only true basis for moral appraisal, clearly points to a conception of ethics in which the ultimate bearer of moral worth is excellence of a peculiarly private and spiritual kind: 'Provided the soul always has the means of happiness within itself, all the troubles coming from elsewhere are powerless to harm it. If anyone lives in such a way that his conscience cannot reproach him for ever failing to do something he judges to be the best, he will receive from this a satisfaction that has such power to make him happy that the most violent assaults of the passions will never have sufficient power to disturb the tranquillity of his soul.'[172]

The upshot of all this is that Descartes' picture of the good life emerges as a sometimes uneasy amalgam of disparate elements. His synoptic vision of ethics as an outgrowth from a complete philosophical and scientific system led him in the direction of an ethics of power and control: of man dominating the natural environment and manipulating his own psycho-physical responses so as to bring his emotional life into line with his rationally planned goals. But reflection on the extent to which human life must remain hostage to the unavoidability of pain and loss led him to retreat into a broadly Stoical kind of resignation, and identify the domain of the ethical with the only sphere wholly and entirely within our control.[173] The dream of power and manipulation gives way to a resigned acceptance of what is unavoidable, and a firm resolve to have the right attitude of submission to whatever comes about:

In view of the condition of human affairs, our demands upon Fortune would be excessive if we expected so many favours from her that we could find no cause for complaint even by exercising our imagination. When there are no objects present which offend the senses, or any indisposition which troubles the body, it is easy for a mind that follows true reason to be contented. For that, we do not need to forget or neglect objects which are not present: it is enough that we try to be dispassionate about those which may cause us distress.[174]

None of this is to prejudge the issue of whether the 'inward turn' represents an advance in our ethical thinking. It could well be argued that according supreme moral value to our inner resolve to do our best according to the dictates of conscience yields a far more humane and sympathetic conception of morality than the aristocratic, success-oriented ideal of the Aristotelians. But to explore that issue would take us too far from our present purpose.[175] What does emerge at the end of our examination of Cartesian ethics is that Descartes finished up resting his claims to show humans how best to live on the central ideal of generosity, defined as the resolute use of the will to follow the dictates of reason. It is in many respects a noble ideal, but as we shall see in the next chapter, it is vulnerable to the charge of glossing over those very difficulties about our complex human makeup which Descartes himself, in his pioneering work on the passions, had been at pains to expose. If, as Descartes often glimpsed, the origin and operation of our inmost drives and feelings is often opaque to the conscious subject, then there will always be a risk that the calm deliberations of reason about how best we should live will themselves be distorted by factors which the agent himself only dimly and imperfectly understands. Descartes himself had come near to laying the foundations for a systematic 'psychotherapy' of the passions – one prepared to delve into our early childhood so as to achieve a true understanding of the dynamics of our adult emotional life. But he never seriously questioned the idea that the thinking subject, endowed with reason, and conscientiously exercising his will to do what seems best, will be able to win through unaided, and grasp the prize of a fulfilling life. 'To pursue virtue in a perfect manner', he wrote in the last part of the *Passions of the Soul*, is 'never to lack the will to undertake and carry out whatever one judges to be the best'.[176] It remains to explore the developments in our own century which suggest that to achieve mastery in our own house, in the way envisaged by Descartes, may be a vastly more complex task than he suspected.

CHAPTER 4

Ethics and the challenge to reason

Nichts ist unwirksamer als intellecktuelle Ideen.
('Nothing influences our conduct less than do intellectual
ideas.')   C. G. Jung[1]

1. THE ECLIPSE OF REASON

L'homme se trouve devant l'irrationnel.
('Man stands face to face with the irrational.') Albert Camus[2]

The traditional project of synoptic ethics aims at the discovery of a
rational life-plan for human happiness; its achievement is the jewel
in the philosopher's crown, the ultimate accolade set on the activity
of philosophizing.[3] For the ancient Greek thinkers, what makes us
essentially human is above all our rationality, and the models of
well-being they offer are shaped by reason in the light of its best
perceptions of what will realize our true nature. The resulting
blueprint is either one where rational activity itself is viewed as the
supreme good, or else one in which reason is seen as the essential
coordinator and controller of the fulfilled life. Many centuries later,
we find in Descartes a view of ethics as part of a philosophical
system whose structure is illuminated by the 'light of reason'; the
end-point of philosophical knowledge is that we should reach a
clear understanding both of the world around us and of our own
human nature, and, armed with the power that understanding
brings, be able to bring about the conditions for a worthwhile life.

From our contemporary standpoint, we cannot approach the
optimistic ethics of the classical and early modern eras without
being aware of a powerful challenge to the traditional doctrine of
reason as the determiner and realizer of the conditions for the good

life. The challenge comes from many directions, but it is in the writings of the existentialists that it appears in its most striking form. Existentialism's most famous precursor, Friedrich Nietzsche, aims through his progressive extolling of the 'Dionysian' element in human nature, to show the radical limitations of the more rational 'Apollonian' perspective.[4] He speaks scathingly of the 'decadence' of Socrates, the very personification, the *fons et origo*, of rational philosophizing: so far from being the hero of the Western tradition, Socrates emerges, in Nietzsche's critique, as a pathological figure, irredeemably damaged by the 'hypertrophy' of the logical faculty. Those who philosophize after the Socratic model, patiently 'following the argument where it leads',[5] are the 'decadents of culture' because they try to insulate themselves from the power and mystery of the Dionysian instinct, wherein lies the 'will to life' – the true key to an existence that has meaning.[6]

In the existentialist thinkers who followed Nietzsche there is a new, counter-Socratic paradigm – the model of 'Irrational Man', to use William Barrett's apt label.[7] What was for the Classical Greek philosophers, and for generations of thinkers in the Western tradition that they inaugurated, the very defining essence of our humanity, becomes, in the new vision, something intensely problematic, even an obstacle to true fulfilment. And with this goes a rejection of philosophy itself, as traditionally conceived. The Socratic model of striving for philosophical wisdom by careful logical analysis is now seen as narrow, cramped and confined: to become fully human (or, in Nietzsche's more radical terms, to transcend the old limits and become 'more than human'),[8] we have to burst the restricting bonds of analytic rationality. The traditional vision of the philosopher gives way to a wider perspective in which self-realization and self-understanding arise from the dynamic operations of the raw will. Music, dance, poetry, sexuality – all these are expressions of the Dionysian spirit which is the key to a 'truer' and 'deeper' consciousness. 'Real knowledge', writes D. H. Lawrence, 'comes out of the whole corpus of the consciousness, out of your belly and your penis as much as out of your brain and mind. The mind can only analyse and rationalize. Set the mind and the reason to cock it over the rest, and all they can do is to criticize, and make a deadness.'[9]

To many, the rhetoric of irrationalism can seem both pretentious and dangerous. For Bertrand Russell, it was the kind of 'rubbish' that 'led straight to Auschwitz'.[10] That reaction may be unfair: if there is any connection at all between the joyful vision of self-realization found in Nietzsche and Lawrence and the methodical cruelty of the Nazis, it is certainly not a direct and straightforward one. Ruthlessness need not be an essential attribute of the critics of rationality, any more than gentleness is necessarily the prerogative of its apostles (to counteract that bromide, it is useful to recall that Russell himself, the champion of analytic rationality, was for a time a supporter of dropping atomic bombs on Russia to force her to agree to the internationalization of such weapons).[11] The connection between moral enlightenment and the careful employment of reason is evidently a complex one: the latter is certainly not sufficient for the former, though one may very plausibly consider, with Russell, that it is at least necessary. Be all that as it may, however, there is another and more pervasive criticism which the rhetoric of irrationalism has to face, namely that it is self-defeating. For in order to be able to articulate any position whatsoever, one must perforce accept at least some of the traditional 'Socratic' constraints – formal consistency, reliance on a framework of meaning-rules and logical operators – since without these nothing significant could be said. If the antagonists of reason are to tell us anything at all, and not merely gesture and grunt, they are necessarily obliged to conform, at least in some measure, to the constraints of coherent discourse.

Yet when these caveats have been entered, there remains something important, and sayable, about the modernist challenge to reason. One way of putting the challenge is that chosen by Heidegger, whose relationship to the traditional Greek mode of philosophizing has something of the flavour of Nietzsche's. Heidegger's reiterated point about the Socratic model of controlling reason is that it lacks the dimension of open responsiveness to the irreducible contingency of our human existence. We are not rationally in charge of nature, whether the nature of the world around us, or that of our own humanity. Rather – this is the clear implication of Heidegger's famous term *Geworfenheit* – we are 'thrown' into existence. The passiveness implicit in this label suggests that we find ourselves precipitated into a raw mode of being: Heidegger's central term for human existence, *Dasein* ('being there') is suggestive of a mode of existence that we cannot fully encompass or control. And the appropriate response to this is not to hanker for the old models of rational dominance found in Classical and Cartesian philosophy, but rather to strive towards an openness, a balanced adjustment to the existential reality in which we find ourselves – the response which Heidegger calls *Stimmung,* or 'tuning'. The contrast between this modulated, harmonic attunement, whose keynotes are openness and wonder, and the dogged drive for rational hegemony is elegantly summarized by one of Heidegger's most insightful expositors:

Heidegger proceeds to challenge Descartes and the Cartesian foundations in all subsequent models of rational, scientific knowing. For Descartes, truth is determined and validated by certainty . . . The self becomes the hub of reality and relates to the world outside itself in an exploratory, necessarily exploitative, way. As knower and user, the *ego* is predator. For Heidegger, on the contrary, the human person and self-consciousness are not the centre, the assessors of existence. Man is only a privileged listener and respondent to existence. The vital relation to otherness is not, as for post Cartesian and positivist rationalism, one of 'grasping' and pragmatic use. It is a relation of audition. We are trying 'to listen to the voice of Being'. It is, or ought to be, a relation of extreme responsibility, custodianship, *answerability to and for* (the Heideggerian term is *Entsprechen*). Of this answerability, the thinker and the poet, *der Denker und der Dichter,* are at once the carriers and the trustees.[12]

The implications of this new vision of philosophical understanding are at once more humbling, and more dangerous, than anything put forward in the traditional ratiocentric conception. More humbling because the old dream of mastery of ourselves and our environment is abandoned. Instead of trying to use reason in order to become, in Descartes' famous phrase, *maîtres et possesseurs de la nature,*[13] instead of arrogantly attempting to control nature and bend it to the demands of the rational will, we take an essentially submissive stance: we give ourselves over to 'the voice of being' (*die Stimme des Seins*), and allow ourselves to come into tuneful accord (*Stimmung*) with that voice. In a certain sense, in terms of the ancient antithesis between 'natural' and 'revealed' truths,[14] the move is towards the latter; there is a shift away from philosophy as rational confrontation, and towards a quasi-theological model of philosophy as devotion and submission.[15] In the words of the old pietist tag which Heidegger was fond of quoting, *Denken ist Danken* – the very act of philosophical thought becomes a submissive act of openness and thanksgiving. Thought 'lets Being be' (*das Denken lässt das Sein sein*).[16] But the move is also a more dangerous one than anything envisaged by the old model of the philosopher as the controlling rational agent. The mastery of nature, and of self, held out to earlier philosophers the dream of immunity from fortune – the insulation of human well-being from our vulnerability to fortune.[17] In the new vision of openness and 'listening', that illusion of security is swept away. The path ahead is a perilous one, which offers no rational guarantees. But precisely in the bold abandoning of ourselves to the mystery of being, with all its perils, lies the hope of salvation. In the words of Friedrich Hölderlin's celebrated poem, quoted by Heidegger in one of his later essays, 'Wo aber Gefahr ist, wächst / das Rettende auch' ('Where there is danger, the agency of salvation waxes strong').[18]

Even among those who may be sceptical about the Heideggerian style of philosophy, there are reasons why his attack on the claims of controlling reason should strike some responsive chords. Within the realm of analytic philosophizing itself there has been, during the present century, a growing disquiet about the traditional claims of ratiocentric philosophy to map out the essential structure of reality. Many, perhaps most, philosophers working today are highly doubtful about the notion of a *definitive* route to the truth, encapsulated in Descartes' bravely announced 'method of rightly conducting reason and reaching the truth in the sciences'. The idea that we can determine the ultimate structure of reality, uncover the universe 'as it really is', now looks distinctly problematic. Relativistic philosophers of science have reminded us of the cultural and historical forces which mediate and condition the 'advances' of science;[19] semantic theorists have stressed the impossibility of stepping outside our conceptual scheme to achieve a 'God's eye view' of reality;[20] post-modernist thinkers have underlined the fluidity and 'contingency' of all human discourse;[21] philosophers of knowledge have lambasted the very project of 'foundational epistemology' as a doomed attempt to base a theory of knowledge on self-evident, self-standing axioms.[22] For these and many other reasons there are grounds to take seriously the Heideggerian strictures on the self-confident ratiocentric project of science and philosophy, as traditionally conceived.[23]

Powerfully suggestive though it is, however, the Heideggerian vision often seems to offer no more than a glimpse of the way forward. In common with the existentialist writers of the mid and late twentieth century who were so indebted to him, Heidegger tells us a lot about what authentic human well-being is *not* (it is not based on rational control, it is not derivable from the results of Aristotelian-Cartesian essentialism), but provides only hints of what it *is*. The forest clearing, the *Lichtung*, which Heidegger envisaged as the quiet place where the voice of Being would be heard, remains a destination glimpsed through the trees, but the conditions for our arrival there are left somewhat vague. Indeed, precisely because reality, for Heidegger, is characterized in such an insistently indeterminate way – it is not scientific reality, it transcends traditional ontological categories, it is mere being, the 'Being of Being' – critics have charged Heidegger with being fonder of uttering portentous phrases than with getting down to the task of constructing a detailed blueprint for authenticity.[24]

The problem is already observable in the existentialist thinkers who preceded Heidegger. Truth, for Kierkegaard, is 'subjectivity'. And what this seems to mean is that any attempt to devise a coherent, objectively assessable answer to the ancient philosophical problem of how we are to live is disqualified from the outset. We know we have to be authentic, to resist the neat answers of rationalism and essentialism, but beyond that there is nothing very clear on offer. We have to 'listen to the voice of being', to avoid the inauthentic and self-deceiving solutions which Sartre labelled 'bad faith'; but the more sceptical critics of the existentialist tradition have asked whether this comes down to much more than the vacuous injunction to be 'laid back' and 'do your own thing'. To such critics, the existentialists seem to lure us down into a murky cellar where any supposed victory over traditional ratiocentrism is bought at the cost of dwelling in darkness too profound for anyone to see what is actually going on (the simile, aptly enough, is one that was first used by Descartes to dismiss the pseudo-profundities of his obscurantist opponents).[25] We seem here to have an unbridgeable chasm, from the edges of which the upholders of the analytic-rational tradition on the one side, and the subjectivist philosophers of Existence on the other, gaze across at each other in mutual incomprehension. If ever there was a case calling for a Hegelian synthesis, preserving the insights of each tradition, but transmuting and 'raising' (*aufheben*) what is inadequate, this would surely seem to be it.[26] For the activity of philosophizing has always drawn its strength from such confrontations or boundary disputes. Where different traditions clash, where different approaches yield incompatible results, the philosopher's task has characteristically been to see how, if at all, the contradictions can be resolved in a deeper, and more comprehensive world-view. To return to the point made earlier, a blank rejection of the claims of reason cannot, ultimately be a satisfying solution, if only because it is self-stultifying; while on the other hand we have all gone too far down the modernist road to allow a simple re-assertion of the ratiocentric view to sound anything other than smug and superficial.[27] What seems required is an approach which will come to terms with modernist insights about the dangers and limitations of 'logocentric philosophy', while at the same time preserving a role for reason which will enable us to do more than mouth slogans about the being of Being.

Yet a patient reading of Heidegger's voluminous writings does in the end turn out to provide the material for a response to the charge of portentous obscurantism. What Heidegger is at pains to stress is that the world is encountered in fundamentally human terms. In our dealings with the world we come across 'gear' or 'tackle' (*Zeug*): 'equipment for writing, sewing, transport, measurement . . .' We encounter a room 'not as something between four walls (in the geometrical, spatial sense) but as equipment for residing'. The being of objects is thus a function of what Heidegger calls their 'readiness-to-hand' or *Zuhandenheit* (for example, a hammer exists not as an object with abstract physical properties, but in the context of its use and function, in terms of our human concerns). This practical slant to Heidegger's ontology makes it im-

portantly different from those rather austere earlier metaphysical
systems (particularly those of the seventeenth century)[28] which had
aimed to delineate the objective essences of things in abstraction
from the human perspective. To exist as a human being is, for
Heidegger, already to be involved in specific projects and concerns; Heideggerian metaphysics thus turns out in the end to be
not an abstract study of being, but rather an enterprise where
understanding and valuing are inextricably intertwined. In
coming to terms with the world we are drawn into a practical
community of other involved agents, and thus into 'solicitous
concern for others' – what Heidegger calls *Sorge*, or 'Caring'.[29]

Though there is much here that bears investigation, I do not
propose to develop further the Heideggerian response to our
ethical predicament (though I shall return to some aspects of it in
later sections of this chapter).[30] Rather than beating the existentialist drum, I shall suggest instead that a more promising way
forward is to turn to the resources of modern psychoanalytic
theory. There are still deep prejudices in many quarters about the
work of the founders of that movement: the theories of Sigmund
Freud are often seen as involving a crudely reductionistic view of
human motivation, while the ideas of Carl Jung sometimes appear to touch the wilder shores of mysticism. I shall certainly not
be nailing my colours to the masthead of either the Freudian or
the Jungian ship, or to that of any one of the many later vessels in
the psychoanalytic fleet.[31] Indeed, I shall risk outraging the specialized territoriality of the movement by drawing freely on insights derived from various sources, Freudian, Jungian, and
Lacanian. Without attempting the probably impossible task of
providing a synthesis, or aiming to reconcile the many differences
of emphasis, I shall adopt an explicitly eclectic stance, extracting
whatever seems to yield results applicable to the task in hand.
The aim will be to uncover the seeds of an approach which comes
to terms with the incapacity of controlling reason to settle the
conditions for human well-being, while at the same time not
abandoning the values of systematic analysis and rational reflection. But before I turn to this task, I need to take a few moments
to prepare the ground. For a large number of thinkers from the

analytic tradition have been so deeply sceptical of the scientific and philosophical claims of psychoanalysis as to put this area virtually off limits to philosophers for much of the twentieth century. This resolutely sceptical stance has, it is true, begun to be seriously eroded in the last decade or so. But it will nonetheless be useful to survey some of the main worries voiced by the detractors of the psychoanalytic movement, in order to clear the way forward.

2. PSYCHOANALYSIS AND ITS CREDENTIALS

Die wenigsten Menschen dürften sich klar gemacht haben einen wie folgenschweren Schritt die Annahme unbewußter seelischer Vorgänger fur Wissenschaft und Leben bedeuten würde.

('Probably but very few people have realized the momentous significance for science and life of the recognition of unconscious mental processes.') Sigmund Freud[32]

Modern analytic philosophy has by now partly grown out of the sport of Freud-bashing that became fashionable among the smugger practitioners of the 'ordinary language' philosophy of the nineteen-sixties. So deeply is our contemporary culture and language pervaded by concepts and attitudes stemming from the psychoanalytic movement, that it would be hard today to find any antagonist jumping in as rashly as the Oxford don who is alleged to have 'refuted' Freud by observing that the expression 'unconscious mind' was simply a contradiction, and that was that.[33] To be sure, many psychoanalytic concepts (especially what one might call the more 'technical' notions such as 'abreaction', 'anaclitic object choice', 'cathexis') remain to most people either obscure or highly problematic (and indeed are the subject of fierce controversy among the theorists themselves); but many others – 'repression', 'rationalization', 'sublimation'– are now pretty much taken for granted in our everyday modes of self-understanding, so much so that the vehement critics of Freud are sometimes found employing them in their very diatribes against psychoanalysis, curiously unaware of all they have accepted. Yet there are, nevertheless, major conceptual problems in the notion of unconscious mentation which demand philosophical scrutiny. Before coming to these (in section 3), it will be useful, in the present section, to deal first with some influential criticisms of the psychoanalytic movement which come instead from an empirical and what may be called a 'sociological' direction.

To begin with, the 'clinical credentials' of psychoanalytic theory (the term is Grünbaum's)[34] have been subject to searching examination: there have been serious specific doubts about the way in which Freud himself managed and evaluated the empirical data supposed to support his views, and more general worries about the extent to which he and his subsequent disciples insulated themselves from the possibility of serious empirical testing of their clinical success rates. What seems clear from these debates, however, is that while the scientific methodology of some, perhaps many, of the clinical practitioners of psychoanalysis is open to criticism, there is no reason in principle why the success or otherwise of psychoanalytic practice cannot be put to empirical test.[35] But now a second and more complex difficulty arises. Since the demise of logical positivism, it has become apparent that the relation between any explanatory theory and the relevant data is not, and cannot be, so tight-fitting as to constitute decisive verification or falsification. If this is a problem with the 'hard' physical sciences, it is *a fortiori* likely to pose an even more serious worry in the psychological arena – or at least in that part of psychology where we are dealing directly with phenomena as complex as the beliefs and desires of the subject, and their interpretation. Because of the complexities of the semantic dimension here, many psychoanalytic theorists have been content with a more anecdotal or narrative approach, citing as support for the theory detailed individual case histories, and arguing that the interpretations offered derive their plausibility from the fact that in the actual experience of patient and analyst alike they are felt to have a deep explanatory power.[36]

The anecdotal approach cannot, of course, yield anything approaching conclusive verification, but as Thomas Nagel has pointed out, reflection on individual cases often provides a peculiarly vivid kind of illumination which it seems extremely hard to explain other than in broadly psychoanalytic terms. Here is one such case, drawn from Nagel's own experience:

At a dinner party, an elderly man of independent means, who had spent his life as a private scholar without an academic position, challenged a psychiatrist who was present to explain why, whenever he listened to the news on the radio, he fell asleep just at the point when the stock market report came on. The psychiatrist, knowing these facts, replied that it probably expressed difficult feelings about his father. 'My *father!*', said the man incredulously, 'My father has been dead for fifty years!' The conversation then went on to other things, but the next day, the man telephoned the psychiatrist to report that later in the evening the memory had come flooding back to him that when, in his youth, he had resisted going into the family business, his father had made him promise at least to listen to the stock market report on the radio every day.[37]

Many people could cite similar examples known to them, which, while falling short of 'clinching evidence', nonetheless seem to provide what are prima facie extremely plausible instances of the operation of unconscious mental processes; and this in turn, in Nagel's words 'makes it credible that more extensive and systematic insights of the same type can be developed by analysts who probe far more deeply and uncover far more material for interpretation'.[38]

Here, though, a more radical criticism has been put forward, one which does not deny the authority and convincingness of the proffered interpretations for the subjects themselves, but which argues that that very power derives from a kind of systematic bamboozling of the patient. Ernest Gellner, one of the psychoanalytic movement's most trenchant critics, cites no less than eight sinister features which he takes to explain the perceived power of psychoanalytic interpretations for those who submit themselves to analysis, and which (if he is right) could undermine the legitimacy of those interpretations. The psychoanalytic patient is (i) utterly passive and vulnerable (he is urged to hold nothing back), yet at the same time, though revealing the most intimate details of his life, is (ii) cocooned on the consulting room couch, in a euphoric state of relaxation which permits total escape from the responsibilities and demands of normal reality. He is moreover (iii) buoyed up by the hope of a 'cure', which will encourage him to accept the authority and healing power of the analyst; yet at the same time (iv) he is prevented from being able to evaluate that power, since he is disoriented by the suspension of the normal dynamic structure of two-way social interaction (the analyst never argues, never judges, never gets angry or excited, only listens). Furthermore, (v) there is a kind of dependence analogous to addiction involved in the psychoanalytic process: the patient is desperately eager for 'progress' – for an improvement in his condition or completion of the therapy, while at the same time the judgements and interpretations of the analyst that might contribute to this process are doled out 'in measured and carefully delayed doses'. (vi) Reinforcing the dependence, the analyst provides a seductively rare commodity, total absorbed attention; but (vii) unlike any other close and intimate relationship involving personal attention, the psychoanalytic one is 'test proof': no sacrifices may be asked of the analyst, no extra time and attention demanded beyond that paid for, no promises, pledges, or other demonstrations of commitment, may be given. Finally, and most powerfully of all, (viii) the patient is in the grip of a 'double bind' with respect to the therapeutic process: on the one hand he must utterly abandon himself to the non-directed process of free association (only thereby can the unconscious defences be penetrated); yet at the same time there is the background knowledge that some analyses 'go well' and others 'badly', and that it is somehow mainly up to the patient to make things 'go well' (for example, the analyst never initiates the sessions – it is always for the patient to get things going). 'Under these contradictory rules', concludes Gellner, 'it can always be ensured and insinuated, tacitly conveyed, that it is [the patient's] fault. Perhaps he is not trying enough? Or equally, with even greater cogency, is it not failing because he is *trying*, exercising his will, when he should be surrendering himself?'[39]

We shall have occasion to revisit Gellner's diatribe at a later stage,[40] but some initial evaluation is in order here. To begin with, it might be objected at a superficial level that all the Gellnerian criticisms show is that the psychoanalytic relationship (like many others: doctor/patient, teacher/student, priest/parishioner) is, by virtue of its power structure, always potentially open to abuse, and always places special responsibilities on those in such positions of authority. That much is of course true, but does not in itself undermine the validity of what goes on in such relationships. Gellner's point however is not just that the psychoanalytic relationship offers scope for abuse, but that its very structure, even when everything is working 'as it should', is designed to erode the patient's ability to retain a detached critical stance with respect to what is going on. Yet it is important to see that, even interpreted in this way, the Gellnerian criticisms do not in themselves undermine the validity of the psychoanalytic process. Indeed, in a certain sense they presuppose it. On Gellner's own admission, his explanations are explanations of that complex relation of dependence of the patient on the analyst which Freud famously called *transference*, and which he came to see as crucial to the psychoanalytic process; transference is, Gellner admits, an 'indisputably crucial and genuine phenomenon'.[41] But what his criticisms imply, and this is the key point, is that though the phenomenon is genuine enough, its causal genesis derives directly from the vulnerability of the patient and the manipulative structure of the psychotherapeutic 'set up' – in such a way that there is no further need to posit the *truth* of psychoanalytic theory to explain the (undeniable) power of what is going on. In a sense the Gellnerian approach is rather like that of dispassionate scientific observers of religious phenomena such as the (regularly announced) miracles at Lourdes. Such observers do not deny that something powerful is occurring, but (quite plausibly, perhaps) attribute most of it to the excited state and acute suggestibility of the supplicants, coupled with certain empirically established results (for example the power of subjective conviction to produce the sometimes indisputably beneficial effects associated with phenomena like 'faith-healing').

At this point the situation seems to be that we have, both in the psychoanalytic and the analogous religious case, a corpus of impressive empirical phenomena relating to important (and often ameliorative) changes in the mental or physical health of those involved. The question is now simply one of 'inference to the best explanation': *is* the truth of psychoanalytic theory (or the truth of the relevant tenets of Catholicism) the most plausible explanation for the results seen? A defender of the psychoanalytic approach might reply here that the relevant inference is indeed supported by the way in which the insights achieved in therapy are seen by the subjects themselves as 'making sense' – as generating deep and lasting resonances which affect the way they understand themselves and their relationships. The concepts, language and interpretative schemas acquired via the psychoanalytic process have, in short, a compelling power which ever after informs the outlook of those who have undergone the process. A perhaps unfairly *ad hominem* but nonetheless striking observation in this connection is that Gellner's own language, even as he criticizes the theory, is deeply imbued with Freudian and psychoanalytic resonances: his very rationalistic explanation of the transference process is couched in terms that, in spite of his scepticism, seem vividly to presuppose the interpretative structures he so insistently condemns:

> Though in one way it may be a great relief *to let go the sphincters of the mind,* on the another hand it cannot but inspire *shame and guilt* to present a mass of material, inevitably *disreputable and undignified* both logically and morally. The normal presentation of the self *must* be selective: it isn't just the *improper parts that are hidden* but so is, perhaps primarily, that total chaos which pervades our stream of consciousness. To free-associate genuinely in the presence of another is like *undressing on a day on which one is wearing badly soiled underwear:* or like receiving someone in a bed-sitter which one hasn't tidied up for weeks. To do it deliberately is to indulge in *an extreme case of that role-reversal* which signals the presence of the Exceptional, an initiation to the sacred.[42]

It does not require a detailed knowledge of the history of twentieth-century ideas to see that not just the tone and the turn of phrase, but the very structure of the thoughts expressed here, the wry self-awareness, the deep understanding of the tensions between adult respectability and infantile helplessness – everything bears the unmistakable imprint of our modern, post-Freudian world-view.

Yet all of this still leaves open the substantive doubt which Gellner has nonetheless managed to raise. The Gellnerian critic can readily admit the compelling power of the psychoanalytic framework (and even wryly demonstrate this in his own writing), while still maintaining that the truths it purports to purvey are suspect. The analogy with religious initiation (explicitly invoked by Gellner in the last sentence of the paragraph quoted) is once more revealing here. In an epoch when theological models of understanding were dominant, the writings even of atheistical critics might have been liable to be infected with the language and presuppositions of the religious outlook; yet for all that, it still remains an open question whether the (alleged) truths of religion *were* the best explanation for the relevant psychological and social phenomena, and for the resonant power of religious ideas in the lives of its adherents.

So long as we remain within the realm of the 'sociology of knowledge', the reflections so far canvassed seem to present us with an impasse. The Gellnerian approach offers us a plausible explanation for the perceived power of psychoanalytic theory to command the allegiance of its devotees; it provides a disquieting analogy with other types of practice and belief system which maintain their dominance through techniques relying on suggestibility and a complex apparatus of authority and control; but at the end of the day the actual truth of the target theory (or, if you will, its epistemic and scientific respectability) remains an open question. It would probably be fruitless, at this point, to try to advance the debate by drawing a dividing line between belief systems which are, and those which are not, objectively and scientifically supported, and then to try to place psychoanalytic theory one or other side of that supposed divide. For if the philosophy of science of the last two decades has revealed anything it is how intensely problematic is the project of trying to establish such a dividing line in any clear and non-question-begging way. Whether in the end psychoanalysis will retain a dominant place in our intellectual culture, whether it will increasingly be accepted as a legitimate route to understanding, or instead be relegated to the epistemic dustbin of superstition and charlatanry, is likely to depend on a complex of factors which it is beyond the power of the philosophical (or other) critic to determine in advance. What the philosopher surely can do, and is entitled to do, is to examine the central concepts of the theory, and scrutinize both their internal consistency and the degree to which they cohere with the other elements of our world-view.

3. THE CONCEPT OF THE UNCONSCIOUS
AND ITS HISTORICAL ANTECEDENTS

Wie das Physische, so braucht auch das Psychische nicht in Wirklichkeit so zu sein, wie es uns erscheint.

('Like the physical, the psychical is not necessarily in reality what it appears to us to be.') Sigmund Freud[43]

We have now arrived at the area where the philosophical criticism of psychoanalytic theory has been most intense, and most potentially damaging. The charge, in brief, has been that there are deep inherent confusions, and even perhaps outright contradictions, in the central concept of psychoanalytic theory, that of the unconscious mind. As is well known, the unconscious is the pivotal notion on which Freudians, Jungians, and almost all the various subsequent branches of psychoanalytic theory, have relied. It plays a crucial role in the importance assigned to dreams and their interpretation, and it is the primary explanatory concept which is invoked in the diagnosis of a whole range of neurotic, disjointed and disturbed behaviour, as well as more familiar and run-of-the-mill phenomena like depression, unhappiness, confusion and problems of motivation. Freud himself was aware that the notion of the unconscious mind would strike many critics as problematic, though he was equally firm that those of his critics who equated the realm of the mental with the realm of consciousness were guilty, as he put it, of an arbitrary *petitio principii.*[44]

But is it so arbitrary? Many philosophers have been taught to believe that there is a strong analytic connection between the concept of mind and the notion of conscious awareness. This strong link is often attributed to Descartes, and in some quarters it has become a ruling dogma – what is sometimes called the doctrine of the 'transparency of the mind'. There are in fact two distinct doctrines which might be suggested by this label. The first, which Descartes certainly did assert, is the thesis that in introspection the mind has a full and complete awareness of its own nature as a thinking thing: 'I can achieve an easier and more evident perception of my own mind than of anything else' (Second Meditation).[45] That doctrine was aptly criticized by Descartes' deviant disciple, Nicolas Malebranche: Malebranche agreed that when we introspect we are indubitably aware of the *existence* of something which is thinking, but went on to argue that there was no reason to suppose that this privileged awareness of existence amounted to a grasp of the *nature or essence* of the underlying substance that was doing the thinking. If anything, Malebranche pointed out, our knowledge of the nature of mind is less, not more, distinct that our knowledge of the nature of bodies. '*Je ne suis que ténèbres a moi-même*: to myself I am but darkness, and my own substance seems something which is beyond my understanding.'[46]

Transparency may be construed in a second way, however, which does not offer hostages to the dubious forces of Cartesian epistemology and metaphysics, namely as the assertion of a straightforward conceptual link between something's being in S's mind and S's being aware of it. This supposed link retains its hold even among critics of Descartes; thus many of those who have no truck whatever with the Cartesian doctrine of the mind as a separate incorporeal substance still tend to go along with the view that it is consciousness which constitutes the essence of mentality. (Precisely what is supposed by many to be wrong with behaviourism, for example, is that by treating a mental state like pain as a complex kind of disposition to act and react in certain ways, we ignore its crucial phenomenological character – its essential nature as a characteristic mode of conscious awareness.)

Closer examination reveals, however, that the equation of the contents of the mind with those items of which I am directly and consciously aware is actually an untenable and confused position, and one moreover which Descartes himself almost certainly did not maintain. In the first place, the term 'consciousness' is not in Descartes' normal philosophical vocabulary. The defining characteristic of the mind, for Descartes, is not consciousness but thought, *cogitatio*; and (despite the over-interpretative moves of some translators) to render this term as 'consciousness' is misleading and anachronistic.[47] It is true, nevertheless, that the notion of direct introspective awareness does play a crucial role in Descartes' account of *cogitatio* : 'I use this term', he observed, 'to include everything that is within us in such a way that we are immediately aware of it.'[48] This of course emerges as a key feature in the setting up of the foundations of knowledge by means of the famous Cogito argument. When I say '*cogito ergo sum*', the privileged status of the premise hinges on the fact that there is something going on within me of which I am directly aware, and which I cannot doubt. It may seem a short step from this to the conclusion that the realm of the mental is to be equated directly with the transparent contents of conscious awareness. Yet even in Descartes, the supposed arch-transparency theorist, there lurks, behind this apparently simple picture, a much more complex account of the mind and its workings. That more complex account goes far beyond the present and continuous flow of transparent items of thought.

To begin with, the Cartesian account of the mind involves the notion that it is stocked with *ideas*. Descartes is sometimes taken to use the terms 'idea' and 'thought' interchangeably, but in fact he carefully distinguishes the two. In the list of definitions of technical terms which he supplies at the end of the Second Set of Replies (printed with the first edition of the *Meditations*), we find the term 'idea' defined not in psychological but in logical terms: an idea is the 'form of any given thought'.[49] In the Third Meditation, the meditator makes an inventory of the ideas which he finds within him, and the resulting list includes many items which are evidently supposed to be 'in' the mind, and yet which need not be directly present to consciousness. One such is the idea of God, which (for those who do not have a taste for metaphysical meditations) *may not ever surface at all*: the idea of God (with the results derived from it) is compared to the idea of a geometrical figure (with its complex attendant properties). One could go through life, says Descartes, without ever contemplating the idea or bringing it into the light of conscious awareness: 'It is not necessary that I ever light upon any thought of God; but whenever I do choose to think of the first and supreme being, and bring forth the idea of God as it were from the treasure house of my mind, it is necessary that I attribute all perfections to him.'[50] What is 'in my mind', then, is not all the same as what is present to consciousness: the two notions are neither extensionally nor intensionally equivalent. The mind is like a treasure house (*thesaurus*) stocked with ideas which may or may not surface as the objects of conscious attention.[51] Descartes lays particular emphasis on this point when speculating on what the mind of an infant is like:

It seems reasonable to think that a mind newly united to an infant's body is wholly occupied in perceiving or feeling the ideas of pain, pleasure, heat, cold and other similar ideas which arise from its union and intermingling with the body. Nonetheless, it has in itself the ideas of God, itself, and all such truths are called self-evident, in the same way as adult humans have when they are not attending to them.[32]

There are interesting ambiguities in this notion of something's being present in the mind without being attended to. It seems plausible to construe much of Descartes' talk of the mind's being stocked with ideas in a *dispositional* way: that is, the mind has a disposition to come up with certain thoughts when suitably stimulated (for example it will see the truth of certain propositions about God, or about triangles, when it reflects on these concepts). In this sense, the stock of my knowledge may be said to include the idea that Paris is the capital of France, without implying that I am actually entertaining this thought at any given time. There is, however, a richer sense, not dispositional but *occurrent*, in which a thought can be said to be 'present' without being attended to – the sense in which the thought that I must buy a ticket to Paris tomorrow can 'hover at the back of my mind' when I am making an appointment to see the dentist today. Reflection on this type of case suggests that the transparency thesis may need to be qualified not just by allowing for unactivated dispositions, but in a more radical way. For since attention is often a matter of degree, the possibility arises of allowing for occurrent mental contents which are just above, or just below the threshold of full conscious awareness. Descartes himself uses in this connection the metaphor of a thought being 'submerged' or 'swamped'; he also speaks of one thought 'obstructing' another. And it is striking that he does not confine these metaphors to the rather special topic of innate forms of knowledge, but also employs them when discussing individual mental episodes. When we prick ourselves with a sharp instrument, the urgency of the painful stimulus may be such as to obstruct everything else that is in the mind.[33] But of course (though Descartes does not make this explicit) the obstruction cannot be total, since (short of actually fainting) we retain, even when subject to agonizing pain, some residual awareness of our surroundings and situation. To change the metaphor, one might say that an intrusive bodily stimulus pushes other mental contents out of focus, or to the outer edge of awareness. Another example Descartes uses in this connection is that of someone who is 'half-asleep' (*semi-somnolens*);[54] the point, presumably, is that in such a state thoughts swim in and out of focus. The upshot of these examples is that transparent conscious awareness ceases to be an 'all or nothing' criterion of the mental; what is going on 'in the mind' becomes a complex matter which admits of degrees of focus, or degrees of immediacy. For a pure disembodied spirit (the 'angel' which Descartes so often discusses),[55] mental life would presumably be a clear flow of utterly transparent conscious episodes; but for human creatures whose minds are 'intermingled' with matter, there will frequently be a fuzziness, a dimming or even swamping of attention, as the intrusive signals from the body make themselves felt.

Mention of the 'intermingling' of mind with body takes us beyond the strict dualism of Descartes' official metaphysics to what I have earlier called Cartesian 'anthropology' – Descartes' account of the nature of that embodied creature of flesh and blood, the *human being*. In the kind of awareness we have of the emotions and passions that arise from our human status, Descartes maintains (as I have argued in Chapter Three) that so far from transparency, a pervasive opacity obtains. In the case of love, for example, Descartes tells us that the (transparent) rational thoughts involved are 'often accompanied by the confused feelings of our childhood which remain joined to them'. To understand exactly what is going on when we feel the passion of love, we have to delve back into the past, even as far as our experiences at the breast at infancy 'when we first came into the world'; and it is this, according to Descartes, which makes our experiences of passionate love 'so hard for us to understand'.[56] A proper understanding of our human nature involves recognition of the extent to which we are not just angelic minds inhabiting bodily mechanisms, but creatures whose deepest and strongest feelings are 'obscure and confused', because intimately tied up with structures and events which are concealed from us as 'thinking beings'.

The stage is now set for disentangling the actual Descartes from the 'transparency theorist' caricature – for acquitting him of the charge of crudely equating the concept of the mind with that of immediate conscious awareness. Descartes' position, as it has so far emerged from our analysis, does in the first place unmistakably allow for items which are 'in' the mind (in a dispositional sense) though not present to conscious awareness. In the second place, even with respect to occurrent mental states, Descartes acknowledges the possibility that the boundary of the mental may be fuzzy and indeterminate, with thoughts alternately rising above and falling below the level corresponding to direct attentive awareness. It is worth remembering here that Descartes often stresses that mental activity can occur in early infancy, and in sleep, even though the degree of awareness involved in such cases must evidently fall far short of the paradigm of full conscious attention.[57] Lastly, with special reference to the passions, when Descartes moves from the incorporeal mind (the subject of his official metaphysics) to his theory of the embodied human being (the subject of his ethics), he allows, even insists, on a considerable degree of opacity in our self-awareness. The upshot is that Descartes' account of the mind is a good deal more sophisticated than is suggested by those commentators who imply that the Cartesian mind is a simple transparent goldfish bowl, with ideas swimming around for inspection in the glass container of consciousness.

If, in the light of this, we consult the work of those writing on the mind in the period following Descartes' death, the Cartesian position appears as considerably more subtle than that of some of its empiricist critics. In his famous attack on Cartesian innateness, Locke bluntly asserted that 'No Proposition can be said to be in the Mind which it never yet knew, which it was never yet conscious of.'[58] Against the disciples of Descartes who subscribed to the theory that we are born with innate ideas imprinted on our minds, Locke retorted that 'to imprint anything on the Mind without the Mind's perceiving it seems to me hardly intelligible'.[59] If we are looking for a philosophical architect of the transparency thesis, then it appears to be Locke, rather than Descartes, who is guilty of making a simplistic equation – regarding the mind as a blank sheet of paper or wax tablet on which clear, and always in principle readable, impressions are stamped. The intuitions of Leibniz, writing only a decade or so after Locke, were rather closer to what we have seen to be the more nuanced and explanatorily richer view of Descartes: for Leibniz, an idea can be imprinted, in some form, in the mind, without our needing to suppose that the mind is 'an open book' in which the printed matter is just there in front of us waiting to be read.[60]

Nevertheless, Leibniz himself was convinced that Descartes, for all his insights into the innate properties of the mind, had still been guilty of serious oversimplification about the mind's nature. As is well known, he drew a distinction between mental activity simpliciter, or what he called 'perception', and reflective awareness of that activity, which he termed 'apperception'. The latter activity, he argued, requires *attention* :

All attention demands some memory, and often when we are not admonished, so to speak, and warned to pay attention to certain of our present perceptions, we let them pass without reflection and even without noticing them; but if someone draws attention to them immediately afterwards, and makes us notice, for example, some sound that has just been heard, we remember it, and we apperceive that we did have some sensation of it at the time. Thus there were perceptions which we did not immediately apperceive . . . Herein lies the great mistake of the Cartesians, that they took no account of perceptions which are not apperceived.[61]

In fact, despite Leibniz's typically triumphalist tone (implying he had spotted something which everyone before him had missed), there is nothing in the actual assertions in this quotation that is not consistent with Descartes' more complex picture of the mind as outlined above. Descartes frequently distinguished between something's being in the mind, and our attending to it;[62] and he explicitly notes that thoughts can be present in a dim and confused manner which falls short of explicit reflective awareness.[63] Leibniz does go on, of course, to articulate a concept of 'perception' that goes way beyond the Cartesian one, allowing that there may be, even in what he calls 'bare monads' (the ultimate substances of which all reality is composed) some germ of perception. Even in animals, even in stones, there is some faint 'perceptual' or representational activity – what Leibniz called *petites perceptions* – in virtue of which every monad is a 'perpetual living mirror' of the whole universe. But to explore this (in my view dubious and problematic) 'panpsychist' trend in Leibniz's thought would take us too far from the present purpose.[64] What emerges clearly in the human case (both for Leibniz and for Descartes) is that there can be mental activity which falls short of full reflective awareness, and that even when the mind is not engaging in rational cogitations there can be confused and fleeting mental activity of a kind which often does not, as it were, reach the transparent surface of consciousness because the relevant kind of attention is absent, or the attention is directed elsewhere.

I do not wish to claim here that there are fully explicit anticipations of the modern doctrine of the unconscious mind in this Cartesian and Leibnizian acknowledgement of the possibility of mental activity not fully integrated into conscious awareness.[65] But what does seem to be the case is that the modern (Freudian) notion,[66] so far from being a radical innovation starkly at odds with earlier views, is a natural and readily intelligible extension of fairly straightforward common-sense beliefs about the mind which are readily apparent in seventeenth-century (and no doubt many other) writers. Contemporary critics of the psychoanalytic movement who charge it with violating a long established paradigm of the mind seem not to have looked carefully enough at what earlier philosophers of mind (such as Descartes and Leibniz) actually said. As far as Locke is concerned, it does appear that he subscribed to a strongly restrictive view of mentality, implying that there can be nothing in the mind that is not present to direct conscious awareness; but in the light of the phenomena pointed out by Leibniz and Descartes (the case of impressions not attended to, and other events at the threshold of awareness), that stipulation seems to be wholly arbitrary.

4. UNCONSCIOUS PROCESSES AND MANIFESTATION

Le cogito philosophique est au foyer de ce mirage qui rend l'homme moderne si sûr d'être soi dans ses incertitudes sur lui-même.

('The philosophical Cogito is at the centre of that mirage which renders modern man so sure of being himself even in his uncertainties about himself.') Jacques Lacan.[67]

Suppose, extrapolating from the above results from Descartes and Leibniz, we acknowledge that conceivably in some animals, probably in human infants, arguably in adults when they are dreaming, and certainly in all of us when we are not attending to what is being presented to our senses, there is something going on in the mind which often is not integrated into full conscious awareness.[68] Can the Freudian concept of unconscious mentation be presented as a natural extension of these cases?[69] It might be objected that there is a crucial difference. For leaving aside the problematic case of animals (not to mention the bizarre reaches of Leibnizian panpsychism applied even to plants and stones), all the other cases mentioned are cases where what is supposed to be going on in the mind can in principle be brought to the threshold of conscious awareness.[70] We *can* wake up and remember our dreams; we *can*, though not fully aware of the music in the next room as we tap away at the word processor, nevertheless quickly become aware of it if we are asked to listen. And even in the case of our forgotten experiences as young children, where despite the greatest effort we appear unable to recall what happened, our preparedness to accept that there was *mental* activity going on seems to depend on the idea that there might be a way, at least in principle, of activating the memory of those events; or alternatively it depends on our holding that it makes sense to suppose that, at the time at least, something was going on which qualified as some sort of conscious awareness. What seems to threaten the conceptual coherence of the notion of the unconscious mind, as used in psychoanalytic theory, is that it appears to invoke mentality in cases where the link between the mental and the possibility of conscious manifestation is severed altogether.

There are two possible answers to this objection, which take us to the core of the philosophical debate over the unconscious. The first, canvassed by Sebastian Gardner, is to argue that the concept of the unconscious can be introduced in a way that does, after all, preserve a general conceptual link with conscious mentality. 'A *general* dependence of the concept of the mental state on that of consciousness does not entail the possession by each *species* of mental state of the feature of consciousness. Psychoanalytically attributed states can lack manifestability and yet not be conceptually independent of consciousness, for the reason that they are necessarily parts of *the mind*, the concept of which *is* connected with that of consciousness.'[71] This suggestion is not particularly easy to understand, but it is, I believe, coherent. Consider the following analogy. There is a property, namely divisibility, which is not countable; nevertheless, it is not conceptually independent of countability, since it is necessarily a property of *number*, the concept of which is connected with that of countability. Or, to take another (perhaps clearer) example, we can imagine a natural kind (say water-skimming fish) which is identified by reference to the species' essential characteristic of spending most of its time on the aquatic surface: it is conceivable that we might be led to classify a sub-species as a water-skimmer (perhaps because of important structural or genetic similarities with the main group), even though the members of the subgroup turned out in fact to spend most of their time below the surface. But though coherent, the suggestion in the case of the unconscious mind has an air of being question-begging; for it seems to rely on the premise that the unconscious states are parts of the *mind*, or species of mental state – which is precisely what those who insist on a strong conceptual connection between mentality and consciousness would deny.

The second, and more promising, line to take for defenders of the concept of the unconscious is to accept the broad conceptual link between mentality and manifestability, but to argue that this condition can in fact be met in the case of unconscious states. This is the line which Gardner himself in the end seems to come round to:

> The data of clinical practice . . . suggest [that] the unconscious can . . . be epistemically fixed through something that we could call the 'quasi-manifestability' of unconscious states. To *some* degree the unconscious is introspectable. People who have undergone analysis for a certain length of time come to be able to recognise events in their unconscious – activations of impulses, onsets of [phantasy] activity and so forth – as they occur. They are then aware of these movements of their mind in such a way that they can identify their content and direction, and can perhaps do something to hinder them, but without being able to fully control (let alone initiate) them.[72]

Gardner concludes, appropriately enough, that unconscious mentality should not be defined in terms of mental states lacking the possibility of manifestation; rather, manifestation is possible, though 'in a finer and more conditional sense'.[73] Not only does this seem persuasive, it also accords quite closely with the line taken in some of his writings by Freud himself, who asserted, in effect, that manifestability was not only possible, but that its actualization was the very essence of the therapeutic process: 'the task of psychoanalytic treatment can be summed up in this formula: everything pathogenic in the unconscious must be transferred into consciousness'.[74] In the famous case of the 'table-cloth lady' (a patient subject to compulsive and obsessive behaviour, namely the summoning of her maid again and again to witness a supposed spot on the table-cloth), the patient had responded to initial questioning by insisting that the ritual was meaningless, and she really didn't know why she did it. But when analysis slowly brought to light the painful events of her wedding night (an impotent husband who after repeated unsuccessful attempts to consummate the marriage, ended the night by marking the sheets with red ink, to avoid, as he put it, 'being disgraced in the eyes of the maid'), the patient, after prolonged embarrassment and hesitation, suddenly came to see that she did, after all, know what her obsession about the stained tablecloth meant.[75] As it appears in psychoanalytic theory, the unconscious is a shadowy area, often stocked with fearful and dark images which the subject initially perceives only dimly, if at all; but the notion that these contents are nonetheless in some sense in the subject's mind is made plausible precisely by the process of guided discovery whereby what is dark is brought into the light. Whether the resulting explanations are satisfying will depend, as with any claim about the human mind, on a host of complex theoretical and empirical considerations. But the charge of a priori conceptual incoherence can be met, and met confidently.

If the above account is accepted, the alleged difficulties in the concept of the unconscious are spectacularly less severe than has appeared to be the case to many philosophical critics. And it is tempting to conclude our discussion on the credentials of psychoanalytic theory by offering a psychoanalytic interpretation for the very intensity of the resistance which the theory has aroused. Freud himself, of course, infuriated his critics by doing just this. He saw himself as the third great revolutionary, after Copernicus and Darwin, who had cut the grandiose self-image of humanity down to size:

> Man's craving for grandiosity is now suffering the third and most bitter blow from present-day psychological research which is endeavouring to prove to the 'ego' of each one of us that he is not even master in his own house, but that he must remain content with the veriest scraps of information about what is going on unconsciously in his own mind.[76]

Not surprising that this most humbling result should provoke the most passionate and determined opposition – what Freud described (not without some justification, writing in the nineteen-twenties) as 'the universal revolt against our science, the total disregard of academic courtesy in dispute, and the liberation of the opposition from all the constraints of impartial logic'.[77] Of course, to tell critics that their very opposition is a symptom confirming the truth of the target theory is a tactic designed to provoke rather than convince, and in itself it will (rightly) not cut much ice with philosophical critics of psychoanalytic theory. Nevertheless, given the extent to which Freudian ideas have by now permeated our ways of thinking about human conduct, there is surely something remarkable about the almost wholesale disregard of those ideas by contemporary practitioners of philosophical ethics. There is, to put it no stronger, something which calls for an explanation in the way so many contemporary moral philosophers pointedly ignore, refuse even to consider, the possibility that psychoanalytic theory might have something to teach them, still writing instead as if humans were transparently self-aware creatures, and the task of ethics were simply that of intellectually analysing the structure of our goals, and rationally working out the best way to implement them.

In the following section I shall explore the challenge psychoanalytic theory poses to the traditional project of philosophical ethics. The initial challenge is to the hegemony of reason, to the picture of the controlling intellect irradiated by the transparent beams of the *lux rationis*. But that gauntlet had of course been thrown down much earlier by Hume, when he famously dubbed reason the 'slave of the passions'.[78] What Hume never questioned, however, was the assumption that when we make our ethical decisions we are at least able to gain relatively uncomplicated access to our passions; and hence, for Hume, reason remains firmly in charge as executor, straightforwardly implementing the means to transparently 'given' ends. Freud's challenge runs a lot deeper, casting doubt on our ability even to access the *materials* for appropriate deliberation; the disenfranchised ego has to be content with 'the veriest scraps'.

Yet the suggestion made above about the ultimate 'manifestability' of unconscious materials points, in the end, to a less threatening result – the possibility that after acknowledging its lack of total mastery, our conscious power of understanding can eventually get to grips with those buried images, drives and fears that at first seemed to deny us mastery in our own house. The results of psychoanalysis drag into the light truths which, once we see them, we can recognize that, in a sense, we knew all along. What at first seemed grotesque and unfamiliar eventually emerges on the surface through a process not radically discontinuous with what happens in the case of all sorts of less troubling phenomena that are part of ordinary human experience: the music in the next room, dimly heard but consciously unregistered, the forgotten but partly recoverable memories of childhood, the weird, elusive, but ultimately encompassable deliverances of dreams. Psychoanalysis, like a revolution that overthrows a long established despot, challenges the sovereignty of the ego, only, in the end, to hold out the promise of a more enlightened autonomy of true self-understanding.

5. PSYCHOANALYSIS AND THE ETHICAL DOMAIN

I regard the (daily, hourly, minutely) attempted purification of consciousness as the central and fundamental arena of morality. Iris Murdoch[79]

In its initial challenge to reason, and in the hope it offers for a new kind of self-understanding, the psychoanalytic approach has inevitable implications for the traditional enterprise of philosophical ethics. Ever since Socrates, the philosophical enterprise has been seen as involving some element of self-examination,[80] and there is a sense in which psychoanalytic theory simply carries that process forward, albeit in a more radically introspective fashion. Ultimately, I believe, it is a mistake to think there is a fundamental discontinuity between psychoanalytic and philosophical modes of searching for the good life. To begin with, if the arguments of the previous section are correct, psychoanalytic theory is not as revisionary, vis-à-vis previous philosophical models of the mind, as is often supposed; the psychoanalytic notion of unconscious mental processes is not, after all, so startlingly innovatory from a purely conceptual point of view. Freud's own parallel with the Copernican revolution of the sixteenth century needs to be handled with some care in this connection. For despite insistently argued claims to the contrary,[81] it is not clear that the advent of the heliocentric account of celestial motion required any fundamental shift in the accepted meanings of terms. Motion, it is true, had previously been measured relative to a supposedly fixed earth, but there was no semantic rule involved here: people had no insuperable difficulty *understanding* what was meant by the new notion of a moving earth revolving around the sun. Among those hostile to the change, resistance may, to be sure, initially have taken the form of an attempt to accuse the new theory of incoherence: since motion is defined as a change of position relative to the earth, 'the earth moves' is a contradiction. But it is unlikely that such a move ever carried conviction. People could readily understand the idea of heliocentric terrestrial motion by extrapolating from the earlier model of geocentric planetary motion. And in much the same way, though initial resistance to psychoanalytic theory has sometimes taken the form of protesting that the notion of unconscious mentation is incoherent, it appears (as argued in the previous section) that we can readily understand what is meant by extrapolating from established and unproblematic phenomena involving mental events below the threshold of focused, attentive consciousness.

Nevertheless, though not necessarily involving any major semantic shift, the changes in thinking brought about by the Freudian revolution, like those wrought by its Copernican predecessor, were still profound. After Copernicus and Galileo, our views about the status of the earth could never be the same. And it is similarly clear, despite the continuities we have outlined,[82] that accepting

the psychoanalytic account of the nature and role of the unconscious does radically transform the way in which we understand
ourselves. The pre-Freudian world, with its broad confidence in
the scope of rational enlightenment, is now no longer a secure
home for us; we could no more return to it than we could to the
flattering security of the Ptolemaic universe. What is curious,
however, is that this transformation has, for the most part, yet to
be reflected in philosophical work on ethics. For the most part,
today's moral philosophers still work within one or more of the
paradigms created respectively by Aristotle, Kant and Bentham,
all of which, as Jacques Lacan has pointed out, blithely presuppose, in one way or another, the uncontroversial hegemony of
reason in determining the conditions for the good life, or in laying
down the rules of right conduct, or in working out the appropriate
way to maximize the good. Nowhere, at least within the analytical
tradition in moral philosophy, has there been any serious attempt
to come to terms with what Lacan has called 'the revolution in
thought that the effect of [psycho]analytic experience brings with
it concerning the ethical domain'.[83] The Lacanian point has been
aptly put by John Rajchman as follows:

Psychoanalysis . . . introduces a new *kind* of problem for ethical reflection:
not the ancient problem that we may live and act in ignorance of what is
truly good for us, but the modern problem that there is something in our
desire that goes beyond what would direct us to what we think we want
for ourselves. In particular, it raises the question of *fortune* in our lives in a
new way, for it links fortune not to the good we can know, but to [that] in
our desire which takes us on paths we can never regulate nor foresee.
Psychoanalysis holds that the 'truth' of our mortal destinies is not one for
which there exists a general wisdom, a general means for adequating
one's living to what is truly good for it. To give a true *logos* for one's life is
thus no longer to know how to wisely master it . . . [84]

There are many aspects to this discontinuity between the world
of traditional ethics and the post-psychoanalytic world. Consider
first the case of Aristotelian ethics. For Aristotle, there was, to be
sure, a problem about fortune, and the devastating effects which it
might have on even the most carefully planned life.[85] But nothing
in the Aristotelian problematic takes us beyond the thought that
the life of reason is (unfortunately) not sufficient for *eudaimonia*: the

terrible tragedies that afflicted Priam in his old age are potent signs
of the fact that the most virtuous human may in the end be cheated
of the crown of fulfilment by the cruel blows of external chance,
over which he has no control. But the post-Freudian worry is
altogether more pervasive and disturbing. It is that the area of
'fortune' – the recalcitrant residue over which rational choice has
no control – extends inwards to the very core of our being. The
complexities of the human psyche, the opaque and intensely
problematic character of our deepest motivations, mean that the
deeper significance of the very goods we strive for, the very plans
we construct, is often obscured even from the strivers and con-
structors themselves. The psychoanalytic perspective uncovers
what is implicit in the tragedy of a Pentheus or an Agamemnon:
'events occur too early, or their effects come to late, for us to be
able to "assimilate" them in the portion of living that is governed
by *prohairesis* (rational choice)'.[86]
      The importance of the temporal dimension is crucial here.
What underlies Lacan's thinking is the Freudian concept of *Nachträglichkeit*, a term which is hard to render in English, but which
conveys the idea of something's being 'deferred' or 'carried over'
from the past, with the added implication that, in the understanding of what occurred, something is retroactively 'added on' or
reinterpreted.[87] The standard picture of the rationally ordered life
is of a straightforward linear progression from past to present and
on into the future, with each decision being made in the light of the
available evidence, building on what has gone before. But Freud's
analysis of psychological development suggests that the events of
infancy, not fully understood or assimilated, can lie dormant until,
for example in puberty, or in later adult life, they are reinterpreted
and restructured. It is not that there was an action or event which
is subsequently remembered and acted upon; rather, as Malcolm
Bowie has put it, 'there was no action at all until the individual's
resurgent sexual feeling triggered it, and action of this latecoming
kind took place in the retroactive mode, as a desire-laden restruc-
turing of the personal past'.[88] In Lacan's reading of Freud, our
relationship to our past (and indeed our future) is always complex
and problematic, always shifting in the light of continual re-
evaluation and reinterpretation. We may now recapitulate a

theme which has surfaced in each of the three preceding chapters, but which now assumes its full meaning: the human ethical predicament operates at the locus of a dynamic interplay between *Nachträglichkeit*, the past that we strive to recover and reinvent, and *Zukünftigkeit*, 'the futurality' which will bestow the 'meaning to come' on what we do now.[89] In Lacan's words:

> Continuity in *anamnesis* [recollection] has nothing to do with. . . . a restoration of duration in which the authenticity of each instant would be destroyed if it did not sum up . . . all preceding ones . . . For Freud it is not a question of biological memory . . . but a question of balancing the scales, in which conjectures about the past are weighed against promises of the future upon the single knife-edge or fulcrum of chronological certainty. In psychoanalysis by our use of language we reorder past contingencies by conferring on them the necessities to come . . . At each turning point, the subject restructures himself, and each restructuring takes place, as Freud puts it, *nachträglich* [retrospectively and retroactively].[90]

This model of human understanding radically undermines the linear, unidirectional account which is presupposed in Aristotle's conception of deliberative rationality. Not of course that the Aristotelian account will not work perfectly well in many contexts. We are cold; we work out that lighting a fire would keep us warm; we build the fire: much of our lives does indeed consist in an ordered linear series of decisions to select the means reason has perceived as most appropriate to further a chosen goal. But in the key areas of human passion and emotion, when it comes to anger, jealousy, fear, ambition and sexual desire, linear rationality seems to fail us. What is amiss is not just that we imperfectly understand the past causes and future consequences of what we are 'choosing' to do and why. For if the structure of our deepest feelings and desires is conditioned by the influences of the dormant past, to the extent that the significance of our actions and choices will often be opaque to us, then the very notion of rational deliberation as a guide to action seems shaky. Unless and until the past is reclaimed, unless we can come to appreciate the significance of our past, and the role it plays in shaping our emotional lives, then the very idea of an ordered plan for the good life will have to be put on hold; to suppose otherwise would be to court the tragedy that haunted the ancient Greek dramatists. *Hubris,* the arrogance of deliberative rationality, trusts in its power to devise a logical framework for decision-making on the basis of 'sorting out' all the relevant information; but the true meaning of that information only becomes apparent through genuine learning, the deeper awareness, enriched by suffering, that finally enables the protagonist to 'learn' only when it is too late:

> Zeus, who ever he may be . . .
> lays down the road for mortal understanding
> setting before us this one sovereign truth:
> *we come to learn, at last, by suffering.*[91]

A similar undermining of the credentials of rationality threatens the structure of both Kantian and Benthamite ethics. In the Kantian case, the notion of the categorical imperative has, of course, long come under searching scrutiny from philosophical critics (centering on whether the test of what can be rationally willed as a universal law can in fact generate the results Kant intended). But the psychoanalytic perspective yields a new kind of criticism – namely that the stern Kantian voice of conscience, which is supposed to command our absolute allegiance, turns out to have its source not in the deliverances of objective rationality, but in the imperious and arbitrary demands of that part of the psyche which Freud called the Superego or *Über-ich* – from that part of ourselves which corresponds, in Jennifer Church's apt phrase, to the 'internalized other'.[92] On the well-known Freudian account, the absolute power of the parent on the young child is eventually internalized as the voice of conscience, its resonance and authority stemming from its dual character as an 'inner' voice, which at the same time seems endowed with independent status, harshly judging the desires and inclinations of the ego. There is a close parallel here with the Kantian idea of the rational will as transcending the inclinations of the phenomenal self – a parallel which has led some to suggest that the Freudian account 'should be seen as accommodating rather than competing with that of Kant', the Freudian superego being 'a naturalistic counterpart to Kant's account of the noumenal self, with the commands of the superego replacing the commands of the will'.[93] It is certainly true that a psychological account of the origins of a moral theory need not automatically undermine its validity (to suppose otherwise would be to commit the 'genetic fallacy');[94] and I shall suggest in a moment that there are important limitations to the scope of Lacan's critique of Kant. Nevertheless, Lacan's strictures do at least raise some stirrings of doubt about the calm confidence which the Kantian places in the credentials of the categorical imperative. For all that Kant's supreme law claims to provide an uncontroversial route to autonomous moral enlightenment, the nagging suspicion begins to surface that the very rigidity of its authority, its very harshness, may turn out to be a complex outgrowth from infantile reactions to parental power, operating in a way that is inherently inimical to the possibility of true rational autonomy. All this is a fairly direct development of Freud's own ideas, where we find a repeated stress on the characteristic 'harshness' of the superego:

[The child's] aggressiveness [towards the heavily controlling parent] is sent back whence it came, that is, it is directed towards his own ego. There it is taken over by a portion of the ego, which sets itself over against the rest of the ego as super-ego, and which now, in the form of 'conscience' is ready to put into action against the ego the same harsh aggressiveness that the ego would have liked to satisfy upon others.[95]

To describe this inherent 'harshness' of conscience, Lacan in a memorable phrase talks of the *gourmandisme* of the superego: the more cruel the conscience becomes, the more inescapably it commands obedience, and yet the very obedience only serves to generate an ever more stringent and searching inspection of the guilty secrets of the ego. Like a sinister parasite, the more you feed it, the more it wants.[96] Or, to use another of Lacan's vivid comparisons, the Kantian dynamic becomes assimilated to that of Kant's darker eighteenth-century contemporary, the Marquis De Sade: our relation to the moral law becomes one of 'erotic servitude'. The law is revealed as 'something fundamentally "other" in our living, which we cannot represent or control in advance'.[97]

Depending on one's literary tastes, it can be easy to be overwhelmed, or alternatively repelled, by Lacan's rhetoric. There are, in any case, limits to the scope of his critique: clearly the appeal of

Kantianism in ethics is not entirely subverted by the Lacanian focus on its sinister psychoanalytic shadow. Thus Marcia Cavell, for example has persuasively argued that 'while the super-ego may explain various neurotic forms of self-punishment, precisely what it doesn't explain, or even make room for, is the moral point of view, which demands just what Freud's reduction of all interests to self-interest won't allow: valuing something because one holds it to be valuable in itself'.[98] What is more, even on a self-interested reading of human nature, the Kantian ideal of respect for persons can hope to survive relatively unscathed: contractarian versions of Kantianism can point to the indisputable fact that all members of a community have an interest in the laying down of ground rules which prohibit unwarranted encroachments on personal liberty. On the socio-political level at least, the Kantian 'constructions of reason' retain their appeal.[99] But at the level of the individual pursuit of the good life, the Kantian distinction between the actual desires of the 'phenomenal self', and the pure rational will of the 'noumenal self' does seem to be put seriously at risk if we adopt the psychoanalytic perspective. For what had appeared as the austere, the 'holy' (Kant's term)[100] requirements of abstract rationality lose their right to command our allegiance if we are indeed unable to sort out the extent to which they arise from the tortuous struggles of a fragmented self to come to terms with the legacy of arbitrary parental power. This (to anticipate) need not rule out the possibility of a higher awareness in which the demands of the inner voice have been examined and explored, and their best elements retained in the goals of a harmonious and reintegrated personality. The 'gentler' formulation of Kant's imperative tells the agent that he must treat '*himself*, as well as all others, never merely as a means but always at the same time as an end in himself'[101] – a principle which it is certainly possible to see as embodying the very ideal of balanced self-awareness and self-respect that is the goal of successful psychotherapy. But the message of psychoanalytic theory is that this can only come at the end of a long journey of self-scrutiny, in which the significance, the powerful resonance, of the many voices we find within us, has been fully examined. In the light of the Lacanian critique, Kantian ethical rationalism, in so far as it relies on an appeal to the supposedly clear and straightforward inner voice of duty, risks, at the very least, incurring the charge of being wedded to a naively oversimplified moral psychology.

The case, finally, of Bentham, provides further grist for the psychoanalytic mill. Again, as with Kant, it would be wrong to suppose that psychological diagnoses of the genesis of a theory can in themselves undermine its ethical credentials. But what emerges from the Lacanian critique of utilitarianism is, once more, a series of radical worries about oversimplification. The utilitarian reformer offers us a neat and tidy world fully accessible to rational scrutiny – one where (as symbolized by Bentham's famous creation, the panopticon) the consequences of every action are manifest, and hence controllable by reward and punishment so as to maximize the general good. Deterrence theory is a supreme exemplification of rational optimism, where the mechanisms of choice are fully transparent, and the social engineer manipulates all for the best by assigning suitable weights to the options presented for rational selection. Sometimes, of course, it succeeds; indeed (as I have argued elsewhere) the glib reformers who proclaim that 'deterrence has failed' are themselves often guilty of confusion and oversimplification.[102] But from a post-Freudian perspective there is, nonetheless, something impossibly naive about the assumption of simple transparency in the mechanisms of desire and motivation:

> The terrible cheerfulness, the indefatigable optimism of the utilitarian reformer would betray a desire to master something he cannot explain: that there exists in our suffering and our gratifications something that cannot be put to use to serve the greatest number ... [A] patient clings to the imperious manifestation of his own desire[s] ... beyond any reasonable manifestation of their utility, beyond anything that can be encompassed in the tabulated world of rewards and punishments.[103]

None of this shows, of course, that general happiness is not a good, or that social policies which will serve that end are not justified. But it does point, nonetheless, to something in the human psyche which is too dark and too complex for its products to be straightforwardly controlled by the application of a utilitarian calculus.

In different ways, the Aristotelian, Kantian and Benthamite models of ethics thus all emerge as relying on an oversimplified moral psychology – one which is inadequate to the intricacies of the human condition. Bernard Williams has recently speculated, in defence of the uncompromisingly poetical style of Friedrich Nietzsche's writings on ethics, that there may be 'something about ethical understanding which means Nietzsche's style suited it – something which resists treatment in traditional analytical terms'.[104] If that is right, at least part of the reason may be waiting to be found in the results uncovered by the psychoanalytic movement. If we take the central problem of moral philosophy to be that of how we should live our lives to the full, in a way adequate to the deepest complexities of our human nature, then psychoanalytic theory uncovers a fundamental flaw in the idea that we can reach that goal by the application of a rationally laid out plan, whether an Aristotelian recipe, a Kantian response to the moral law, or a Benthamite reliance on the felicific calculus. All these approaches presuppose that the end is clearly in sight, and that what has to be done is to arrange the pieces in the appropriate way – for Aristotle, by developing suitable habits of virtue, for Kant by exercising our rational will in the right manner, for Bentham by carefully working out the consequences of our actions. These may all be plausible candidates for necessary conditions for the achievement of our goal, but they can never, of themselves, be sufficient. For what the psychoanalytic approach implies, in direct opposition to the premise of these ratiocentric theories, is that our innermost nature, and hence the structure of any possible recipe for its fulfilment, is *not* clearly in sight.

Before we can begin on the project of seeing how we should live, we first have to embark on the task of trying to understand ourselves. That much, at least, is fully in accord with a long classical tradition stretching from the famous injunction at Delphi right down to Pope's *Essay on Man*: 'Know then thyself'. But what is new is the insistence that that process has to begin with an attempt to come to terms with the darker side of our nature – the side which is not revealed by simple introspection and rational weighting of 'what on balance we most want', but which will be grasped only at the end of a long process of recovery, rehabilitating those parts of the self which are initially submerged beneath the level of ordinary everyday awareness. Descartes, the apostle of rational control, once confided to his private diary that he saw himself as wearing a mask: *larvatus prodeo*.[105] Only in the post-Freudian era have we begun to come to terms with a radically new problem for ethics, what Lacan called the problem of *démasquage*.[106] In the process of analysis, the subject aims finally to unmask himself, to be at last faithful to the hidden truth of his desire, to recover the dissociated fragments of the self, and in so doing transform his self-understanding. It is to the details of this complex process of recovery and transformation that we must now turn.

6. THE TRANSFORMATION OF THE SELF

> *O Mensch! gib acht!*
> *Was spricht die tiefe Mitternacht?*
> *Ich schlief, ich schlief –*
> *Aus tiefem Traum bin ich erwacht;*
> *Die Welt ist tief*
> *Und tiefer als der Tag gedacht.*
>
> *Oh Man, attend!*
> *What does deep midnight's voice portend?*
> *Long did I sleep*
> *But now my deep dream finds an end:*
> *The world is deep*
> *Deeper than day can comprehend.*
> Friedrich Nietzsche[107]

Nietzsche's extraordinary poem vividly anticipates the psychoanalytic vision of a human psyche far too deep and complex to be encompassed by the grasp of calm analytic rationality. Yet if we are tempted to follow Nietzsche into the deepness of the night, this need not mean abandoning or devaluing what is clearly visible by day. Despite the challenge to ratiocentric ethics posed by psychoanalytic theory, one can certainly cite many human activities and institutions whose point, with respect to human flourishing, is fully or largely accessible to rational scrutiny. Political forums which allow maximum scope for informed and equal rational debate, social arrangements (career structures, leisure facilities) which offer the opportunity for humans to realize their diverse talents and develop their best potentialities – all these are in

principle grist for the rational mill, assessable ingredients the kind
of reasoned life plan envisaged, for example, in the grand Aristotelian design. But these elements (to make a crude but nonetheless serviceable distinction) all mostly relate to human beings in
their public, social role. They concern, roughly, what I have
earlier called 'committee ethics'[108] – evaluation of the kinds of
social and political structures which one could imagine a group of
rational agents debating in connection with the allocation of
public resources, or the general arrangements for running an
equitable and efficient society. Yet alongside this, there is that
intensely private sphere of close personal relations which, for most
of us, forms the very core of a worthwhile life. These are relations
involving uncertainty, vulnerability, powerful drives and emotional commitments, deep physical and psychological needs – the
relations that belong to the area of love, sexuality, romance,
marriage, the family and parenthood. It is in this area that, if the
psychoanalytic approach is correct, the structure of our deepest
desires and aspirations is fundamentally opaque to pure unaccom-
modated reason.

The point at once needs qualifying. To be sure, the goods
involved in our private relationships are often clear and palpable:
to function as human beings we need the comfort, support and
enrichment that mutual emotional interdependence brings. And
to this extent, the place of such goods in an overarching vision of
the good life is accessible to rational scrutiny. But what is not
similarly accessible is something which lies beyond these generalities: the power and resonance which informs each of the relevant
relationships in a uniquely particular way, at the deepest level of
our pre-rational drives and feelings. Traditional models of rational
control are wholly unable to accommodate the significance of this
inner dimension.

To see why this should be so, let us return once more to that
oldest of philosophical topics, the relation between reason and the
passions. In traditional synoptic ethics, the rational life plan is
threatened by the phenomenon of *akrasia*, or lack of control:
through weakness, or fear, or impetuosity, or under the influence
of strong and immediate appetites, we choose the lesser good, or
even the bad, when the greater good is staring us in the face.

Reason is, incomprehensibly, absurdly, 'dragged around like a slave by the passions'. It is no accident that the orthodox moralists of the synoptic tradition all in one way or another attempted either to override such 'weakness', or, more radically, to deny its very possibility. For Plato, *akrasia* just could not happen: when all the relevant information is available for rational scrutiny, there is simply no room for any action other than choosing the best course.[109] For Aristotle (struggling to resist the Platonic conclusion but nonetheless unable entirely to escape from its shadow) akratic behaviour can only come about when knowledge is somehow suspended or clouded at the moment of choice.[110] For the Stoics, the life of the philosophical sage (informed by reason) is immune from the possibility of *akrasia*, since rational understanding of the universe and of human life has generated a privileged state of *ataraxia*, or philosophical calm, in which the passions simply cannot get a foothold.[111] For Spinoza, a passion simply ceases to be a passion (in the sense of something that can lead to akratic behaviour) when we achieve a clear and distinct rational understanding of its causes.[112]

In their different ways, all these manoeuvres see the passions as essentially alien to the true nature of man; and a corollary of this is that they can find no place for them in the truly fulfilled human life. Reason confronts the passions as opaque, alien, absurd, and simply liquidates them, or locates them outside the bounds of what is coherently intelligible in human action. Modern analytic philosophers, by contrast, have been quite ready to acknowledge the possibility, and existence, of akratic conduct (indeed, its analysis has been the subject of continuing debate in the philosophy of mind); but they have not, for the most part, begun to digest its deeper and more disturbing implications for the traditional project of philosophical ethics. It is only the psychoanalytic movement that has attempted to come to terms with the irrational part of our humanity, and what it means for the conduct of our lives, in anything like a systematic way. The two most important elements here, stemming from the work of Freud and of Jung respectively, seem to me to be these: firstly, that we should be prepared to confront the non-rational elements of our makeup in a radically new way; and secondly, that we need to undergo a process of rediscovering the self,[113] not through denial or control of those non-rational elements, but by a complex process of recovery and rehabilitation.

Coming to terms with the non-rational parts of ourselves, is not to be confused with a bland acceptance of the existence of irrational drives and impulses. That much is available to anyone who has taken on board the fact that humans are not pure minds inhabiting bodies, but organic, evolving creatures who have inherited behavioural and motivational structures from our non-rational ancestors. To say that is not to minimize the importance of the Darwinian insight: realizing our essential continuity with the rest of the animal world is probably the first vital step towards moving away from an artificial ethics which sees 'reason' as a self-contained, isolated faculty subject only to its own rules of operation, essentially 'in charge' as it drives the chariot of subhuman desires and bodily instincts. In this sense, evolutionary theory prepares the way: Darwin's role is that of John the Baptist to the Freudian gospel. But *il y a fagots et fagots,* to use the phrase from Molière that Freud was fond of quoting; there is knowledge and knowledge.[114] If it was just a matter of the imparting of information, understanding the operation of the non-rational parts of ourselves would be a swift and easy matter. The psychoanalytic process aims to achieve a radically new *perspective* on our inmost desires and drives – one which, quite literally, reinterprets our past and present actions and choices, and does so in a way that was necessarily hidden from anyone using the old model of the mind as a transparent arena where the drama of 'reason versus the passions' is played out in the open sunlight.

To make this clearer, consider the particular problem of human sexual conduct. To any but the most austere ascetic, sexuality must have a fairly central place in any plausible recipe for human fulfilment. But from the grand perspective of ratiocentric ethics, its importance is pretty opaque. In general terms, to be sure, its function as a means of procreation gives it point; but beyond that, it has no rationally accessible 'justification', as it were, beyond being an instrument of pleasure – and, at that, an often messy and risky one which, from a hedonic viewpoint, could as well be replaced by substitutes from the pharmacological cupboard. In

Huxley's nightmare utilitarian vision of a 'Brave New World', sex is 'as good as *soma*' (the imaginary all purpose, side-effect free, pleasure drug); but equally, from that perspective, *soma* is as good as sex.[115] Scrabbling around for a richer justification, ratiocentric ethicists might come up with pious busbyisms about the importance of sex as an 'expression of mutual affection', but while it can, of course, be just that, honest self-examination reveals that there is an element of bad faith in tying down its significance in this way – in filleting it so that it becomes a tidy and digestible dish on the rationally planned menu for the good life. Such an approach conceals, or glosses over, what Lacan aptly calls the *Unheimlichkeit* (the strangeness, the lack of 'at-home-ness') of erotic passion:

> In what Freud called our 'sexuality' or our 'libido' there is something fundamentally rebellious or inassimilable to our well-being or *eudaimonia*. It is not a matter of the virtues of a domestic or civic service to the aims of a *physis* that would reflect it. It is not something which, when moderated and restricted to appropriate occasions, serves to harmonize us with the world of our activities. On the contrary, it is fundamentally traumatic, and introduces something 'beyond' our participation in such activities. For Freud, our *eros* is at odds with our *ethos*; its occurrence in our lives is always *unheimlich*.[116]

Sexual passion can of course figure importantly in a loving relationship, but it is no accident that erotic gratification fails to find a central place in Aristotle's vision of *philia*, mutually respectful love between equals. Clearer eyed on these matters than we are, with our debased, Hollywood-generated culture, the Greeks realized that *eros*, sexual passion, was only contingently, if at all, related to long-term mutual affection, fidelity and reciprocal esteem: some *philoi* might perhaps be erotically involved, but the ends of *philia* as such can be served equally well, probably better, by conversation, or sharing a meal or a glass of wine, or attending a concert or play together. At the level of instrumental generalities (construed merely as an instrument of pleasure or as a problematic enhancer of affection) nothing explains the importance of sexuality in our lives – how it gives colour and vividness to our experience, how its absence torments us, how its presence tantalizes, soothes and irradiates our inner being. For someone to risk a career, or endanger a valued marriage, for its delights, often fleeting, some-

times dangerous, frequently quick to sour, is, from the standpoint
of the rationally ordered life, a mystery:

> Enjoyed no sooner than despised straight;
> Past reason hunted; and no sooner had,
> Past reason hated, as a swallowed bait,
> On purpose laid to make the taker mad;
> Mad in pursuit, and in possession so;
> Had, having, and in quest to have, extreme;
> A bliss in proof, and proved, a very woe;
> Before a joy proposed; behind a dream:
> All this the world well knows, but none knows well
> To shun the heaven that leads man to this hell.[117]

To take stock so far: nothing about the functional or instrumental role of sexuality fully explains its importance in our lives, and
nothing from the resources of ratiocentric ethics can enable us to
come to terms with that importance. Imprudent decisions taken
under the influence of sexual passion are thus either swept away as
a mystery, dismissed as an awkward hangover from our apelike
past, classified as 'akratic' (with all the non-explanation that implies), or else perhaps (as in the Stoic tradition) ground underfoot
and suppressed in a vain attempt to achieve an ideal trans-human
state of philosophical calm.

What I shall call 'transformational analysis' takes a radically
different course. I use this term partly because it is not a technical
term in the psychoanalytic literature, and it therefore suits my
purpose of not committing myself to the jargon or specific doctrines of any one school. The term does, however, have Jungian
overtones (though it is not a label Jung explicitly employs); but,
paradoxically perhaps, these overtones are quite consistent with
my present, 'non-doctrinal' purposes. Jung provides a remarkably
undogmatic general overview of the kinds of transformation which
can be effected by the psychoanalytic process – an account which
does not require exclusive allegiance to any one of the motivational theories which various rival psychoanalytic schools have
(often implausibly) presented as the unique key to the human
psyche. In a relatively early paper, 'Problems of Modern Psychotherapy', Jung tentatively divides the psychoanalytic process of
self-discovery into four broad stages, and it is worth examining

these in a little detail, to see just how radically the process differs from the evasive manoeuvres of the ratiocentric ethicist described above.[118]

The first stage is an acknowledgement of precisely the fallibility, vulnerability and dependence that is an integral part of the strange openness we experience in our emotional lives (perhaps most striking in the area of sexuality), and a source of the power which the relevant passions can exert over us. It is only by giving up, in the first instance, our pretensions to rational control that we open the way for deeper, transformed, self-understanding. 'Until a person can confess himself fallible and human', says Jung, 'an impenetrable wall shuts him out from the living experience of feeling himself a man among men. Here we find the key to the great significance of the true, unstereotyped confession . . . as is shown by the saying from the Greek mysteries, "Give up what thou hast, and then thou wilt receive".' As it manifests itself in the psychoanalytic process, this move is the very opposite of the impulse towards rational control:

The psychoanalytic aim is to observe the shadowy presentations – whether in the form of images or of feelings – that are spontaneously evolved in the psyche and appear, *without his bidding*, to the man who looks within. In this way we find once more what we have repressed or forgotten. Painful though it may be, this is itself a gain – for what is inferior or even worthless belongs to me as my shadow, and gives me substance and mass. How can I be substantial if I fail to cast a shadow. I must have a dark side if I am to be whole; and inasmuch as I become conscious of my own shadow, I also remember that I am a human being like any other.[119]

The first stage of the process of transformation is thus one of listening rather than declaring, of waiting rather than controlling, of attending rather than commanding. Despite obvious differences of approach, there is more than a little convergence here between this Jungian stress on self-surrender, and the Heideggerian insistence on the importance of openness and 'listening' in the attempt to confront the mystery of human existence.[120]

The second stage of transformational analysis is often discussed by Jung with reference to the Freudian notion of transference – the return by the patient to that childish state of dependence, where the role of the analyst becomes inextricably bound up with memories and phantasies which the patient has about his father or mother. Because of the still very strong scepticism which many analytic philosophers have about its scientific credentials,[121] I wish to avoid getting into the complexities of Freudian theory; and in any case, understanding what Jung means by the second stage of the transformation process does not strictly require it. Jung's own preferred label for the second stage is that it is the phase of 'explanation'. Essentially, what is involved is not so much the transference process itself, but what it leads to – an understanding that feelings of anxiety, vulnerability and dependence are an inescapable part of human psycho-sexuality. Plumbing the depths of our vulnerability, accepting that even as adults our relationships bear the stamp of earlier needs (sometimes frustrated, sometimes reciprocated in the wrong way, always involving the abject dependence of the child) – this, as Jung describes it, is 'the most effective antidote imaginable to all idealistic illusions about the nature of man'. It is important, however, not to misunderstand this as a reductionistic move, cutting man down to a stereotyped model of a darkly motivated child, driven by raw infantile sexuality. To interpret things 'entirely from the shadow side', to 'reduce them to their origins in dreary filth', argues Jung, is a distortion: it is a mistake to suppose that 'what is radiant no longer exists because it has been explained from the shadow side'. To acknowledge the shortcomings of the human condition (shortcomings from the perspective of an ideal of pure rational control) need not lead to self-abasement or despair; rather the way is open to an understanding that what gives sexuality its power over us is intimately bound up with our status, not as pure angelic souls, but as creatures of flesh and blood, dependent beings raised and nurtured by other dependent beings. This is the beginning of true morality, a morality which is free from sentimentality and illusion (the sentimentality of overblown 'romantic' love, the illusion of rational control), and which is founded on a sense of acceptance – what Jung calls 'adaptation and patience with our own shortcomings'.[122]

The second stage thus leads on to the third, the process of moral reconstruction, which Jung (here writing in his most undogmatic and eclectic mode) now describes in Adlerian terms. In essence, this stage involves an appeal to the patient's desire to resume control over his moral destiny, a drive towards 'normalization and health' which represent 'the most desirable goals and the most suitable fulfilment for a human being'. In some respects this is the antithesis of the Freudian model: 'if the unconscious is held to be a mere receptacle for all the evil shadow things in human nature, including even primeval slime deposits, we really do not see why we should linger on the edge of this swamp into which we once fell ... The patient must be prodded into other paths, and this always requires an educating will'.[123] But the stress here is not so much on 'will' as on 'educating'. Transformational analysis emphatically does not aim at the subjugation of the psyche to the pure Kantian rational will; against this model of traditional *fortitudo moralis*, austerely directing us along the iron road of duty, Jung adopts the more humane Aristotelian model of carefully developed habits of feeling and action: 'the period of education makes us realize that no confession and no amount of explaining will make the ill-formed tree grow straight, but that it must be trained with the gardener's art upon the trellis before normal adaptation can be attained'.[124] At this stage, there is a kind of convergence between the aims of psychoanalysis, as interpreted by Jung, and those of traditional Aristotelian-style ethics. So far from being, as it is sometimes portrayed, an unended revisiting of the painful traumas of the past, the process of 'transformational' analysis aims to move forward to a phase of healing and growth. There is of course a major difference from the Aristotelian blueprint, arising from the fact that Aristotle optimistically presumes a favoured childhood in which the right habits have been laid down; ignoring the complexities of human psychic development, he is content to observe laconically that it is not easy to right the effects of early damage.[125] The notion of a systematic redemption, or reclamation of the past, so crucial for what gives the psychoanalytic movement its appeal, is simply missing in the ratiocentric world of the *Nicomachean Ethics*. But for all that, the two approaches come together in so far as the goal in each case is the realization of a harmonious and fulfilled life – a life of 'normality' in the sense of one which allows our natural capacities to grow in a maximally healthy way, so that we can reach our full potential as human beings.

It is only, however, in the fourth stage of the process as described by Jung, that the full implications of the concept of 'transformation' become apparent.[126] Jung introduces his account of
this stage with some manifestly Nietzsche-inspired reflections on
the perils of 'normality'. The notion of restricting our potentialities
to some presumed typical or average pattern is anathema to those
whose gifts and inclinations lead them to aspire above the ordinary: 'for them restriction to the normal signifies the bed of
Procrustes, unbearable boredom, infernal sterility and hopeless-
ness . . . [T]he very thought that you want to educate them to
normality is a nightmare; their deepest need is really to be able to
lead "abnormal" lives.'[127] Associated with this reflection is the
insistence that the fourth and 'final' stage of the transformational
process can never, in fact, represent some ultimate phase where
the human psyche has 'arrived' at an equilibrium state. Human
life, for those who cannot rest content with conformism and
conventionality, is an unending quest, a journey whose point (as
indeed Aristotle suggests) lies in the activity rather than the destination; moreover, as Jung puts it, 'a man can hope for satisfaction
and fulfilment only in what he does not yet possess; he cannot find
pleasure in something of which he has already had too much'.[128]
From this, though it is not strictly entailed, it is natural to move on
to the thought that the process of transformation must be a
dialectical one, in the sense envisaged (though in different ways) by
both Plato and Hegel. Rather than grasping an ultimate result, the
last word delivered from on high, the human mind struggles
upwards by a constant process of reaction and counter-reaction:
each insight brings about a change, and that change generates a
new perspective from which we struggle to achieve yet further
insights, and so the process goes on. In the Jungian case, this
ancient theme is initially developed in terms of the relationship
between patient and doctor. The doctor cannot hope to 'instruct'
or 'convince' the patient if he remains a detached, authoritarian
figure: 'you can exert no influence if you are not susceptible to
influence'. Each change in the patient's outlook will produce
changes in that of the doctor; the process of transformation is not
the imposition of an externally devised 'cure', but rather the
realization of a dynamic, two-way process.

In the work of Freud and his disciples, this process, or something superficially like it, makes its appearance as the phenomenon of 'counter-transference': the dependence of the patient, who projects his own infantile phantasies onto the person of the doctor, in turn evokes a reciprocal process in which the doctor counter-projects his own phantasies onto the patient. But it is vital to see that the Jungian conception of the transformation of the self goes far beyond these clinical explanatory models. One reason the point needs underlining is that some of the still widespread resistance to psychoanalytic accounts of the mind and of personal development almost certainly derives from the clinical setting in which the relevant theories were devised. It is anathema to the philosopher to hand over the search for wisdom and fulfilment to a white-coated expert. Not only does the modern Protestant soul revolt against this implied submission to a new secular priesthood; beyond that, the whole philosophical project, as conceived from Socrates through Descartes and on downwards, seems threatened if our autonomous authority to search for the truth is entrusted to another's care. The perception of psychoanalysis as a branch of psychiatry, as dealing with those who are mentally disturbed – at least neurotic, if not positively unbalanced – has exacerbated these tensions between philosophical ethics and psychological theory; it is as if the latter is perceived as (at best) the appropriate resource when things go badly wrong with the mind and its workings, while when all is 'in order', the way is clear for straightforward ethical ratiocination of the traditional variety.[129] It seems likely that many philosophers will continue to resist the insights of the psychoanalytic movement, or at any rate dismiss them as peripheral to their own work, until they are persuaded that they have a general applicability to the human predicament, one which extends beyond the clinical setting, and *relates to all of us, not qua patients, but qua human beings.*[130] It is here that what Jung has to say about his fourth 'transformational stage' is of crucial value. For in this final phase, the very division between patient and doctor, between 'learner' and 'expert', is eroded away:

What was formerly a method of medical treatment now becomes a method of self-education, and therewith the horizon of our modern

psychology is immeasurably widened. The medical diploma is no longer
the crucial thing, but human quality instead . . . All the implements of
psychotherapy developed in clinical practice . . . are now put at our
service . . . for our self-education and self-perfectioning. Analytical
psychology is no longer bound to the consulting room; its chains have
been severed. We might say that it transcends itself and now advances to
fill that void which hitherto has marked the psychic insufficiency of
Western culture.[131]

Despite the grand, perhaps grandiose, phrasing, what is unmistakably offered here is a sober vision of the psychoanalytic method
as extending beyond the consulting room and reaching the wider
territory of philosophical ethics – impinging on the task, which all
of us face, of discovering how to live our lives in the way that is
truest to our human nature. Psychoanalysis, in the Jungian vision,
becomes available not just to the sick but to the healthy as well, 'or
at least to those who have a right to psychic health, and whose
illness is at most the suffering that tortures us all'.[132] The resulting
conception of ethics will have to operate in a way that gives up
many of the traditional assumptions about the straightforward
authority of reason in determining the good life. But for all that, its
continuity with the traditional ethical project is shown by the fact
that it offers a way of pursuing the ancient question, 'How should I
live?', in a manner consistent with the equally ancient injunction
'Know Thyself'. If the route to such self-knowledge is now revealed
as unprecedentedly arduous, involving a recovery of the lost phantasies of early childhood, a journeying down to the depths of our
emotional vulnerability and dependence, a confrontation with the
menacing shadows of our pre-rational fears and desires – all this
can hardly, in the end, be such a surprising or outrageous result.
For we knew all along (for all that philosophical ethics has so often
denied it, or pretended otherwise) that we did not spring into the
world fully armed with the faultless weapons of unsullied rationality. The child, as Wordsworth knew, is 'father of the man'; the
project of knowing who we are cannot avoid the struggle to
understand what made us so. And as Wordsworth came to understand, we may have to accept that those ingredients encompass far
more than the 'natural piety' portrayed in over-idealized pictures
of our infancy.[133] The search, what we may call the 'psycho-

ethical' search, is a search for wholeness. But 'I cannot be substantial if I fail to cast a shadow; I must have a dark side, if I am to be whole.'[134]

7. AKRASIA AND TRANSFORMATIONAL ANALYSIS

Tis one thing to know virtue, and another to conform the will to it.[135] David Hume

Though Jung does not apply his results to the traditional problem of *akrasia*, the materials are, I believe, ready to hand for such an application– or rather for a reinterpretation of the traditional problem in a way which enables us to achieve an invigorated understanding of the psychological and ethical dynamics of what happens when people find themselves failing to act on their rational perceptions of the good. To do this, I shall outline an imaginary case (though patience is needed for a paragraph or so, since it will take a little time to unfold the exact sense in which it can be construed as involving *akrasia*). Consider a committed family man, call him 'Cecil',[136] unequivocally involved in the rewarding project of building a trusting relationship with his partner and cementing the stable structures of mutual reliance and affection necessary to provide a secure and healthy emotional environment for their children. One day, to the astonishment of friends and colleagues, Cecil throws it all over: he announces that he is 'in love' with his secretary, leaves his wife and family, and sets up house with his new mistress. He announces a 'new life', and for a period appears infused with fresh energy. He talks of feeling 'half his age', enthusiastically introduces his glamorous new partner to friends and colleagues, apparently oblivious to the fact that they find his girlfriend superficial, selfish, vain, and sadly lacking the intelligence, warmth and compassion of his former partner. After six months, the passion starts to fade; no longer starry-eyed, the new pair show signs of impatience and disappointment. Public bickering replaces former extravagant displays of mutual fascination; unresolved arguments and sleepless nights of anger and recrimination replace the eager sexual passion that infused the relationship in its early stages. Within a year, the new pair have split up. Our hero attempts to return to his wife and family, but is rebuffed. He lapses into a state of deep depression, realizing that he has sacrificed what is most valuable in his life for a chimera.

To avoid several possible misunderstandings, let me stress that this is not meant to be a 'typical' case, nor is it meant to trivialize the anguish that often leads to marital breakdown, or to suggest that all divorce is irrationally motivated, or that all separations are undertaken under the influence of unreflective passion. What is being presented is just one stylized scenario (though some of the elements will nonetheless be familiar enough to reflective observers of the vicissitudes of late twentieth-century monogamy). I have pitched the story in a fairly exaggerated way precisely to make it a clear case of dissonance between the agent's overall considered conception of the good, and his actual conduct. Looking back on his behaviour years later, our saddened hero confides to friends that he cannot now explain it on any rational model. 'I was just bowled over', is all he can say; 'it was an infatuation – it seemed at the time as if there was nothing else I could do.' Now the point about such a case is that, viewed from the perspective of traditional ratiocentric ethics it appears entirely mysterious. Here is someone wantonly abandoning the greater good for the lesser– sacrificing palpable and deeply rewarding long-term goods for what now appears, against the backdrop of any rational life plan, infinitely less valuable short-term gratification.

One could go on to pitch the rest of the story in 'psychiatric' terms, supposing that Cecil subsequently undergoes a breakdown, takes to drink, loses his job, and ends up a lurid subject for the Sunday papers, found asphyxiated, clad in silk stockings and a rubber mask. But though this type of case is no doubt of great clinical interest, it is too outlandish to support the idea (developed in the previous section) of the psychoanalytic quest as integral to the traditional project of philosophical ethics. The more 'abnormal' or pathological the story, the easier it is to make the defensive move of saying that psychoanalytic thought has relevance only to those who are seriously disturbed. The outlandish cases, like the tortured character of 'Ratman' famously described by Freud, do of course exist, at one end of the spectrum;[137] while at the other may perhaps be found individuals whose nurturing as infants was so finely balanced, and who have made such a smooth and untroubled transition from childhood to adulthood, as to make the world appear to them, psychologically speaking, as 'rather a jolly place'.[138] But most of us, surely, occupy a place somewhere in between. Let us suppose instead, then, that Cecil continues, despite his sadness, to function normally: he carries on working adequately at his job, he continues to do his best to discharge the duties of a concerned parent, he is still able to conduct his life with dignity, and to treat his friends and colleagues with decency and respect. But for all that, he continues to be tortured by the mess he is in, by the unaccountable 'mistake' that spoilt his life.

In what sense can the fateful episode be called akratic? Here it is worth recalling the comment of Bernard Williams (discussed in Chapter Two, section 3, above): 'Whether an episode was [one] of *akrasia* . . . may depend crucially on later understandings. A married man having an affair with another woman and trying to bring it to an end may find himself wavering in that attempt and seeing his lover when they had decided not to meet. If he ends up with his wife, he may well see those episodes as *akratic*. But if in the end he and his wife separate and he goes to live with his lover, it may be that those episodes will not count as *akratic*, but rather as intimations of what were going to prove his truly stronger reasons.'[139] The case envisaged in the last clause of this quotation is importantly different from Cecil's, but it brings out the crucial importance of the time dimension for a proper understanding of certain central cases of *akrasia*. Failure to act on one's considered vision of the good is not a description that can be straightforwardly applied within a fixed time-frame, since one's very understanding of whether that vision is a sound one may have to wait upon information which only becomes available later. But the point is not just one about hostages to contingency. Of course the future is uncertain; but Cecil's problem is not just that he backed the wrong horse, that he took a gamble which, as luck would have it, did not work out. The problem is a deeper, structural one, about Cecil's self-awareness. He may be tempted to rationalize it– to say something like: 'Well, the affaire was very exciting and gratifying at the time, and I was swept away by passion; unfortunately things didn't work out, and I came to realize that my lover wasn't really suitable for me; I regret it all now, but sadly human beings *are* subject to strong and uncontrollable passions; I wish now I could have seen things more clearly, but I didn't, and that's that.' Yet this bland piece of self-analysis signally fails (as he is half-aware in his clearer moments) to do justice to Cecil's enduring torment – the feeling that his life has lost direction and purpose, the sense he has that he has allowed his very integrity and sense of selfhood to slip away.

Let us now suppose that our hero is persuaded to seek the help of psychoanalysis in an effort to understand how he has reached his present predicament. In sketching out an imaginary case such as this, it will perhaps be difficult or impossible to provide a convincing picture of the insights eventually achieved, precisely because the process of coming to terms with the inner hidden self is an intensely individual business, and one which involves lengthy and systematic self-examination. Drawing an analogy with a claim made by Descartes with respect to his *Meditations*, we may say that what is involved is a set of practical exercises to be gone through, rather than a set of static results to be evaluated in terms of their formal structure.[140] Let it be admitted, then, that an element of faith, a measure of at least provisional trust, is required if the process is even to get underway. Those resistant to the whole business cannot be coerced, by rational argument, to give it their support. But at the least one can paint the scenario in such a way that the description of the process diverges from the bitter Gellnerian parody we outlined earlier.[141] Suppose that Cecil is lucky enough to find a highly skilled, deeply concerned and ethically sincere therapist. In such a case (to beg some questions for a moment), Gellner's eight negative conditions (set out in section 2, above) can plausibly be transformed into their much healthier analogues. (i) The 'vulnerability' of the patient, so far from involving a damaging passivity, becomes a source of fruitfulness, allowing him to open himself to the buried roots of his psyche in early childhood. (ii) The 'euphoria' of the consulting room gives way to a commitment to hard work, a long and complex process of interrogation, the reviving of lost memories, the careful analysis and discussion of dreams, desires, fears and phantasies. (iii) The anxious demand for a 'quick cure' is replaced by a rejection of easy answers, an acceptance that the therapist's ultimate goal is to allow the subject to recover his own inner strength, to lead his own life with enriched self-awareness. (iv) The 'authoritarian' dynamic of the consulting room gives way to the realization that the perceived 'power' of the therapist is only a stage to be gone through by the subject in trying to understand his own projections and anxieties. (v) The drug-like dependency on the therapist's tantalizingly measured 'doses' of interpretation is transformed into a genuine interaction, a sense of mutually concerned cooperation. (vi) The 'absorbed attention' of the therapist is seen not as a ruse, but as reflecting the need for hard concentration in order to master the manifold complexity of the subject's individual history. (vii) The therapist's withholding of insistently demanded 'demonstrations' of concern turns out to be a route to freeing the subject from his infantile demands, yet without negating the value of what *is* given – scrupulously professional commitment which respects the boundaries of personal integrity. And finally (viii), the 'double bind'– the subject's being required to abandon himself 'abjectly' to the psychoanalytic process yet at the same time being 'loaded' with responsibility for the outcome – this is replaced by an interactive structure which promotes genuine healing, allowing the whole person to achieve true responsibility by breaking free from the grip of anxiously controlling rationality.

But since further propaganda, on either side, cannot cut much ice, it is time to move from generalities to particulars. Let us suppose (again to beg some questions) that in the painful and anguishing process of dredging up his childhood fears and anxieties, Cecil begins to discern for the first time that his mother, whom he had always tended to see as a doting and devoted (even over-devoted) parent, was in fact someone rather vain, selfish and superficial. His conception of himself as a child, as someone who had securely basked in maternal attention, slowly undergoes a hideously revealing transformation. In Lacanian terms, his former ideal of his life as nourished and harmonious now carries a charge of terror he cannot fully understand – he is plunged into a world in which 'the good itself appears as a grimace of the real'.[142] A process of hard dialogue with the past now opens up. Through repeated discussion of episodes from his childhood which he has not thought about for years, through the agonizingly slow revival

of half-forgotten memories, through the accumulating analysis of
dreams which (though he previously considered himself someone
who dreamed only hazily and infrequently) now crowd vividly
upon him each night, through waking reflection on the tears and
angry outbursts that he is astonished to find himself producing in
the consulting room, Cecil now begins to glimpse that the ecstatic
delight his mother had always taken in his achievements was
deeply suspect – motivated less by a genuine altruistic concern
than by something more sinister and manipulative, more related
to her own self image, her desire to show off to her friends, than to
his own long-term welfare. Not in any sudden revelation, but
through long and painful self-interrogation, he begins to see that
he has a deep, unfulfilled need for the unconditional maternal love
which he never fully enjoyed. And now, after many long months of
work, the 'projection' (in Jungian terms) begins to be lifted.[143] The
ill-fated infatuation with his secretary is thrown into new and vivid
relief: the very features which so inexplicably aroused him – the
superficial glamour, the vanity and triviality – were, he now sees,
strange shadowy representations of the maternal persona which
overwhelmed and dominated the vulnerable and trusting infant
that he once was.

The result is a profound paradox – one that entirely escaped his
earlier rationalizations about his disastrous affaire. His earlier view
was that he simply 'fell in love', was 'bowled over' by the attractions of his mistress. He considered his emotions in the context of a
static time-frame, as if his mind was a transparent goldfish bowl in
which 'beliefs', 'desires' and 'goals' floated around as self-sufficient, straightforwardly identifiable elements, waiting to be acted
on. He never integrated these elements into the context of the long
psychic history that gave them *meaning*, that explained their power
and resonance. Part way along the path to recovery of self-awareness he may still be rationalizing – accepting reluctantly the
childhood frustration of his insistent need for love, but still thinking
perhaps that his affaire was explicable in a relatively straightforward way, as a kind of 'subconscious' attempt to recover the love
he never fully enjoyed. But he is still not yet fully aware of the
complex operation of the shadows cast by the forgotten pains of
childhood. The paradox that he how begins to grasp is that certain

aspects of the 'bad' maternal persona were, unbeknownst to him, being 'introjected' into the structure of his adult desires. What drew him on into his bizarre and 'inexplicable' affaire was a complex web of unfelt, unanalysed needs for security and genuine affection, strangely fixated on a person whose personality mirrored the *damaging* aspects of the attention he received as a child– one whose very unsuitability for the role of a truly caring lover paradoxically invested her with a compelling attraction.

Of course this kind of scenario would have to be filled in with a host of fine detail to make it remotely plausible in a real-life context. But even this brief outline should be enough to yield the central philosophical point. Our imaginary hero's transformational analysis has led to a radical re-perception of the inner structure of his fateful infatuation. What had earlier appeared as a mysteriously akratic act, an unexplained failure of the self to follow its rational perception of the balance of goods, is now seen 'coloured in', irradiated with the full vividness of the inner mental life that before was lost in the shadows. Seen in the context of the deep and unrealized needs of his childhood, the 'infatuated' decision to pursue his flighty and superficial mistress now emerges as all of a piece with the complex structure of his early life: to the child in him (though this is to simplify and make explicit what was highly complex and never explicitly apparent at the moment of action), the decision which mystified his friends and colleagues was, though not consciously grasped by him at the time, a strangely compulsive reworking of the past, a confused and largely unconscious attempt to recover the elusive yet damaging *shadow* of the maternal affection he never securely enjoyed.

This 'transformational' account of *akrasia* is not of course meant to solve all the issues which have perplexed philosophers in connection with that fascinating problem (and indeed, there may be not one but many problems of *akrasia*, corresponding to its many different manifestations, so that any single solution would almost certainly be incomplete).[144] But at least it opens a space between two inappropriate models to which we may be tempted to assimilate what happens when we fail to act to further our own best grasp of the good – models which both turn out on analysis to be better described as cases of *pseudo-akrasia*. On the one hand there is the case of 'allowable indulgence'– the person who says 'I may as well stay in bed for another ten minutes, though I should "really" get up'. Such a case is not a true failure of rational control; for reason has in fact quite properly worked out that some temporary self-indulgence of the desires can perfectly well be permitted, since it is quite compatible with the more or less effective realization of long term goals. At the other extreme, equally divergent from true *akrasia*, there is the case of 'involuntary weakness'– the person who is in the grip of a compulsion or addiction so great that they are quite literally incapable of stopping themselves giving in to an irrational impulse. Again, this is not a truly akratic situation, since the weakness which is of crucial concern from the standpoint of moral psychology is the kind of weakness in action that attracts blame and self-recrimination, not unavoidable, involuntary behaviour. The weakness that is so puzzling from the ethical point of view has a disturbing *strangeness*: it is the case of the person who finds that her knowingly chosen actions are somehow at odds with her rational grasp of the best option, yet who cannot fully explain what has gone wrong.

The facts uncovered in the Cecil case involve a systematic redescription over time of the untoward event, and a transformed grasp of its significance. In stage one, the stage of the ill-fated infatuation, Cecil's decision to abandon his family was not fully perceived by him as akratic; it presented itself, rather, in a shifting guise, sometimes appearing as rash and impetuous, sometimes, for someone 'in love', as apparently the best thing to do. In stage two, the stage of depression and regret, it begins to emerge as akratic but, with hindsight, mysterious: our hero cannot fully grasp how the rational course of his life was disrupted by the attractions of someone whose appeal he now feels was illusory. Only at the end of the transformational process is the mystery solved: the light refracted through the distorting prism of his forgotten early childhood invested the object of his desire with a false colouring; or (to put the matter in a way closer to its actual complexity) a genuine coloration, derived from the unsatisfying characteristics of his actual mother, blended with the (unanalysed) frustrated adoration of her as experienced by his infant self, and resonating with the (objectively unappealing) characteristics of his present beloved, was introjected into the present structure of his desires, making the object before him unbearably attractive.

Mapping out the phenomenon in this way inevitably involves a measure of intellectualizing, and cannot serve as a substitute for the actual process of self-discovery which has to be gone through in each individual case. But it may perhaps be enough to give some idea of the richness of the resources available from a psychoanalytical perspective in comparison with those employed from the standpoint of the traditional ratiocentrism. In a sense, of course, the solution first canvassed by Socrates emerges as not wholly mistaken. Akrasia does indeed turn out to involve a certain sort of failure of knowledge. But what is involved is light years away from the Socratic notion of a purely cognitive error (or even – though it is in some respects nearer the mark – from the more sophisticated Aristotelian notion of desire impeding the operation of the practical syllogism).[145] Moreover, and in more general terms, if we take Socrates and his methods as paradigmatic of the ratiocentric approach, then it is worth observing that the transformational analyst's methods and aims are about as distant as they could possibly be from those of the father of philosophy. Socrates, using the methods of pure rational analysis (supplemented with some self-deprecating irony) typically ends his dialogues by announcing to his bemused interlocutors that, while they thought they knew something (for example, what justice, or piety, was), they will now have to admit their total ignorance. Sometimes, indeed characteristically, the admission of ignorance is forced by a brutal confrontation with a mystifying paradox. Thus, in the case of *akrasia*, we thought we knew that people sometimes knowingly choose the lesser good, but now (Socrates triumphantly proclaims) we must realize, like it or not, that this can't happen! The exercise is essentially a destructive one (the aggression implicit in Socrates' self-images, those of the tormenting fly and the stingray,[146] is no accident): the sharp weapons of philosophical analysis are used to leave us in a state of baffled numbness – *aporia* – with a vague sense that if we were just a bit cleverer, or our logic was as subtle or elegant as that of Socrates, we might have been able to get further. The transformationalist's approach is exactly the opposite. Firstly, the tools employed are not those of pure logic; reason is involved, but it can only get to work once we have been prepared to open ourselves to the darker side of our nature, what lies beneath the calm surface of intellectual analysis and debate. Secondly, rather than aiming to produce bafflement, to trap the victims in inconsistencies and rub their noses in their own ignorance, the exercise starts from a frank and freely acknowledged gap in our understanding: I can see I made an irrational decision, but I can't fully explain why. And thirdly, the end-product is diametrically opposed to the Socratic result. Socrates aimed to show his victims that they didn't after all really know what they confidently thought they knew.[147] The transformationalist, at the end of the process of guided self-examination, aims to reveal just the opposite– that we do after all know what we thought we didn't. What was opaque and baffling can after all be understood; something is brought to the surface that was before only a murky shadow. What we thought was a blank now slowly materializes before our eyes– and in a strange sense, though dimly and not in all its vivid colours, we were somehow aware of it all along.

8. REASON, INTEGRATION AND SELF-AWARENESS

He who binds to himself a joy
Does the winged life destroy.

William Blake[148]

For all its complexity, the psychoanalytic process just described might possibly be interpreted in ultimately rationalistic terms: all that has happened, it might be supposed, is that reason, albeit by means of a long and tortuous psychological progression, has been given better information to work with. This is perhaps how Freud, in many ways, after all, still the rationalist, sometimes saw it: 'where Id was, there shall Ego be'.[149] Dragged painfully into the daylight, the sorry remnants of our psychological past are laid out for clear-eyed inspection by the *lux rationis*. The 'psycho-ethical' quest, on this reading, would emerge in the end as broadly in line with the 'ratiocentric' tradition we have traced out in earlier chapters.

In one respect, such a reading must have an important element of truth. Whatever the insights into our psychic and ethical nature offered by psychoanalytic theory, they cannot plausibly be thought to lead to the conclusion that we should abandon our rational attempts to make sense of our lives. When Voltaire dryly observed that 'to prefer reason to felicity is very senseless',[130] he was deliberately drawing a paradoxical contrast; for, despite all the problems we have been at pains to uncover throughout this book, the soundness of the old Aristotelian definition of our nature cannot be faulted. Man, *anthropos*, the human being, is, *par excellence*, the 'rational animal'; to wish away our reason is to wish away our greatest gift, to abdicate our very title to humanity.

But the 'transformational' route to self-awareness described in the previous two sections suggests there is a truth beyond what can be stated via the old model of the light of reason inspecting the data and drawing its conclusions. Full self-awareness must involve more than widening the scope of deliberative reason; it requires a new *kind* of understanding, one mediated not by the grasp of the controlling intellect, but by a responsiveness to the rhythms of the whole self. To revert to the Heideggerian language examined at the start of this chapter, it is a matter of listening, of attunement, of a readiness to 'let being be'. In a rare departure from his technocratic program for the scientific manipulation of our bodily responses, Descartes is reported to have observed on one occasion that in matters of health, 'nature, with her perfect internal awareness of herself knows better than the doctor who is on the outside'.[131] And there may be a parallel here with the psyche: the ancients believed in *vis medicatrix naturae*, the healing power of nature; what psychoanalytic theory suggests, at any rate in its Jungian mould, is the *vis medicatrix animae*, the healing power of the psyche to achieve its own equilibrium and wholeness.

This is not a matter of the Platonic charioteer letting go the reins and allowing the horses to career out of control. Such ratiocentric models just do not allow proper scope for understanding what is at stake, for they offer us only a compartmentalized picture in which reason either remains firmly in charge, or else is taken over and dragged around by irrational forces. There is an intense *anxiousness* that such models betray– the fear that unless reason remains fussily and tensely at the helm, our lives will lose direction. Yet even a moment's reflection should reveal that what most gives our lives direction – the springs of human creativity, inventiveness and imagination – are in an important sense beyond reason's power wholly to encompass and regulate. This is as true in the sciences as in the arts, as true in matters of the intellect as in matters of the emotions. How often, on waking up in the morning, does the scientist find that a tightly knotted puzzle has begun to unravel; the novelist that the 'blocked' final chapter has begun to take shape? Of course the hard struggle and intellectual labour of realizing the details of the vision still remains; but the brain, unbeknownst to the anxious waking self, has been active in sleep. The beauty, rhythm and creativity of the human soul works its magic, and bestows its precious gifts without our direct bidding.[152]

Psychoanalytic theory has famously stressed the healing and illuminating activity of the mind in sleep, but the point just made goes beyond the tiresome debates about whether dreams can be said to have 'meaning' or whether they can be properly put to use in the consulting room. Indeed, the central issue does not really hinge on the phenomenon of dreaming as such. For even those who sincerely (if mistakenly) deny that they dream, and even those who acknowledge that they do, but consider dream material to be an insignificant jumble, must accept that there is more to the creative power of the mind than what can be willed into being by careful intellectual concentration. Even if we confine ourselves to what happens when we are awake, it is clear that the thoughts traced out by our conscious intellect are 'produced' by a staggeringly complex process of whose workings, as we ponder and deliberate, we are largely unaware. Yet for all that, many try to cling to the image of themselves as thinking beings who are always 'in charge', who are somehow *directing* their thought-processes from beginning to end.

We need a renewed humility here – the kind of humility that, paradoxically, the very apostle of the autonomous *res cogitans* managed to achieve. In the Third Meditation, Descartes recognizes the utter weakness and dependency of the thinking ego: the Cartesian meditator, *qua* thinking thing, is forced to acknowledge that it depends on a power far greater than itself, so much so that it could not even continue to exist from moment to moment without being supported by the unseen substance that sustains and preserves it.[153] Descartes, of course, was referring to the supreme power of God, without which everything would slip out of existence. But there is a secular analogue. The rational thinking self, as it ponders and deliberates from moment to moment, is, as Descartes saw, something extraordinarily thin and fleeting – a series of isolated moments of cogitation: 'I am, I exist, that is certain. But for how long? For as long as I am thinking. For it could be that were I totally to cease from thinking, I should totally cease to exist.'[154] The fragility and momentariness of the Cogito requires divine conservation to give it an enduring identity. Translating this into a less metaphysical and more biological idiom, we might say nowadays that beneath the deliberations of our reason, sustaining their continuity and grounding their identity, is an awesomely powerful nexus of psycho-physical structures and processes; it is these that provide us with our enduring sense of self, with the memories and patterns of recognition that enable us to locate ourselves in narrative with a history, with the imaginative and creative drives that urge us to recover our past, and take us forward to the future – in short with everything that makes us truly ourselves. Unless we regain some sense of attunement with that totality, of which our intellectualizing is only the thinnest of surfaces, we will be clinging to the most pitiful illusion – that our flickering cogitation from moment to moment makes up all of what we are. We will be like the *philosophe en méditation* pictured in Rembrandt's painting – turning away towards the flickering fire in his damp and stone-flagged chamber, while behind him, unnoticed, the brightness of the sun streams through the window, irradiating his whole being.[155]

The search for integrity, for allowing ourselves to recover, accept, and transform what we are, does not at all mean abandoning our rational birthright. For a human being who has achieved psychic balance, there will always be a dynamic interplay between the creative forces of the unconscious mind and the power of the self-conscious intellect, mapping, organizing, shaping, making coherent and testable patterns out of the flux of imaginative insight that wells up inside us. Nietzsche's night, 'deeper than day can comprehend', is nevertheless bound in with the day, in the spinning pattern of alternating light and darkness that sustains our life.

Much of our philosophical ethics, to be sure, will and should continue to operate in the light, concerned with the constructions of reason, the continuing project of building together a fair and productive social framework within which our lives may be lived. But true ethical value grows from the inside outwards; its core is the structure of passionate commitment and personal love that gives ultimate meaning to what we do.[156] Unless we are sure of who we are, unless we understand the sources of ourselves in our childhood, then all our solemn pronouncements on the good life will be hollow and unstable; for it is as children, like it or not, that we all learned to love, and life without love, and a true understanding of its psychic roots, cannot be fully human. There is no short cut here, no way that reason can productively forge ahead without first securing the ground of true self-awareness. To try to take refuge in abstract philosophical inquiries into the 'general good' is to enter the plea which the poet William Blake harshly described as 'the plea of the scoundrel, the hypocrite and the flatterer'; behind the hyperbole lies the insight that without what Blake called the 'minute particulars' that give meaning to our personal lives, the rest will risk being a sham.[157]

The search for self-awareness is not an easy one. We may hanker, as Socrates did, for a supremely authoritative inner voice, or, as Descartes did, for an external divine guarantee. In the starker light of modernity all we know is that we must continue to struggle, for however far we think we have come in the search, we can never be wholly sure that we are not impostors.[158] But expulsion from an illusory paradise need not be cause for despair. There are worse ambitions than to be like Milton's Adam and Eve, as they set out on their journey from Eden:

> Some natural tears they dropd, but wip'd them soon;
> The World was all before them.[159]

The destination is uncertain. But what is at stake is the attempt to achieve an ethics freed from reliance on the anxious frettings of controlling reason, where our rationality can instead be put to the service of a growing self-awareness. By the very act of embarking on the journey, we can achieve courage to endure, and hope of joy.

Notes

1 Compare the opening quotation of Chapter 2, below, and the other references cited there; For more on the 'hybrid' nature of human beings, see Chapter 3, section 4.

I PHILOSOPHY AND HOW TO LIVE

1 Jean-Paul Sartre, 'Question de Méthode' [1957], in *Critique de la raison dialectique*, p. 20.

2 Eustachius a Sancto Paulo, *Summa Philosophiae Quadripartita* [1609], Preface to Part II.

3 The *Summa* is divided into four parts, the first dealing with logic, the second with morals, the third with types of soul (vegetable, animal, sentient and rational) and the fourth with 'abstract and spiritual things'. It was evidently a favoured textbook, and at least five subsequent editions appeared during the following three decades, some (e.g. the 1620 edition) with the variant title 'Summa philosophica quadripartita'.

4 The scientific status of psychoanalytic theory has received considerable philosophical attention; see for example S. Hook (ed.), *Psychoanalysis, Scientific Method and Philosophy*, and see further chapter 4, section 2, below. Recent work in the theory of language and meaning has addressed implications of Freudian ideas, e.g. for the concept of intentionality (see M. Cavell, *The Psychoanalytic Mind: From Freud to Philosophy*); and in the philosophy of mind there has been a growing interest in what Freud has to say about self-deception and the role of the imagination (see for example David Pears, 'Motivated irrationality, Freudian theory and cognitive dissonance', in Wollheim and Hopkins (eds.), *Philosophical Essays on Freud*). But the ethical implications of psychoanalytic accounts of the human mind have received relatively scant attention; notable exceptions are the pioneering work of Richard

Wollheim (see *The Thread of Life*, esp. chs v–vii), and more recently Sebastian Gardner, *Irrationality and the Philosophy of Psychoanalysis*. See also I. Dilman, *Freud and the Mind*.

5 For the relationship of philosophy to its history, see further J. Cottingham, 'Plus una vice agendum: Cartesian Metaphysics Three and a Half Centuries On', and B. Williams, 'Philosophy and its Historiography', both in J. Cottingham (ed.), *Reason, Will, and Sensation*.

6 The notion of *Nachträglichkeit* is over-simplified here, but it will be explored further in chapter 2, section 3, and chapter 4, section 5. For the general importance of the time dimension for the understanding of human life, compare Wollheim: 'A person leads his life at a crossroads: at the point where a past that has affected him and a future that lies open meet in the present' (*The Thread of Life*, p. 31).

7 Prefatory letter to the 1647 French edition of the *Principles of Philosophy* (AT ix 20: CSM i 190). For key to abbreviations, see Note on references, p. xiii, above.

8 Some of the implications of this conception will be explored in chapter 2, sections i and 4.

9 Zeno's phrase 'a good flow of life' (*eurhoia biou*), and the formula of his successors 'living in accordance with nature (*homologoumenos te physei zen*) are preserved in the compilations of the anthologist Stobaeus (early fifth century AD); see Long and Sedley (eds.), *The Hellenistic Philosophers*, no. 63A and B.

10 Dante Alighieri, *La Divina Commedia: Paradiso* [*c*. 1300], Canto i (translated J. Cottingham).

11 Alexander Pope, *An Essay on Criticism* [1711], 267.

12 *Principles of Philosophy*, Lettre-préface a l'édition française [1647]: AT ixb 14: CSM i 186.

13 'Through this philosophy we could know the power and action of fire, water, air, the stars, the heavens, and all the other bodies in our environment, as distinctly as we know the various crafts of our artisans, and use this knowledge . . . to make ourselves as it were the lords and possessors of nature' (*Discourse on the Method* [1637], part vi, AT vi 62: CSM i 142–3).

14 The passage cited in the previous note continues with the hope that with the aid of the new Cartesian philosophy 'we might free ourselves from innumerable diseases, both of the body and the mind, and perhaps even the infirmity of old age'. For Descartes' views on medicine, see also the *Conversation with Burman* [1648], AT v 178–9: CSMK 353.

15 Descartes' 'crowning project' was to be the articulation of the 'highest and most perfect moral system (*la plus haute et la plus parfaite morale*) which presupposes a complete knowledge of the other sciences, and is the ultimate level of wisdom (*le dernier degré de la sagesse*)' (*Principles*,

Lettre-préface, AT IXB 14: CSM I 186). For more on 'le traité de morale qui aurait couronné l'œuvre', see G. Rodis-Lewis, *La morale de Descartes*, p. 4, and Descartes, *La Morale*, ed. Grimaldi, Introduction; see also J. Cottingham, *A Descartes Dictionary*, s. v. 'morality'. Descartes' conception of ethics will be dealt with fully in chapter 3, below.

16 'Gaudium . . . inconcussum et aequale, tum pax et concordia animi'. Seneca, *De Vita Beata* [*c.* AD 40], III, 4.

17 From among many possible examples, compare the 'science of morals' developed by Richard Cumberland who was influenced by the views of Descartes, as well as those of the Cambridge Platonists. Cumberland speaks of the 'countless things that can be picked out from a knowledge of the universe for the material of particular precepts directing the foundation of morals' (*De Legibus Naturae* [1672], ch. 1; in D. D. Raphael (ed.), *British Moralists*, section 106). Writing in a rather different tradition some seventy years later, the German theologian and philosopher Christian Crucius defines ethics as 'the science that explains rationally both the divine laws and the rest of the general rules for the achievement of good ends, thus showing the way as far as possible to attain human perfection and happiness' (*Guide to Rational Living* [*Anweisung vernünftig zu leben*, 1744], section 159; in J. B. Schneewind (ed.), *Moral Philosophy from Montaigne to Kant*, vol. II, p.577).

18 *Physics* [*c.* 330 BC], bk. II, ch. 8 (trans. Hardie and Gaye). For more on teleology in Aristotle, see R. J. Hankinson, 'Philosophy of Science', in J. Barnes (ed.), *The Cambridge Companion to Aristotle*, ch. 4.

19 Bacon, *De dignitate et augmentiis scientiarum* [1623], III, 5 (in *Works*, ed. Ellis and Spedding, p. 473); Descartes, *Meditations* [1641], Fourth Meditation, AT VII 55: CSM II 39. See further ch. 3, section 1, below.

20 *Objections and Replies* [1641], Fifth Replies (AT VII 375: CSM II 258).

21 This theme will be developed in chapter. 3, section 2.

22 The vividly proleptic image surfaces in the midst of Aristotle's confident assertion of natural teleology: *Physics* (bk II, ch. 8).

23 *In Memoriam* [1850], liv. Though Charles Darwin's *The Origin of Species* did not appear until nine years later, Tennyson's poem clearly anticipates the idea of a struggle for existence in which countless individuals and species perish:

> Are God and Nature then at strife,
> That Nature leads such evil dreams?
> So careful of the type she seems,
> So careless of the single life . . .
>
> 'So careful of the type?' but no.
> From scarped cliff and quarried stone
> She cries, 'A thousand types are gone
> I care for nothing, all shall go.'

Tennyson took a keen interest in the work of many of Darwin's predecessors, such as Charles Lyell's *Principles of Geology* (1830–3) and Robert Chambers' *Vestiges of Creation* (1844).

24 'We should refer every choice to 'the health of the body and the calm of the soul' (ἐπὶ τὴν τοῦ σώματος ὑγίειαν καὶ τὴν τῆς ψυχῆς ἀταραξίαν), since this is the 'end of the blessed life' (τοῦ μακαρίως ζῆν τέλος); *Letter to Menoeceus* [290 BC], 127, in Long and Sedley, *The Hellenistic Philosophers*, 21B(1).

25 *Letter to Menoeceus* 122 (in Long and Sedley, *The Hellenistic Philosophers*, 25A).

26 We may note in passing that there is a parallel fallacy to the 'pan-axial' fallacy which Spinoza does *not* manage to avoid: this is the *pan-psychist* fallacy – the attempt to explain (not value but) *consciousness* in terms of some pervasive property of the universe as a whole (rather than as an emergent property of some things in it). For Spinoza the totality of being has the attribute of thought; his near contemporary Leibniz was, in a different way, equally attracted by panpsychism (see Leibniz, *Monadology* [1714], sections 60–70, in *Philosophical Writings*, ed. Parkinson, pp. 188ff.), and the idea still has its adherents (cf. T. Nagel, 'Panpsychism', in *Mortal Questions*).

27 Ludwig Wittgenstein, *The Blue and Brown Books*, [1958], p. 18.

28 To assess the effects of Hume's philosophy on what I have called the 'synoptic' conception of ethics would be a highly complex task. I shall confine myself to two brief points of interest. (i) The successful development by Hume (and others such as Francis Hutcheson) of a 'moral sense' theory, grounding morality in sentiment as opposed to reason, was clearly inimical to the kind of grand deductive schema for ethics which some rationalist moral philosophers had espoused (compare note 17 above). Nevertheless, though supporting his arguments via a (supposedly) empirical methodology rather than on the basis of a grand metaphysics, Hume does in fact end up offering a systematic blueprint for the good life based on a theory of the virtues that are adapted to the natural demands of our human makeup and the requirements for a happy society. In this sense he may perhaps be construed as a 'synopticist', albeit of the more modest secularized kind distinguished towards the end of section 2 of the present chapter. (ii) Perhaps more important for subsequent ethical theory than for Hume himself was his supposed prohibition on the move from 'is' to 'ought' judgements (though commentators disagree as to whether he did in fact consider such a move to be always unjustifiable; see Hudson (ed.), *The Is / Ought Question*). Whatever the correct interpretation, there is no doubt that much twentieth-century philosophy has made a very sharp distinction between factual and evaluative language, and this may

have generated some background resistance both to the 'synoptic' notion of a universal philosophical system linking ethics with science, and even to the more modest project of deriving evaluative conclusions from a theory of human nature. Cf. note 36, below.

29 For the notion of a 'scientia generalis' or 'mathesis universalis' ('universal discipline'), see Descartes, *Rules for the Direction of the Understanding* [1629], Rule IV (AT x 378: CSM I 19). Compare Leibniz, 'Of Universal Synthesis and Analysis', in *Philosophical Writings*, ed. Parkinson, p. 17. See further, Cottingham, *The Rationalists*, 36ff. and 64ff.

30 See John Skorupski, *English-Language Philosophy 1750-1945*, p. 131.

31 Perhaps typical of the rise of the 'academicized' conception of moral philosophy was G. E. Moore's highly influential *Principia Ethica* (1903). Moore, to be sure, did issue pronouncements on the good life ('by far the most valuable things . . . are the pleasures of human intercourse and the enjoyment of beautiful objects'; p. 188); but the Moorean theory of goodness as simple and indefinable implied, in the words of a recent commentator, 'that judgments of intrinsic goodness by their very nature admit of no evidence, for or against' (Tom Regan, 'Moore', in L. Becker (ed.), *Encyclopedia of Ethics*).

32 I leave on one side the development of so-called 'Continental' philosophy in the twentieth century, much of which took a rather different course; some of the contributions of those writing in the existentialist tradition will be addressed in chapter 4, section 1, below.

33 The phrase is Skorupski's: *English-Language Philosophy*, ch. 4.

34 Compare the famous closing sentence of the *Tractatus Logico-Philosophicus* [1921]: 'Wovon man nicht sprechen kann, darüber muss man schweigen' ('What we cannot speak of we must pass over in silence'); for the notion of what can be said, and the limits of the sayable, see *Tractatus* 6.53.

35 Compare A. J. Ayer's fourfold classification in chapter 6 of *Language, Truth and Logic*: 'There are, first of all, propositions which express definitions of ethical terms . . . Secondly there are propositions describing the phenomena of moral experience, and their causes . . . Thirdly there are exhortations to moral virtue. And lastly there are actual ethical judgements.' Only class one, on Ayer's view, constituted a legitimate terrain for the moral philosopher; the second was the province of 'the science of psychology or sociology'; the third consisted of mere 'ejaculations or commands'; and the fourth were simply expressions of feeling.

36 Midgley argues that moral philosophers since Moore have represented the notion of value as 'floating free, a kind of mysterious exotic pink balloon, a detached predicate, high above all possible attempts

to entrap it and connect it with life by any conceptual scheme whatever': *Beast and Man*, p. 194. See further J Cottingham, 'Neo-Naturalism and its pitfalls'.

37 For examples of work during this period which refutes the caricature, compare Alasdair MacIntyre's writings, including *A Short History of Ethics* (1966), where some of the ideas were beginning to surface which would later flower in his groundbreaking *After Virtue* (1981). Among other interesting counterexamples are P. T. Geach, 'Good and Evil', in P. Foot (ed.), *Theories of Ethics* (1967), and G. E. M. Anscombe's seminal 'Modern Moral Philosophy' (1958).

38 Samuel Scheffler, 'Against the System', *Times Literary Supplement*, 16 February 1996.

39 See Michael Smith, *The Moral Problem*, p. 2. Smith's opening proposition is that 'philosophers are surely right to give meta-ethical questions a certain priority over questions in normative ethics'. It should be added however, that Smith's interests go beyond 'pure analysis' since he argues that a dominant interest in the meaning and analysis of moral language is needed in order to 'legitimate' philosophical incursions into normative ethics (*The Moral Problem*, p. 3).

40 *A Theory of Justice*, p. 21.

41 E. Craig, *The Mind of God and the Works of Man*, ch. 1.

42 *A Theory of Justice*, section 9, p. 46.

43 *A Theory of Justice*, section 20, p. 121.

44 *A Theory of Justice*, ch. 1. For criticism of the kind alluded to, see R. M. Hare, 'Rawls' Theory of Justice' in N. Daniels (ed.), *Reading Rawls*.

45 Cf. Rawls, *A Theory of Justice*, ch. 1.

46 *A Theory of Justice*, p. 12.

47 It should be stressed that this is not, in itself, intended as a *criticism* of the Rawlsian project, most of which, as its author underlines, is not intended to provide an account of ethics in its entirety, but only of that part of morality which is concerned with the theory of social justice.

48 J. S. Mill, *Utilitarianism*, ch. 4.

49 For preference utilitarianism, see for example J. Harsanyi, 'Morality and the Theory of Rational Behaviour', in A. Sen and B. Williams (eds.), *Utilitarianism and Beyond*, pp. 54ff. Compare also R. B. Brandt, *A Theory of the Good and the Right*. It should be noted, however, that, while defining an individual's good in terms of desire-satisfaction, Brandt allows only *rational* desires to count– i.e. those which would remain after exposure to all the relevant empirical information and logical reasoning; the theory of the good is thus constrained in important ways. Brandt also holds that when one is concerned with promoting the good for *others*, the preference-satisfaction view needs to give way to a more traditional hedonistic or happiness-maximizing account.

50 *A System of Logic* [1843], final chapter. In *On Liberty*[1861], Mill notes that he regards utility as 'the ultimate appeal on all ethical questions, but it must be utility in the largest sense, grounded on the permanent interests of man as a progressive being' (ch. 1, section 11).

51 The phrase is Mill's: *System of Logic*, final chapter.

52 The general flavour of this kind of 'liberalism' with respect to substantive values is aptly characterized by Paul Grice in an informal aside on the intellectual climate of post-war Oxford: 'We are independent and we are tolerant of the independence of others, unless they go too far. We don't like discipline, rules . . . self-conscious authority, and lectures or reproaches about conduct (which are usually ineffective anyway, since those whom they are supposed to influence are usually either too sensitive or not sensitive enough). Above all we dislike punishment, which only too often just plays into the hands of those who are arrogant or vindictive. We don't much care to talk about "values" (pompous) or "duties" (stuffy . . .). Our watchwords (if we could be moved to utter them) would be "Live and let live, though not necessarily with me around" or "If you don't like how I carry on, you don't have to spend time with me"' (*The Conception of Value*, pp. 57–8n.).

53 For the notion of 'neutral' liberalism, as contrasted with one which embodies more substantive conceptions of the good, such as a strong commitment to autonomy, see Will Kymlika, 'Liberal Individualism and Liberal Neutrality', *Ethics* 99 (July 1989), pp. 883-905. See also J. Raz, *The Morality of Freedom*, ch. 5.

54 Compare comments made earlier on the 'thin' theory of the good in Rawlsian ethics. In his later writings, John Rawls suggests that rational argument about social justice might need to be supported by an 'overlapping consensus' among those who may hold radically divergent conceptions of the good. See 'On the idea of an Overlapping Consensus', *Oxford Journal for Legal Studies* (1987), pp. 1–25.

55 For the second line, see Raz, *The Morality of Freedom*, ch. 13.

56 Iris Murdoch, *Metaphysics as a Guide to Morals* [1992], p. 297.

57 Further evidence of this is the burgeoning of 'applied ethics' since the 1970s; see 'Introduction', p. 1, above.

58 Aristotle, *Nicomachean Ethics* [325 BC], bk I, ch. 7.

59 For a comprehensive sample of recent work in virtue ethics, see R. Crisp (ed.), *How should one live?*

60 T. Hurka, *Perfectionism*, pp. 30-1.

61 Martha Nussbaum, 'Aristotle, Nature and Ethics', in Altham and Harrison (eds.), *World, Mind and Ethics*, p. 108.

62 Bernard Williams, 'Replies', in Altham and Harrison (eds.), p. 201. The debate between Williams and Nussbaum has many ramifications which are too complex to be evaluated here.

63 Martha Nussbaum, 'Aristotle, Nature and Ethics', p. 123.

64 John Kekes, *Moral Wisdom and Good Lives*, p. 209.

65 Some of which, I should add, are readily acknowledged in Kekes's discussion; *Moral Wisdom and Good Lives*, p. 209.

66 See the opening chapters of Martha Nussbaum's groundbreaking study *The Fragility of Goodness*.

67 Reflection on this may suggest that there is something about the very language and style of contemporary moral philosophy, in its abstract intellectualist mould, that makes it ill suited to conduct an inquiry into the conditions for human happiness that will have the right kind of depth to be truly illuminating. The problem of finding the right *style* for an authentic moral philosophy, though it has begun to be addressed in recent work (see, for example, Williams, 'Replies'), seems to me very far indeed from having found an adequate solution.

68 R. Campbell, *Truth and Historicity*, p. 2.

69 Though there is no explicit reference to the work of Freud and his disciples in the arguments of Kekes, referred to above, he does seem to acknowledge the kind of problem I am underlining here when he talks of 'our desires, hopes, fears, aversions, memories, *fantasies*, plans, disappointments, and so on' as 'anomalies that refuse to fit into the account we are trying to impose on them' (*Moral Wisdom and Good Lives*, p. 211; emphasis supplied).

70 'But man's craving for grandiosity is now suffering the ... most bitter blow from present-day psychological research which is endeavouring to prove to the "ego" of each one of us that he is not even master in his own house, but that he must remain content with the veriest scraps of information about what is going on unconsciously in his own mind.' Sigmund Freud, *Introductory Lectures on Psychoanalysis* [*Vorlesungen zur Einführung in die Psychoanalyse*, 1916–17], ch. 18.

2 RATIOCENTRIC ETHICS

1 Alexander Pope, *An Essay on Man* [1744], Epistle II, 3–4, 7–8, 13–18. For an earlier variation on this theme compare Blaise Pascal, *Pensées* [*c.* 1660], ed. Lafuma, no. 678 ('l'homme n'est ni ange ni bête'), and, earlier still, Augustine, *De civitate Dei* [413–26], ix, 13 ('homo medium quoddam ... inter pecora et angelos').

2 Seneca, *Epistulae Morales* [*c.* AD 64], 16 3.

3 Plato's philosopher-guardians spend the bulk of their lives in abstract intellectual contemplation (*theoria*), required only occasionally to 'descend' to the political arena to take their turn in political administration; their life, described as 'far more enviable than that of any Olympic victor', will be one whose wealth consists 'not of money but of the happiness of a right and rational life' (*Republic* [*c.* 380 BC], 465d,

521a). The intellectualist flavour of (much of) the *Republic* is not to be found in all Plato's writings; see further the second paragraph of section 2, below (and see also notes 39 and 58, below).

4 Cf. Aristotle, *Nicomachean Ethics* [*c.* 325 BC]: happiness depends on man's proper function, the 'activity of the soul in accordance with reason or not without reason' (bk I, ch. 7: 1098a7). Aristotle's notion of practical reason (and his sporadic attraction to the more theoretical Platonic model) will be discussed in section 2, below.

5 The image (probably dating from the third century BC) is recorded in the *Lives of the Philosophers* (*c.* third century AD) by Diogenes Laertius: 7, 39–41 (in Long and Sedley, *The Hellenistic Philosophers*, 26B).

6 Diogenes Laertius, 7, 134 (and other texts cited in Long and Sedley, 44B-F).

7 Diogenes Laertius, 7, 143 (in Long and Sedley, 53X).

8 For more on this see the commentary in Long and Sedley, p. 319.

9 Marcus Aurelius, *Meditations* [*Ta eis heauton, c.* AD 175], X 6.

10 See chapter I, section I.

11 Diogenes Laertius, 7, 87–9, in Long and Sedley 63C (with omissions; trans. J. C.). Zeno of Citium (335–263 BC) was the founder of the Stoa; his pupil Cleanthes (331–232) was its second head; and Chrysippus (280–207) its third head (and probably the most important for the subsequent development of Stoic thought). Similar accounts of the salient features of Stoic ethics can be found in several others sources; compare the following from Cicero's *De Finibus* [45 BC], III, 73: 'No one can make true judgements about good and evil without a grasp of the rational principles of nature and divine life, and an understanding of whether or not the nature of man accords with that of the cosmos. Without a knowledge of the principles of physics, no one can see the supreme significance of the ancient ethical maxims of the sages, such as "yield to the times", "follow God", "know thyself" and "nothing in excess". Such knowledge alone reveals the relevance of the power of nature when it comes to cultivating justice and maintaining friend-ships and the other ties of affection.' For commentary on this passage and much valuable information about Cicero's presentation of sto-icism, see the edition of M. R. Wright, *Cicero on Stoic Good and Evil.*

12 Long and Sedley, *The Hellenistic Philosophers*, pp. 57ff.

13 　　　multa minuta modis multis per inane videbis
　　　corpora misceri radiorum lumine in ipso
　　　et velut aeterno certamina proelia pugnas
　　　edere turmatim certantia nec dare pausum
　　　conciliis et discidiis exercita crebris;
　　　conicere ut possis ex hoc, promordia rerum
　　　quale sit in magno iactari semper inane.

De rerum natura [*c.* 60 BC], 2, 116–22 (trans. J. C.). Here and later on in this chapter, I offer verse translations of Lucretius which aim to be reasonably accurate but sometimes depart from a literal word for word rendering in the interests of fluency.

14 The Epicurean universe is a predominantly deterministic one, though the trajectories of the atoms are subject to occasional random 'swerves' (*De rerum natura*, 2, 216–50).

15 *De rerum natura*, v 1203.

16 The fact that the moral prescriptions emerging from both Stoic and Epicurean philosophy have so much in common, despite the different metaphysics, gives some support to the view of Julia Annas, one of the most insightful recent commentators on Greek ethics, that 'ancient ethical theories can be legitimately studied in a relatively autonomous way'. Since '[there is an ethical] structure common to philosophers whose metaphysical principles are mutually conflicting', it follows that 'what is thus shared cannot be dependent on the metaphysical principles' (*The Morality of Happiness*, p. 15). Annas goes on to point out that many of the ethical arguments of the earlier Stoics aim to establish the content of ethics independently of any wider cosmic perspective: 'what we get from the wider perspective is increased understanding of a subject whose content has already been established without the wider perspective' (p. 165). Annas allows that Stoic ethical prescriptions (e.g. that virtue is sufficient for happiness) acquire added resonance when we come to see that they are 'underwritten by the nature of the universe', but insists that this cannot make any 'actual difference' to the content of the thesis that virtue suffices for happiness, or provide any new motive to be virtuous ('if I understood and lived by the ethical theory, I already had sufficient motive to be virtuous'; p. 166). Annas's view of the matter clearly has much to commend it (and it is certainly in tune with the 'compartmentalized' approach to ethics that characterizes present day moral philosophy (see above, chapter 1, sections 2 and 3)); occasionally, though, it perhaps seems to risk underplaying the *holistic* dimension that characterizes the way in which Classical ethical theories were typically supposed to operate. Thus, increasingly as Stoic thought develops (and most prominently in the later Stoics), there is an interplay between inquiries into how human life should be lived and awareness of the wider cosmic perspective in which human life is set. I have argued (in chapter 1) for the importance of this 'synoptic' strategy for the understanding of ancient ethical theories. I will only add here that what I have called the 'holistic' dimension need not be construed in terms of a rigidly deductive schema; the emphasis should be placed on the *interplay* of the cosmic and the personal, rather than on a formal logical demonstration of

the latter from the former. (See *The Morality of Happiness*, p. 710, where Annas makes a convincing case against forcing ancient theories into a hierarchical pattern in which supposedly self-standing 'cosmic' premises are supposed to be laid down in advance, and then to do all the logical work in justifying or supporting the resulting ethical insights.)

17 For the Epicurean notion of *ataraxia*, see Epicurus, *Letter to Menoeceus* [*c.* 290 BC] 127–32 (translated in Long and Sedley, p.124); the notion is discussed in detail in Julia Annas, *The Philosophy of Happiness*, pp. 238ff. For the Stoic ideal of tranquillity (*summum bonum animi concordia*), see Seneca, *De Vita Beata* [*c.* AD 58], VIII, 6 (compare also *Letters*, 92.3, quoted in Long and Sedley, 63F).

18 This theme is extensively explored in E. R. Dodds's groundbreaking study, *The Greeks and the Irrational*.

19 Friedrich Nietzsche, *The Birth of Tragedy* [*Die Geburt der Tragödie*, 1872], trans. Kaufmann, section 1. I am here simplifying somewhat, since as unfolded by Nietzsche the concept of the Apollonian is not simply identified with the power of transparent rationality, but is partly related to the creative powers of the unconscious mind: Apollo is the 'ruler over the beautiful illusion of the inner world of fantasy'. The world of our dreams is a 'creation of which every man is truly an artist'; the 'profound delight and joyous necessity' experienced in our dreams stems from the same creative source that powers all art (ibid.).

20 *The Birth of Tragedy* , section 2.

21 See above, chapter 1, section 4.

22 For more on this, see chapter 1, section 3, above.

23 Cicero, *De Finibus* [45–44 BC], III 7 (trans. Wright, p. 41).

24 Cf. chapter 1, section 4, above, and chapter 4, section 1, below. The term 'post-modern' is a rather slippery and unsatisfactory one, but I use it to indicate a collection of views developed amongst others by Jean-François Lyotard (*La Condition post-moderne* [1979]) and most closely associated in the anglophone world with Richard Rorty. Rorty's aim is to deflate the pretensions of earlier philosophers to provide a rationally defensible overview which 'limns the true structure of reality'; we need to give up the notion that 'all contributions to a given discourse . . . can be brought under a set of rules which will tell us how rational agreement can be reached'. In place of the traditional view of the philosopher as a kind of 'cultural overseer who knows everyone's common ground', he offers a more modest conception of philosophy as a kind of 'hermeneutics', aiming not at an 'objective', rationally determined route to the truth, but frankly acknowledging that our interpretations can operate only within the assumptions of a particular culture. (See *Philosophy and the Mirror of Nature*, pp. 299ff.) For

a discussion of Lyotard and the post-modernist movement, see E. Matthews, *Twentieth-Century French Philosophy* , ch. 8, section 4.

25 Friedrich Nietzsche, *Unzeitgemässe Betrachtungen* [1873], translated as *Unmodern Observations*, ed. W. Arrowsmith, p. 88. The importance of this Nietzschean notion is tellingly explored in Bernard Williams, 'Descartes and the Historiography of Philosophy' in J. Cottingham (ed.), *Reason, Will and Sensation*, pp. 19ff.

26 *Epistulae Morales*, 76, 9–10 (in Long and Sedley, *The Hellenistic Philosophers*, 63D).

27 Compare the celebrated terms 'rationalism' and 'empiricism', hallowed by long usage in the historiography of philosophy, but (as increasing scrutiny in recent decades has shown) often concealing important variations in approach and emphasis, and often used to refer to philosophers whose ideas overlap far more than the conventional picture of two distinct and opposing philosophical camps would suggest. For more on this, see J. Cottingham, *Rationalism*, chapter 1, esp. pp. 9ff.

28 Compare Hume's famous remark that 'Tis not contrary to reason to prefer the destruction of the whole world to the scratching of my finger' (*A Treatise of Human Nature*, bk II, part iii, section 3; Selby Bigge edn, p. 416). For more on Hume's position, compare the text cited at note 66, below; see also chapter 1, note 27, above.

29 *Republic*, 441e.

30 The plight of a city where policy depends on the rapidly fluctuating moods of the people is directly compared by Plato to the plight of an individual whose life is dominated by the passions (*Republic*, bk VIII, 555–61).

31 Thus, drawing an analogy with the harmonious state, Plato defines temperance in terms of the 'unanimity and concord' of reason, spirit, and the desires, 'where there is no conflict between the ruling element and its two subjects, but all are agreed that reason should be ruler' (*Republic*, bk IV, 441–2; cf. 430–1).

32 Compare Martha Nussbaum: '[T]here is no reason [according to the conception which appears in book IV of the *Republic*] why the *content* of a life plan should not include appetitive activities as intrinsically valuable components that get selected and arranged alongside the others. There is also no reason to suppose that reason will organize the agent's life around the activity of reasoning' (*The Fragility of Goodness*, p. 139). Nussbaum goes on, however, to point out that by the end of the *Republic* Plato has 'rejected many of the most common human activities, including all appetitive activities, as lacking in true or intrinsic value' (ibid.). For an unorthodox view of Plato which sees him as having a fairly neutral conception of the good life (subject to its

providing for the orderly satisfaction of chosen goals), see T. H. Irwin, *Plato's Moral Theory*, 226–48.

33 *Republic*, 421b5; cf. note 3, above.

34 *Republic*, 517c1–5; 517b1.

35 For Plato's view that only the few have the innate aptitude for the life of the philosopher-ruler, see *Republic*, bk III, 412–15.

36 Compare Socrates' demonstration that the life of the philosopher-ruler is 729 times better than the life of the tyrant: *Republic*, 587e.

37 *Republic* 540a5–10.

38 The philosopher-rulers, enjoying the pure air of the upper world of philosophical contemplation, are to be compelled 'to go down, each in turn, to live with the rest, and let their eyes grow accustomed to the darkness' (*Republic*, bk VII, 520c).

39 What I have described as Plato's view is based on the picture found in the early Socratic dialogues and in (parts of) the *Republic*. It is however possible to see in other texts a more sympathetic attitude to the emotions; thus Nussbaum argues that in the *Phaedrus* Plato dramatically recants his earlier intellectualism (*The Fragility of Goodness*, ch. 7).

40 J. S. Mill, *Utilitarianism* [1861], chapter 2. But see J. Skorupski, *John Stuart Mill*, p. 306, for a possible defence of Mill against the circularity charge.

41 Compare *Phaedo*, 66–8, where Socrates argues that the life of the philosopher is vastly superior to that of the mere *philosoma* or body-lover; while we are alive, we will be 'nearest to the truth if as far as possible we have no communion with the body which is not absolutely necessary, and if we are not affected by its nature but keep ourselves pure from it, until God himself shall set us free' (67a).

42 It is no accident that Plato's philosopher-guardians are to live without family or close personal ties (*Republic*, bk V, 462–3); compare the critical comments of Aristotle on this point, *Politics*, 1262a. For more on the role of personal commitments and emotional ties in the good life, see J. Cottingham, 'Partiality, Favouritism and Morality'; see also 'Partiality and the Virtues' in R. Crisp (ed.), *How Should One Live?*

43 *Nicomachean Ethics*, book x, ch. 7 (1177b).

44 A *zoon politikon*, literally, an animal that lives in a *polis*, or city-state; Aristotle, *Politics* [c. 330 BC], book I, ch. 2 (1253a2).

45 *Practike tis [zoe] tou logon echontos*: *Nicomachean Ethics*, book I ch. 7 (1098a3–4). Some translations wrongly put 'active' instead of 'practical', which, as Broadie points out, is a distortion (*Ethics with Aristotle*, p. 35, n. 31).

46 'Though you could cut off a vine-shoot with a carving knife or a chisel or other tool you would do the job best if you used a pruning-knife made for the purpose, which, surely we may call its function . . . The

function of a thing is that which only it can do, or that which it does best' (*Republic*, 353a).

47 'Just as the good i.e. [doing] well for a flautist, a sculptor and every craftsman, and in general, for whatever has a function and [characteristic] action, seems to depend on its function, the same seems to be true for a human being . . . What could this be? For living is apparently shared with plants, but what we are looking for is the special function of human being; hence we should set aside the life of nutrition and growth. The life next in order is some sort of sense-perception; but this too is apparently shared with horse, ox and every animal. The remaining possibility, then, is some sort of practical life of the [part of the soul] that has reason.' *Nicomachean Ethics*, book i, ch. 7 (1097b25–1098a3). The translation is by Irwin, except for the final sentence (for which see note 45, above).

48 Compare T. Nagel, 'Aristotle on *Eudaimonia*', in Rorty (ed.), *Essays on Aristotle's Ethics*.

49 *Nicomachean Ethics*, 1177b26. For more on the complexities of Aristotle's attitude to *theoria*, see Sarah Broadie, *Ethics with Aristotle*, ch. 7.

50 In the well-ordered state, 'the desires of the inferior multitude will be controlled by the wisdom of the superior few' (bk iv, 431d1). Compare the graphic description in bk viii, 559ff. of what happens when a 'brood of conflicting desires' gets possession of someone's soul; the image of the 'many-headed beast' comes in book ix, 588c8 (see also the reference at note 65, below). In addition to the (multiform) appetitive element, Plato acknowledges a 'spirited' element in the soul (connected with virtues like courage and the desire to avoid what is shameful), whose activities can be benign; but whose role is strictly limited to that of a pliant 'auxiliary' to reason, corresponding in the political sphere to specialist agencies serving the guardians and dedicated to the internal and external security of the state (*Republic*, 416ff.; 441e5).

51 '*To men hos epipeithes logo, tod' hos echon and dianooumenon.*' (*Nicomachean Ethics*, book i, ch. 7, 1098a4–5).

52 Book i, ch. 13 (1102b30).

53 Book i, ch. 13 (1102b 16–18).

54 πάντα ὁμοφώνει τῷ λόγῳ (1102b28).

55 'To understand the relationship between virtue and happiness on Aristotle's view, it is important to note that ἐγκράτεια (*enkrateia*), or self-control, that subordination of appetite to the moral will, which is for Kant the highest expression of a moral nature, is for Aristotle a mere *pis aller*: the very moral struggle which arises when our human passions pull against the demands of right action is, to the Aristotelian way of thinking, already a sign that all is not as it should be. Far from

earning extra points on the scale of goodness, self-control is a second best virtue, rescuing (but in no sense transfiguring or validating) the life of the individual whose emotional and behavioural habits have not been properly and harmoniously laid down' (J. Cottingham, 'Partiality and the Virtues', in Crisp (ed.), *How should one live?*, p. 61).

56 Strictly speaking, our table is incomplete, since there are in fact not four but eight logically possible cases. The full table would look like Table 2 (below). The first four rows correspond to those discussed by Aristotle. But in addition we have (row 5) the character who is 'self-controlledly bad' (that is one whose bad principles are threatened by residual good appetites, but who manages determinedly to stick to his bad principles (for example the professional blackmailer who manages to suppress affectionate impulses for his victims). Then there is (row 6) the character who is 'weakly bad' – who fails to stick to his bad principles because of residual good feelings (for example the blackmailer who weakly gives in to impulses of affection for his victims). Finally, (rows 7 and 8) are the remaining logically possible cases (less interesting from the ethical point of view), where the behaviour fails to conform either to chosen goals or to appetites; this, presumably, can only happen where there is some physiological malfunction or external compulsion (in other words we are dealing with involuntary conduct rather than ethical states or dispositions of character).

Table 2

	Character	Goal	Appetite	Conduct matches goal?
1	Virtuous	good	good	yes
2	Self-controlled	good	bad	yes
3	Uncontrolled	good	bad	no
4	Vicious	bad	bad	yes
5	Self-controlledly bad	bad	good	yes
6	Bad but weak	bad	good	no
7	[involuntary bad conduct]	good	good	no
8	[involuntary good conduct]	bad	bad	no

57 This conception of non-human animals is almost certainly over simplistic, but it is beyond my purpose to explore that here. For a fascinating discussion of some of the issues, particularly as they arose in the ancient Greek context, see R. Sorabji, *Animal Minds and Human Morals*.

58 I should here renew the caveat made earlier about the label 'Platonic': I am identifying one important strand in Plato's thinking that emerges in only some of his works, e.g. in certain passages in the *Republic* – and some commentators have interpreted even these differently; cf. section 3, and notes 32 and 39, above. Were there space here for a less schematic account, it would be worth paying attention to the tensions found even in Plato between the extolling of the exclusively intellectual life and the demands of practical living which require not only 'intelligence and truth', but also a 'sound and just character, accompanied by temperance' (*Republic* 490b). Overall, however, I tend to agree with the verdict of Christopher Rowe that 'In the *Republic*, Plato's talk is largely, if not exclusively, about the need to repress our non-rational drives' ('Philosophy, Love, and Madness', in C. Gill (ed.), *The Person and the Human Mind*, p. 229). See also note 125, below.

59 Aristotle, *Eudemian Ethics*, 1214b10–11.

60 *Ethice arete*, often awkwardly translated 'moral virtue'; see the introduction by Jonathan Barnes to the Penguin translation of the *Nicomachean Ethics*. Aristotle connects the root of 'ethics' with the word for habit, *ethos* (bk ii, 1103a18).

61 For complexities in Aristotle's account of the part that is 'responsive to reason', and difficulties with his analogy with childhood obedience to parental guidance, see Broadie, *Ethics with Aristotle*, ch. 2, esp. section 2.

62 The man of practical wisdom (*phronesis*) deliberates 'not about some restricted area but about what makes for living well in general (*pros to eu zen holos*)'; *Nicomachean Ethics*, bk vi, ch. 5 (1140a28).

63 'Actions should express right reason (*orthos logos*)' (bk ii, ch. 2, 1103b33); 'virtue is a disposition concerned with choice, lying on a mean . . . this being determined by reason, and in the way that the person of practical wisdom would determine it' (bk ii, ch. 6, 1106b36ff).

64 Val Plumwood, *Feminism and the Mastery of Nature*, p. 107.

65 *Phaedrus*, 230a3–6 (freely translated).

66 David Hume, *A Treatise of Human Nature* [1739–40], book ii, part iii, section 3.

67 This radical position is perhaps better attributed to Socrates, rather than to Plato. I cannot enter here into the complex question of how far the views of Socrates, as presented in some Platonic dialogues, correspond to the considered philosophical position of Plato himself. Some commentators have argued that as his philosophy developed Plato moved away from, or at least qualified, the intellectualism he inherited from his teacher. His theory of the tripartite soul, for example, seems to allow for genuine cases of reason being overcome

by the passions (compare the example of Leontion, in *Republic* 339e–440a). The question of whether we can distinguish between those of Plato's works where 'Socrates' expresses views of the historical Socrates, and those where he is a spokesman for Plato's own distinctive views, is interestingly discussed in T. Penner, 'Socrates and the early dialogues', in R. Kraut (ed.), *The Cambridge Companion to Plato*. See also note 70, below.

68 *Protagoras*, 358c–d; trans. Guthrie (with modifications). For detailed discussion of this argument, see Irwin, *Plato's Moral Theory*, ch. 4.

69 Though generally translated 'weakness of will' (or sometimes, with a somewhat archaic flavour, 'incontinence'), the Greek term *akrasia* literally indicates a lack of control, being made up of the negative prefix '*a*', plus the cognate noun from *kratein*, 'to rule' (the root from which we get some of our political vocabulary – cf. demo*cracy*, auto*cracy*).

70 Or 'contradicts things that appear manifestly' (Irwin's translation); *Nicomachean Ethics*, 1145b29. It is significant that Aristotle speaks of Socrates rather than Plato. Though one can never be wholly certain when Plato is expounding the philosophical views of the actual historical Socrates, as opposed to using him as a mouthpiece for his own views, there is good reason to think that the denial of *akrasia* (and indeed the general tendency to intellectualize ethics) is genuinely Socratic in origin. For a detailed and sophisticated treatment of the various Socratic and Platonic analyses of mental conflict, as well as those found in Aristotle and the Stoics, see A. W. Price, *Mental Conflict*.

71 For some of the details, see the passage quoted at note 72, below, and, for some of the complications, note 74, below.

72 'Within "having knowledge but not using it" we can see a difference in the having, so that there is such a thing as having knowledge in a way and yet not having it, as with someone who is asleep or mad or drunk. Now this is exactly the condition of a man under the influence of passions; for outbursts of anger and sexual desires and other such passions do actually alter our bodily condition, and sometimes even produce fits of madness. Clearly, then, akratic people are like people who are asleep or mad or drunk . . . That a man *says* knowledgeable things is no proof that he knows them. Men under the influence of these passions may utter scientific proofs or recite the poems of Empedocles, but they do not understand what they are saying' (*Nicomachean Ethics*, bk VII, ch. 3, 1147a11; translated in J. Ackrill, *Aristotle the Philosopher*, pp. 146–7).

73 *Nicomachean Ethics*, 1147b15.

74 In his detailed explanation of *akrasia*, Aristotle imagines a universal principle (like 'nothing X [e.g. fatty] should be tasted'), which,

coupled with the minor premise 'this is X', should lead me not to eat; but at the same time there is another universal ('all sweet things are nice'), which, coupled with the premise 'this is sweet', and accompanied by a strong appetite, leads me to taste. Aristotle observes that 'since the last premise is a belief about something perceptible, and controls action, this must be what the incontinent person does not have when he is being affected' (1147b10). The phrase 'the last premise' is somewhat obscure, and might mean either that the akratic man fails to realize that this chocolate bun in front of him is fatty, or perhaps that he somehow fails to draw the conclusion that he should not eat it. For a meticulous analysis of possible interpretations of this passage, and a complex reconstruction of a possible defence of Aristotle, see S. Broadie, *Ethics with Aristotle*, ch. 5, esp. section 3.

75 Unless he is a speed junkie, pathologically quite out of control. But again, this is not the typical or interesting case. Before putting his foot down, the akratic driver will characteristically check the mirror to see if there are any police cars in the vicinity; he urgently wants the thrill of driving fast, but is not so far in the grip of a psychological compulsion as to be beyond reflecting on what he is doing.

76 The phrase is Broadie's: *Ethics with Aristotle*, ch. 5.

77 The sexist metaphor, incidentally, is appropriate enough to Aristotle, who, notoriously, considers women to be unsuited for the attainment of full ethical and political virtue (cf. *Nicomachean Ethics*, 1162a19–27; *Politics*, 1159b28ff.); but it may seem discordant when applied to Plato, given his proposals for the equal status of women as philosopher-guardians (cf. *Republic*, 451–2). Recent critics have argued, however, that the arrangements for female guardians set out in the *Republic* cannot rescue Plato from the charge of having a general tendency to devalue women; see especially V. Plumwood, *Feminism and the Mastery of Nature*, pp. 76ff.

78 In his fine analysis of the emotion expressed in Shakespeare's love poetry, Leishman comments on its 'passionately hyperbolical vehemence, intransigence . . . sweepingness' (*Themes and Variations in Shakespeare's Sonnets*, p. 213).

79 For the Greek conception of *hubris*, the 'capital sin of self-assertion', see E. R. Dodds, *The Greeks and the Irrational*, p. 48.

80 William Shakespeare, *Romeo and Juliet* [*c.* 1594], II, vi, 9.

81 Bernard Williams, *Shame and Necessity*, p. 45. I have to some extent taken this quotation out of context, since it forms part of a philosophical discussion about the location of the problem of *akrasia* (whether as an issue in ethics or in the philosophy of mind) which is not germane to my present purpose.

82 *Moral Luck*, ch. 2. Though the example is loosely based on that of the painter, it is not supposed to hinge on the truth of any of the actual historical circumstances affecting the real Gauguin's life.

83 Robert Burns, 'To a Mouse' [1785].

84 See above, chapter 1, section 1.

85 See Karl Popper, *Conjectures and Refutations* [1963], ch. 1.

86 'It is perfectly true, as philosophers say, that life must be understood backwards. But they forget the other principle, that it must be lived forwards. And if one thinks over that proposition, it becomes more and more evident that life can never really be understood in time, simply because at no particular moment can I find the necessary resting place from which to understand it backwards' (from Søren Kierkegaard, *Journals*, in the entries for the year 1843; in Dru (ed.), p. 127). Compare the discussion of *Nachträglichkeit* in chapter 4, section 5, below; the psychoanalytic project of recovering the past suggests a less pessimistic conclusion than Kierkegaard's.

87 Jean Grimshaw, 'Ethics, Fantasy and Self-transformation', in A. Phillips Griffiths (ed.), *Ethics*.

88 Note that there are certain courses of action, for example adulterous behaviour, which Aristotle already condemns in advance as cases of vice (1107a10), so that he is not lumbered with the implausible claim that there is a 'right amount' of such passion-dominated behaviour, or a 'right time' for its indulgence. In our contemporary ethical culture, however, the suggestion that we can rule out as inherently vicious all contra-monogamous erotic desires is one which it is difficult, without bad faith, to sustain. This is not because the relevant prescriptions are incoherent, but because our modern conceptions of marital virtue are confused and unstable; our contemporary culture lacks convincing and accepted models of chastity and sexual fidelity which can carry the right kind of emotional force to serve as clear guides for action. For more on this theme, see J. Cottingham, 'Religion, Virtue and Ethical Culture'.

89 Indeed his original point is not necessarily linked to the use to which I am putting his suggestion. See note 81, above.

90 Quoted by the philosopher Porphyry (late third century AD); in Long and Sedley, *The Hellenistic Philosophers*, 25C.

91 *Nicomachean Ethics*, book II, ch. 6 (1106b21).

92 'The aim of being without passions (*apatheia*) was contrasted with the ideal of moderation in passions (*metriopatheia*) adopted by the Peripatetics in dependence on Aristotle, who had held that it was wrong to feel either too little or too much fear, anger, or other emotion' (F. H. Sandbach, *The Stoics*, p. 63). In common with several more recent commentators, Sandbach goes on to observe that the contrast can be

exaggerated, since the Stoics did not wish to eliminate feelings entirely: if the 'moderate' passion of the Peripatetic corresponds to a 'correct' feeling (one informed by an enlightened estimation of the value of the objects of desire), such a feeling 'could perhaps not be regarded by a Stoic as a passion at all'. Despite this qualification, Sandbach goes on to make the apt point that 'what a Peripatetic would regard as a correct amount of anger or of fear would seem excessive to a Stoic' (*The Stoics*, p. 64).

93 Stobaeus, 2.88, in Long and Sedley, *The Hellenistic Philosophers*, 65A.

94 Julia Annas, *Hellenistic Philosophy of Mind*, p. 116. Annas cites the famous illustration of Chrysippus: a man acting emotionally is like someone running instead of walking. He is going faster than the situation prudently demands, but he is not being 'dragged about' in the way Plato's conflict model suggests; rather, he is in a state (for which he is fully responsible) where he has misperceived what the situation requires. Such is the intuitive appeal of the 'inner conflict' model, however, that defenders of the Stoic point of view often reverted to it. Annas goes on to note that Cicero, for example, 'persists in treating the Stoic ideal of banishing *pathe* as a more rigoristic version of other theories' demand to moderate the *pathe*' – a move which leads to an 'edifying muddle' (*Hellenistic Philosophy of Mind* p. 118).

95 Brad Inwood, *Ethics and Human Action in Early Stoicism*, p. 154.

96 Annas, *Hellenistic Philosophy of Mind*, p. 114.

97 For a full discussion of some of the difficulties, see Inwood, ch. 5.

98 Plutarch, *De Virtute Morali* 446, in Long and Sedley, *The Hellenistic Philosophers*, 65G. Though Plutarch's original text does not specify who were the proponents of the 'wavering thesis', Long and Sedley, along with other modern commentators, plausibly suppose that the Stoics are meant.

99 Inwood, *Ethics and Human Action in Early Stoicism*, p. 138, following the original criticism of Plutarch; see however Annas, *Hellenistic Philosophy of Mind*, p. 117.

100 See C. Gill, 'Did Chrysippus misunderstand the Medea?', *Phronesis* vol. 28 (1983).

101 Paul, *Epistle to the Romans* [*c.* AD 50], 7:19.

102 William Shakespeare, *Measure for Measure*, [1604], Act III, scene I.

103 Annas, *Hellenistic Philosophy of Mind*, p. 114.

104 Stobaeus, 2. 90 (in Long and Sedley, *The Hellenistic Philosophers*, 65E).

105 This is particularly true of the later Stoic writers; compare Seneca: 'Quid est beata vita? securitas et perpetua tranquillitas' ('What is the blessed life? Security and perpetual tranquillity'). *Letters*, 92.3, in Long and Sedley, 63F.

106 Epictetus, *Discourses* [*c.* AD 100], 8.

107 The notion of the 'widening circle' was developed by the later Stoic Hierocles [second century AD], quoted in Stobaeus, *Florilegium*, 84, 23. Cf. Epictetus, *Discourses*, 2.10. For a discussion of the Stoic concept of *oikeiosis* which is involved here, see Annas, *The Morality of Happiness*, pp. 267ff.

108 Susan Wolf, 'Moral Saints', *Journal of Philosophy*, 79 (1982) 419–39; reprinted in Peter Singer (ed.), *Ethics*, p. 347.

109 Diogenes Laertius, 7, 101–3, quoted in Long and Sedley, *The Hellenistic Philosophers*, 58A. In some of the Stoic writers, the category of the 'indifferent' was broken down into importantly distinct sub-categories: some indifferent things were regarded as 'to be taken' (see Stobaeus, 2, 79 and 82, quoted in Long and Sedley, 58C). For discussion of these distinctions, see Annas, *The Morality of Happiness*, pp. 167ff.

110 The three types of 'good feeling', χάρις, εὐλάβεια, and βούλησις are listed in Diogenes Laertius 7, 116 (in Long and Sedley, 65F).

111 Annas, *Hellenistic Philosophy of Mind*, p. 115.

112 Annas suggests that the Stoic can care 'in the normal way' for things with non-moral value, yet not 'wrongly value them in a way which could lead you to give morality less than its proper, overriding place' (*Hellenistic Philosophy of Mind*, p. 115). This may be so, but the considerations I advance in the text suggest that the richness and urgency of typical human 'caring' is going to be hard to accommodate within the Stoic picture of the good life.

113 Ay, in the very temple of Delight
Veil'd Melancholy hath her sovran shrine,
Though seen of none save him whose strenuous tongue
Can burst Joy's grape against his palate fine.
(John Keats, 'Ode to Melancholy' [1820])

114 'Since *eupatheiae* are defined via ideal conditions, it is not very surprising that we have no very intuitive idea of what they would be like' (Julia Annas, *Hellenistic Philosophy of Mind*, p. 115).

115   ulcus enim vivescit et inveterascit alendo
inque dies gliscit furor atque aerumna gravescit,
si non prima novis conturbes volnera plagis
volgivagaque vagus Venere ante recentia cures . . .
    etenim potiundi tempore in ipso
fluctuat incertis erroribus ardor amantum . . .
Unaque res haec est, cujus quom plurima habemus
tum magis ardescit dira cupidine pectus.
(Lucretius, *De rerum natura*, IV 1068ff.; freely translated J.C.)

116 Martha Nussbaum, 'Words Not Arms', in her edited collection *The Poetics of Therapy*, p. 82.

117 'Epicureans from Polystratus to Lucretius tirelessly urge on us that only the rational activity of philosophy will make us happy, for we need the exercise of the rational soul in order to organize our lives, and make sense of the products of the irrational soul' (Annas, *Hellenistic Philosophy of Mind*, p. 151).

118 To give one example, the deliverances of dreams are characterized as essentially delusive rather than revelatory of important underlying truths about the emotions; cf. Lucretius, *De rerum natura*, IV 961ff.

119 Compare the purple passage where Lucretius extols the power of reason (*'rationis potestas'*):

> Reason alone, why doubt it, has the power
> When life is one long struggle in the gloom,
> To free us. For as children fear the dark
> So we by day fear things no more to dread.
> The fear of mind and darkness of the soul
> No beams of sun, nor the bright shafts of day
> May cast aside, but reason and the shape
> Of nature seen even as she truly is.
>
> *De rerum natura*, II 53ff. (trans. J. C.).

120 ἄφοβον ὁ θεός
ἀνύποπτον ὁ θάνατος
τἀγαθόν μὲν εὔκτητον
τὸ δὲ δεινὸν εὐεκκαρτέρητον

Philodemus, *Adversus sophistas*, 4 (in Long and Sedley 25J). The adjective in the second line ἀνύποπτον means literally 'unsuspected', or (in this context) 'nothing to be suspicious about, nothing to worry about'. An alternative version has ἀναίσθητον – 'nothing to feel in death' or 'death is total unconsciousness' (cf. Epicurus, *Letter to Menoeceus*, 124, in Long and Sedley 24A).

121 'Sed nil dulcius est, bene quam munita tenere / Edita doctrina sapientum templa serena'; *De rerum natura*, II, 7–8.

122 Nussbaum herself, later in the article cited, fully acknowledges this strand in Epicureanism; indeed, the phrase 'godlike self-sufficiency' is her own (*The Poetics of Therapy*, p. 83). It will be clear to readers of this and other works of Nussbaum that my thinking on these matters, despite some differences of interpretation, is deeply indebted to her work.

123 For this theme, see Annas, *The Hellenistic Philosophers*, pp. 196–9.

124 Aristotle, with his schema for the moderation of the emotions, is by far the least guilty of this charge, though as we have seen, even he falls into serious difficulties about the relationship between reason and the feelings; see above, section 2.

125 A fascinating text in this respect is the passage in *Republic* book IX, where Plato strikingly anticipates the Freudian insight into the sig-

nificance of dreams, describing the 'desires which emerge in our dreams, when the reasonable and humane part of us is asleep and its control relaxed, and our bestial nature, full of food and drink, wakes and has its fling and tries to secure its own kind of satisfaction'. But this apparent acknowledgement of the dangerous power of unconscious forces is immediately retracted by a calm insistence that the man of 'sound and disciplined character' will be able to go to sleep 'with an untroubled temper, with the other two parts of him [spirit and desire] quietened, and his reasoning element stimulated', so that he will be in a position to 'grasp the truth undisturbed by visions of wrong-doing' (571c–572a). For some interesting discussions of Plato's account of the 'lawless desires', see Jonathan Lear, 'Plato's Politics of Narcissism', in Irwin and Nussbaum (eds.), *Virtue, Love and Form*. For other possible parallels between Plato and Freud, compare A. W. Price, 'Plato and Freud', in C. Gill (ed.), *The Person and the Human Mind*, ch. 11.

3 THE ETHICS OF SCIENCE AND POWER

1 Francis Bacon, *Novum organum* [1620], book 1, section 81; trans. in *Works*, ed. Spedding and Ellis, p. 280.

2 Blaise Pascal, *Pensées* [*c.* 1660], no. 206 (in *Œuvres*, 11, 27).

3 For an illuminating exposition of some of the basic ingredients of this traditional picture, see Charles Taylor, *Sources of the Self*, parts 1 and 11.

4 In the well known Aristotelian schema, there are four types of cause or explanation, formal, material, efficient and final. To provide the *formal* cause is to specify something's essential nature – 'what it is to be something'. The *material* cause specifies something's constituents or ingredients; the *efficient* cause is the motive or productive agency that brings something about ('that from which the first origin of change proceeds'); and the *final* cause is what something is for, or 'that for the sake of which' something comes about. See Aristotle, *Physics*, book 11, ch. 3; *Posterior Analytics*, book 11, ch. 11; *Metaphysics*, book Delta, 1013a29. For more information on these notions as used in the seventeenth century, see J. Cottingham, *A Descartes Dictionary*, s. v. 'cause'.

5 See further the passage from Aristotle's *Physics* quoted in chapter 1, section 2, above (reference at ch. 1 note 18).

6 For a discussion of the philosophical issues involved here, see A. Woodfield, *Teleology*, and C. Price, 'Functional Explanations and Natural Norms'.

7 Paracelsus, *Sämtliche Werke*, 1, 12, 148ff. (in Jacobi (ed.), p.183).

8 See further Geneviève Rodis-Lewis, 'Descartes' life and the development of his philosophy' in J. Cottingham (ed.), *The Cambridge Companion to Descartes*, p. 26.

9 See Descartes' early treatise, *Le Monde* [1633], AT xi 36: CSM i 92; Descartes withdrew the treatise from publication on hearing of the condemnation of Galileo by the Inquisition. For his caution in this respect, see letter to Mersenne of April 1634 (AT i 285: CSMK 42–3); for further details, see J. Cottingham, *Descartes*, pp. 11–12. For abbreviations used in referring to works of Descartes, see p. xiii above.

10 Fourth Meditation, AT vii 55: CSM ii 39. Some twenty years earlier, in 1623, Bacon had observed that 'the search for final causes is sterile, and like a virgin consecrated to God brings forth no fruit': *De dignitate et augmentiis scientiarum*, iii, 5 (in Bacon, *Works*, p. 473).

11 For Descartes' rejection of the scholastic apparatus of 'substantial forms' and 'real qualities', see letter to Morin of 13 July 1638, AT ii 200: CSMK 107. For a general discussion of this aspect of the seventeenth-century revolution, see J. Cottingham, *The Rationalists*, pp. 4–6.

12 *Il Saggiatore* ('The Assayer'), in Galileo, *Opere*, vi, 232.

13 *Principles*, part ii, art. 64 (AT viii 79: CSM i 247).

14 Compare Descartes' scathing comments on the value of traditional classificatory models like the 'tree of Porphyry' in the *Search for Truth* [*c.* 1641], AT x 516: CSM ii 410.

15 'The [scholastic] philosophers maintain that above the clouds there is a kind of air much finer than ours, which is not composed of terrestrial vapours as our air is, but constitutes a separate element. They say too that above this air there is yet another body, much finer again, which they call the element of fire . . . But in explaining these elements, I do not use the qualities called 'heat' 'cold', 'moisture' and 'dryness' . . . for they can all be explained without the need to suppose anything in their matter other than the motion, size, shape and arrangement of its parts' (Descartes, *Le Monde*, ch. 5, AT xi 23–6: CSM i 88–9).

16 Compare Robert Boyle: 'If it be demanded how snow dazzles the eyes, they [the schoolmen] will answer that it is by the quality of whiteness . . . and if you ask what whiteness is, they will tell you that it is a real entity, which they term a quality' (*The Origins of Forms and Qualities* [1672], in *Selected Philosophical Papers*, p. 16).

17 For the notion of simple structural patterns underlying a wide range of phenomena, and expressible merely in terms of 'order and measure', see Descartes, *Regulae* ('Rules for the Direction of Our Native Intelligence') [*c.* 1628], Rule Four, AT x 378: CSM i 19.

18 *Le Monde*, ch. 6 (AT xi 34: CSM i 91).

19 As Stephen Gaukroger has aptly pointed out, although the mathematical and mechanical approaches to science go together in Descartes, forming a 'potent combination', they are not necessary concomitants; some seventeenth-century mechanists (for example Hobbes and Gassendi) provided little if any mathematics to support

the mechanical models they offered; conversely, some mathematical theorists (compare Kepler) made no use of physical mechanisms. See S. Gaukroger, 'Descartes: Methodology', in G. H. R. Parkinson (ed.), *The Renaissance and Seventeenth Century Rationalism*, pp. 176–7.

20 *Principles of Philosophy*, part I, art. 70; for more on this, see J. Cottingham, 'Descartes on colour'.

21 'Those long chains composed of very simple and easy reasonings which geometers customarily use to arrive at their most difficult demonstrations gave me occasion to suppose that all the things which come within the scope of human knowledge are interconnected in the same way.' (*Discourse*, part ii, AT VI 19: CSM I 120. Compare also Fifth Meditation, AT VII 71: CSM II 49.)

22 *Discourse*, part iv (AT VI 41: CSM I 131).

23 Substantial forms and real qualities were the stock in trade of scholasticism (cf. notes 15 and 16, above). The role of 'occult powers' is rather more complex. It has recently been argued that appeal to such powers was a feature not so much of scholastic philosophy as of certain forms of 'renaissance naturalism' that attempted to supplant it. See S. Gaukroger, 'Descartes: Methodology', pp. 174ff. For Descartes' hostile attitude to occult powers and forces, see *Principles of Philosophy*, part IV, art. 187. For an interesting discussion of some ambiguities in the notion of an occult quality during this period, see K. Hutchison, 'What Happened to Occult Qualities in the Scientific Revolution'.

24 'The nature of matter or body consists . . . simply in its being something which is extended in length, breadth and depth' (*Principles of Philosophy*, part II, art. 4); 'I regard the minute parts of terrestrial bodies as being all composed of one single kind of matter, and believe that each of them could be divided repeatedly in infinitely many ways, and that there is no more difference between them than there is between stones of various different shapes cut from the same rock' (*Meteorology*, AT VI 239: CSM I 187n.).

25 Consider how this works. A stick, dropped, falls towards the earth; landing on a bonfire it is consumed into smoke and ashes. Traditional explanations appealed to natural kinds and definitions of essences: it is of the nature of terrestrial matter to move downwards, and the subsequent conflagration is accounted for by reference to the natural properties of the airy and fiery elements. This is no doubt a crude oversimplification of the kinds of scholastic explanation on offer, but the central feature which informs them all is the appeal to natural kinds, to the essential properties of the various substances involved. In the new Cartesian science, by contrast, forms, essences and substances play no role whatever. Despite the official talk of 'corporeal substance', with its 'principal attribute of extension' (*Principles*, part I,

art. 63), Descartes' explanation of the event in question invokes simply a very small number of abstract principles – the principle of the conservation of rectilinear motion and the principle of deflection of smaller and slower bodies by larger and faster ones – together with a series of mathematical formulae for calculating the outcomes of various possible cases of the collision of particles. The account, throughout, is a purely quantitative one (see further *Principles of Philosophy*, part II, arts. 45–52). As Descartes observed in his early treatise *Le Monde*, 'when flame burns wood, though others imagine the form of the fire, the quality of heat and the process of burning to be different things, I . . . am content to limit my conception to the motion of its parts . . . It suffices to conceive of these motions in order to understand how the flame has the power to consume the wood and to burn . . . and the same also suffices to enable us to understand how the flame provides us with heat and light . . . It is this motion alone which is called "heat" and "light" according to the different effects it produces' (AT XI 7–9: CSM I 83–4). For a full account of the Cartesian laws of motion, see D. Garber, 'Descartes' physics', in J. Cottingham (ed.), *The Cambridge Companion to Descartes*.

26 Third Meditation, AT VII 40ff.: CSM II 28ff.

27 For Descartes' monistic theory of material substance, see AT VII 14: CSM II 10; see also Cottingham *The Rationalists*, pp. 84ff., and *A Descartes Dictionary*, s. v. 'body'.

28 *Principles of Philosophy*, part II, arts. 4, 36, 37.

29 *Principles* part II, art. 36 (AT VIIIA 61: CSM I 240).

30 *Le Monde*, ch. 6 (AT XI 34: CSM I 91).

31 Cf. J. Cottingham, 'The Cartesian legacy'.

32 Introducing his scientific programme in the *Discourse*, Descartes declares 'I noticed certain laws which God has so established in nature, and of which he has implanted such notions in our minds, that after adequate reflection we cannot doubt that they are exactly observed in everything which exists or occurs in the world' (AT VI 41: CSM I 131). Compare the following comment from Richard Rorty's *Philosophy and the Mirror of Nature*: 'The notion that our chief task is to mirror accurately, in our own glassy essence, the universe around us is the complement of the notion, common to Democritus and Descartes, that the universe is made up of very simple, clearly and distinctly knowable things, knowledge of whose essences permits commensuration of all discourses' (p. 357). Though this represents a standard view of the Cartesian project, it will emerge later in this section that it is in important respects a misleading one.

33 Letter to Mersenne of 27 May 1630, AT I 152: CSMK 25. Cf. Sixth Replies: 'God did not will that the three angles of a triangle should be

equal to two right angles because he recognized that it could not be otherwise; . . . it is because he wills that the three angles of a triangle should necessarily equal two right angles that this is true and cannot be otherwise' (AT VII 432: CSM II 291). For an excellent account of the historical origins of the doctrine, and its broader philosophical significance, see Richard Campbell, *Truth and Historicity*, esp. ch. 5.

34 See S. Gaukroger, *Cartesian Logic*, ch. 2.

35 Letter to Mersenne of 15 April 1630, AT I 146: CSMK 23. For Descartes, just because we humans cannot grasp something is no reason to conclude that it is beyond the power of God. God thus turns out, on Descartes' conception, to be in a real sense *incomprehensible*: our soul, being finite, cannot fully grasp (French, *comprendre*; Latin *comprehendere*) or conceive him. For more on the doctrine of the incomprehensibility of God, see J.-M. Beyssade, 'The idea of God and the proofs of his existence', in Cottingham (ed.), *The Cambridge Companion to Descartes*, pp. 174ff.

36 'The utmost effort of human reason is to reduce the principles productive of natural phenomena to a greater simplicity . . . But as to the causes of these general causes, we should in vain attempt their discovery . . . The most perfect philosophy of the natural kind only staves off our ignorance.' *An Enquiry concerning Human Understanding*, pp. 30–1.

37 See *Principles of Philosophy*, part II, art. 64.

38 I use the term 'post-Humean' in accordance with what may be called the 'traditional' interpretation of Hume as a philosopher who undermined the idea of science as the discovery of necessary connections in the world. For an alternative interpretation, see J. Wright, *The Sceptical Realism of David Hume*.

39 This theme is developed further in J. Cottingham, 'The Cartesian Legacy'.

40 *Principles of Philosophy*, part IV, art. 188.

41 For how this task was addressed by Spinoza and Leibniz, see J. Cottingham, *The Rationalists*, ch. 5.

42 *Principles*, part III, art. 3.

43 *Conversation with Burman*, AT V 168: CSMK 349.

44 *Principles*, part III, art. 3.

45 Letter to 'Hyperaspistes', August 1641 (AT III 431: CSMK 195).

46 AT VII 375: CSM II 258. See further J. Cottingham, *The Rationalists*, pp. 177ff. As used in the eighteenth century, the term 'deist' sometimes referred to those who held the existence of God could be established by reason alone, without recourse to revelation; but it also often implied belief in a God who 'leaves the universe to its own devices' without any kind of intervention; for this reason, deism was

often stigmatized by orthodox thinkers of the early modern period as the royal road to atheism. For more on Descartes' position in this respect, see J. Cottingham, *Descartes*, pp. 100, 106.

47 Letter to Elizabeth of 4 August 1645, AT IV 265: CSMK 257.
48 Letter to Elizabeth of 6 October 1645, AT IV 316: CSMK 273.
49 Fourth Meditation, AT VII 62: CSM II 43.
50 See chapter 1, section 1 and chapter 2, section 1, above.
51 For important anticipations of the new Cartesian vision in the ideas of the Epicureans, see chapter 1, latter part of section 2, and chapter 2, section 1.
52 Cf. Bernard Williams, *Descartes: The Project of Pure Inquiry*, ch. 8.
53 *Principles of Philosophy*, part II, art. 39.
54 Letter from More to Descartes of 23 July 1649 (AT V 383).
55 Letter from Descartes to More, August 1649 (AT V 405: CSMK 382).
56 Though Descartes' own scientific apparatus is in actual fact not quite as straightforward as his reductionist rhetoric here suggests; for some of the complications, see J. Cottingham, 'Force, Motion and Causality: More's Critique of Descartes', in J. Rogers and J-M. Vienne (eds.), *The Cambridge Platonists*.
57 This will shortly need qualifying: Descartes' developed view turns out to be that whilst we are, *qua* thinking beings, set apart from the physical world, we are nevertheless, *qua* human beings, intimately related to it (see section 4, below).
58 '[Ces notions générales touchant la physique] m'ont fait voir qu'il est possible à parvenir à des connaissances qui soient fort utiles à la vie, et qu'au lieu de cette philosophie spéculative, qu'on enseigne dans les écoles, on en peut trouver une pratique, par laquelle, connaissant la force et les actions du feu, de l'eau, des astres, des cieux et de tous les autres corps qui nous environnent, aussi distinctement que nous connaissons les divers métiers de nos artisans, nous les pourrions employer en même façon à tous les usages auxquels ils sont propres, et ainsi nous rendre comme maîtres et possesseurs de la nature' (*Discourse*, part VI, AT VI 61–2: CSM I 142–3).
59 *Discourse*, part IV, AT VI 32–33: CSM I 127.
60 Indeed it was sometimes wholly rejected. Thomas Hobbes and Benedict Spinoza are perhaps the most striking examples here: Hobbes adopted a resolute materialism, while Spinoza, though acknowledging the distinctness of the *attributes* of thought and extension, located them in a single substance. See Hobbes, *Leviathan* [1651], part I, and Spinoza *Ethics* [*c.* 1665], part V, preface (in *Opera*, ed. C. Gebhardt, vol. ii, p. 280: *Collected Works*, ed. Curley, vol. i, p. 596).
61 Cartesian dualism has been the target of unremitting hostility throughout our own century. The story begins with the behaviourist

programmes of the emerging science of psychology; it is taken up in the work of mid-century linguistic analysts like Gilbert Ryle, with his scathing attack on the Cartesian 'dogma' of 'the ghost in the machine'. From another quarter, Wittgenstein's philosophy of mind systematically attacks the notion of the mental realm as consisting of privately accessible subjective states. The counter-Cartesian revolution continues, though in a rather different form, in the nineteen sixties, with the development of a materialist philosophy of mind, in which mental states are bluntly equated with electro-chemical states of the central nervous system. And finally, the new discipline of cognitive science, which mushroomed in the nineteen eighties, seems to put the last nail in the Cartesian coffin: mental states, on this most recent view, are functional or organizational states to be understood on analogy with computer programs. The issue of the relation between the mental and the physical realms cannot, however, be regarded as finally settled: some aspects of what might broadly be called a Cartesian approach continue to exert a residual influence on the work of such thinkers as Thomas Nagel (cf. *Mortal Questions*, ch. 12) and Colin McGinn (see *The Subjective View*, pp. 140ff.).

62 Sixth Meditation, AT vii 78: CSM ii 54.

63 The title of the Sixth Meditation is 'Of the real distinction between mind and body'; in the argument that follows, the meditator distinguishes himself *qua* thinking thing both from body or matter in general, and from the particular human body which is his own. (The fact that Latin lacks both a definite and an indefinite article means that Descartes' use of the term *corpus* ('body') is sometimes ambiguous between these two; see further, J. Cottingham, *A Descartes Dictionary*, s. v. 'body'.

64 There are important qualifications to be made here, but these will be left until section 4.

65 Cf. the comparison with 'les divers métiers de nos artisans': *Discourse*, part vi (AT vi 62: CSM i 142).

66 'It is only the will, or freedom of choice which I experience within me to be so great that the idea of any greater faculty is beyond my grasp; so much so that it is above all in virtue of the will that I understand myself to bear in some way the image and likeness of God.' Descartes goes on to say that 'God's will does not seem any greater than mine when considered as will in the essential and strict sense' (Fourth Meditation, AT vii 57: CSM ii 40).

67 *Principles of Philosophy*, Preface to the French Edition (1647), AT ixb 14–15: CSM i 186.

68 *Discourse*, part iii, AT vi 23: CSM i 122.

69 AT vi 28: CSM i 125. In an earlier letter to his friend Marin Mersenne, written soon after he had withdrawn his *Le Monde* from publi-

cation on hearing of the condemnation of Galileo, Descartes wrote 'I desire to live in peace and to continue the life I have begun under the motto *Bene vixit qui bene latuit*' ['a good life is one which is lived to the end without attracting untoward attention'] (April 1634, AT I 286: CSMK 43).

70 To Chanut, 20 November 1647, AT v 86–7: CSMK 326.

71 Letter of April 1638, AT II 35: CSMK 97.

72 'The author does not like writing on ethics, but he was compelled to include these rules because of people like the Schoolmen [the adherents of traditional scholastic philosophy] who would else have said that he was a man without any religion or faith and that he intended to use his method to subvert them' (*Conversation with Burman* [1648], AT v 178: CSMK 352–3).

73 AT VI 25: CSM I 123.

74 The nearest Descartes gets to discussing our duties in the public arena is in the letter to Elizabeth of 15 September 1645 – though even here the starting point is that 'each of us is a person distinct from others whose interests are accordingly in some way different from those of the rest of the world' (AT IV 293: CSMK 266).

75 *Discourse*, part iii, AT VI 25–6: CSM I 123–4.

76 See section 6 of the present chapter. The sixteenth century had seen a powerful renaissance of Stoic thought. L. Zanta, who provides a thorough account of some of the key figures in this movement, points out that though certain elements in Stoic ethics chimed in well with Christian doctrine, the neo-Stoic movement could nevertheless be seen as potentially subversive of religious faith: 'le stoïcisme, avec son culte exclusif de la raison, ouvrait la porte à la morale laïque, à la religion naturelle . . . Le néo-stoïcisme est en définitive un rationalisme chrétien, dans lequel le christianisme n'apparaît pas toujours comme essentiel, mais plutôt comme surajouté.' (L. Zanta, *La renaissance du stoïcisme au* XVIe *siècle*, pp. 334, 337.)

77 Letter of 4 August 1645, AT IV 264–6: CSMK 257–8. There are other provisos in the letter, notably the requirement that we 'maintain a firm and constant resolution to carry out whatever reason recommends'; this corresponds to what will become a central emphasis in Cartesian ethics, its stress on the power of the will (see section 6 of this chapter).

78 Nor, indeed, (as we shall see later on in section 5) is Descartes by any means always sympathetic to the Stoics; see further J. Cottingham, *A Descartes Dictionary*, s. v. 'passions', and the introduction by G. Rodis-Lewis to Descartes' *Passions of the Soul*, trans. Stephen Voss.

79 AT VI 27: CSM I 124.

80 See above, chapter 2, section 1.

81 *Discours de la méthode pour bien conduire la raison et chercher la vérité dans les*

sciences ('Discourse on the method needed for the good conduct of reason and for reaching the truth in the sciences'; AT VI 1: CSM I 111).

82 Part v, AT VI 44–5: CSM I 133.

83 Part v, AT VI 47ff.: CSM I 134ff.

84 Part vi, AT VI 62: CSM I 143.

85 Ibid. For the experimental emphasis in Descartes' scientific methodology, see AT VI 64–5: CSM I 144, and J. Cottingham, *A Descartes Dictionary*, s. v. 'experience'.

86 The opening synopsis announces Descartes' aim of '*making further progress* in the investigation of nature than has hitherto been achieved' (*aller plus avant* en la recherche de la nature qu'il n'y a été). (Emphasis supplied)

87 'Il n'y a rien qui soit *entièrement* en notre pouvoir que nos pensées' (AT VI 25: CSM I 123; emphasis supplied).

88 Letter to Regius of January 1642 (AT III 493: CSMK 206). Cf. Letter to More of 5 February 1649: 'I understand [incorporeal substances, like the human mind, and God, and angels] to be like virtues or powers which can act on extended things although they are not themselves extended, just as fire is in white-hot iron without itself being iron.' (Intelligo [substantias incorporeas, sc. mentem humanum & Deum & angelos] tanquam virtutes aut vires quasdam, quae quamvis se applicent rebus extensis, non idcirco sunt extensae; ut quamvis in ferro candenti sit ignis, non ideo ignis ille est ferrum.) (AT v 270: CSMK 361.)

89 'Know then thyself, presume not God to scan / The proper study of Mankind is Man.' (*An Essay on Man* [1744], Epistle II, lines 1–2.)

90 Cf. David Hume: 'There is no question of importance whose decision is not compriz'd in the science of man' (*A Treatise of Human Nature*, [1739–40], Introduction, paragraph 3). For this orientation in Kant, see *Critique of Pure Reason* [1781], Introduction, section VII. Compare also Locke, *Essay concerning Human Understanding* [1689], book I, ch 1; Spinoza *De Intellectus Emendatione* [*c.* 1660], para. 38 (in *Works*, ed. Curley, vol. I, p. 19); Leibniz, *New Essays on Human Understanding* [*c.* 1704], Preface (in *Philosophical Writings*, ed. Parkinson, pp. 148ff.).

91 These are the predominant themes in Descartes' correspondence dating from the late sixteen-twenties and sixteen-thirties (AT I 17ff.: CSMK 5ff.); see especially the letter to Huygens of 5 October 1637 (AT I 434ff.: CSMK 66–73).

92 See *Principles of Philosophy*, Part IV, arts. 188ff.

93 Cf. Aristotle, *Nicomachean Ethics*, book I, ch. 7 (1097b33ff.).

94 See the *Traité de l'homme* composed in the early sixteen-thirties (AT XI 119ff.: CSM I 99ff.) and the *Description du corps humain*, composed in 1647–8 (AT XI 223ff.: CSM I 314ff.).

95 AT xi 120: CSM i 99.

96 'Il ne faut point concevoir aucune âme végétative, ni sensitive, ni
    aucune principe de mouvement ou de vie que . . . la chaleur du feu
    qui brûle continuellement dans son coeur, et qui n'est point d'autre
    nature que tous les feux qui sont dans les corps inanimés' (AT xi 202:
    CSM i 108). For more on this see J Cottingham 'Cartesian dualism',
    in Cottingham (ed.), *The Cambridge Companion to Descartes*, pp. 245ff.

97 For the notion of the mind as a 'complete thing' (*res completa*) see
    Fourth Replies [1641], AT vii 223: CSM ii 157.

98 John Locke, who was influenced by Descartes' theory of the mind,
    was careful to distinguish between the concept of a *person* (the bearer
    of consciousness) and the concept of a *man* or *human being* (see *Essay
    concerning Human Understanding* [1689], book ii, ch. xxvii, section 21).

99 *Discourse*, part v, AT vi 59: CSM i 141 (emphasis supplied).

100 Fourth Objections, AT vii 203: CSM ii 143.

101 Letter to Regius of January 1642 (AT iii 493: CSMK 206).

102 Thus if one asks a philosopher today for an example of a mental
     state, one is as like as not to get some such answer as 'a toothache' –
     surely, on reflection, a quite bizarre item to invoke as an illustration
     of the domain of the mental!

103 'Sine [facultate sentiendi] totum me possum clare et distincte intel-
     ligere' (Sixth Meditation, AT vii 78: CSM ii 54).

104 Sixth Meditation, AT vii 81: CSM ii 56.

105 *Principles of Philosophy*, part i, art. 32.

106 For the so-called Cartesian doctrine of the 'bête machine', see *Dis-
     course*, part v (AT vi 57–8: CSM i 140).

107 Some commentators have argued that Descartes failed, in the end,
     to sustain a convincing theory of human nature; see S. Voss, 'De-
     scartes: The End of Anthropology', in J. Cottingham (ed.), *Reason,
     Will, and Sensation*, pp. 273ff.

108 So far as I know, the use of the term 'trialism' in this connection was
     first introduced in my 'Cartesian Trialism' (1985); cf. J. Cottingham,
     Descartes, pp. 127ff. Notwithstanding some subsequent misunder-
     standings, I made it clear in the places cited that the threefold
     classification was not meant by Descartes to be an *ontological* one; it
     relates, rather, to the irreducibility of our distinctively human *at-
     tributes* to the attributes either of pure thought on the one hand or of
     extension on the other. A more 'realist' (and in my view mistaken)
     interpretation of the mind-body union is offered by Martial Guer-
     oult, who construes it ontologically, as a '*substance psychophysique*'; see
     Descartes selon l'ordre des raisons, vol. ii, pp. 201ff.

109 Letter of 21 May 1643 (AT iii 665: CSMK 218).

110 *Principles*, part i, art. 48.

111 Ibid.

112 See above, chapter 2, esp. section 4.
113 'What belongs to the union of the soul and the body is known only obscurely by the intellect . . . but it is known very clearly by the senses . . . Metaphysical thoughts, which exercise the pure intellect, help to familiarize us with the notion of the soul; the study of mathematics . . . accustoms us to form very distinct notions of body. But it is the ordinary course of life and conversation, and abstention from meditation . . . that teaches us how to conceive the union of the soul and body' (Letter to Elizabeth of 28 June 1643, AT III 691–2: CSMK 227).
114 *Passions of the Soul*, art. 212.
115 Sixth Meditation, AT VII 81: CSM II 56.
116 *Passions of the Soul*, art. 211.
117 'L'âme peut avoir ses plaisirs à part. Mais pour ceux qui lui sont communs avec le corps, ils dépendent entièrement des passions: en sorte que les hommes qu'elles peuvent le plus émouvoir sont capables de goûter le plus de douceur en cette vie' (*Passions of the Soul*, art. 212).
118 Descartes' work on the passions is aptly described by Geneviève Rodis-Lewis as 'a ground-breaking study concerning a modality specific to the union between soul and body' (Introduction to Descartes, *The Passions of the Soul*, ed. S. Voss, p. xv). See also Rodis-Lewis's *L'anthropologie cartésienne*, Introduction and chapter 1.
119 Letter to Silhon, March or April 1648: AT V 135.
120 '. . . la notion telle quelle de la Physique, que j'ai tâché d'acquérir, m'a grandement servi pour établir des fondements certains en la Morale' (letter to Chanut of 15 June 1646, AT IV 441: CSMK 289).
121 AT XI 326: CSM I 327. The idea that the passions involve both physiological and psychological aspects was an ancient one, going back to Aristotle. The sixteenth-century Coimbrian commentators on Aristotle had classified the passions as 'affects of the soul in common with the body' (*affectus communes animae cum corpore*). (*Commentarii de anima*, I, I, cited in E. Gilson, *Index Scolastico-Cartésien*, no. 322.) The early seventeenth-century scholastic philosopher Eustachius, whom Descartes had studied as a schoolboy, defines a passion as 'a movement of the sensitive appetite arising from the apprehension of some good or evil, accompanied with some unnatural bodily change' ('unnatural' here denoting an abnormal or excessive physiological response, such as increased heart-rate). (Eustachius, *Summa philosophiae quadripartita*, II, 100–1, cited in Gilson, *Index*, no. 321.) It is, of course, a matter of common-sense observation and personal experience that many emotions are accompanied by physiological changes (embarrassment, for example, by flushing). Descartes, however, will bring the details of his mechanistic physiology to bear on a new account of how the passions may be controlled and modified.

122 Descartes' use of the French *passion* corresponds to the standard scholastic Latin term *passio*, (from the verb *patior*, to suffer), which in turn corresponds to Aristotle's term πάθος, similarly derived from the ordinary Greek verb for to suffer. For standard definitions of the term in scholastic philosophy, see preceding note.

123 *Passions of the Soul*, art. 27.

124 Compare the list in the *Principles of Philosophy*, part I, art. 48. Descartes distinguishes the passions from other kinds of sensory and appetitive states by the fact that the passions are 'referred to the soul', while other items in the list (such as 'smells, sounds and colours') are 'referred to external objects', and others again (such as 'hunger, thirst and pain') are 'referred to our own body' (*Passions*, art. 29).

125 *Passions*, art. 32. See J. Cottingham, *A Descartes Dictionary*, s. v. 'pineal gland'.

126 *Treatise on Man* [*Traité de L'Homme*, 1633], AT XI 143–78: CSM I 102–7.

127 Cf. D. Dennett, *Consciousness Explained*.

128 *Passions of the Soul*, art. 212.

129 Cf. Sixth Meditation, AT VII 88: CSM II 60.

130 Descartes, of course, is no evolutionist with regard to the structure of the soul: it is 'specially created' by God (see *Discourse on the Method*, part V, AT VI 59: CSM I 141). But all our material and physiological structures are derived 'from the potentiality of matter' (ibid.), and the general line Descartes takes with respect to complex physical structures is an evolutionary one (cf. *Le Monde*, ch. 6, AT XI 34: CSM I 91). Moreover, what Descartes says about animal and indeed human physiology (see *Description du Corps Humain*, part I, AT XI 223ff.: CSM I 314ff.) seems to allow for the emergence of patterns of at least behavioural response in the human species. However, the general point about our being 'lumbered' with patterns of psychophysical response is in any case independent of whether their genesis was the result of divine creation or natural evolution.

131 To Mersenne, 18 March 1630 (AT I 134: CSMK 20). Descartes' reflections in this regard were partly stimulated by the writings of some of his renaissance predecessors. In article 27 of the *Passions* he refers to the work of the sixteenth-century philosopher Jean-Luis Vives, who in his *De Anima et Vita* [1538] had cited an example of a morbid condition in which laughter was aroused by certain foods.

132 *Passions of the Soul*, art. 50.

133 See above, chapter 2, sections 2 and 3.

134 Letter to Chanut of 6 June 1647 (AT VI 57: CSMK 322–3). For the notion of 'folds in the brain' (a kind of crude mechanical anticipation

of the modern notion of neural pathways) see *Conversation with Burman*, AT v 150: CSMK 336.

135 See above, chapter 2, section 4 (where the Stoic views are discussed, together with possible Epicurean anticipations of such Cartesian 'therapy').

136 It is fairly common, for example, for commentators on the Freudian notion of the unconscious mind to say that Freud broke from the *Cartesian* thesis that mentality and consciousness are equivalent; cf. S. Gardner, *Irrationality and the philosophy of psychoanalysis* , p. 207. Margaret Wilson, in her *Descartes*, attributes to Descartes 'the doctrine of epistemological transparency of thought or mind' (p. 50), though she does go on to discuss certain aspects of Descartes' philosophy of mind which are in potential conflict with that doctrine (cf. p. 164).

137 The resident was one of Descartes' important correspondents in his later years, Hector-Pierre Chanut (later to become French ambassador to Sweden).

138 'Ce sont ces sentiments confus de notre enfance, qui, demeurant jointes avec les pensées raisonnables par lesquelles nous aimons ce que nous en jugeons digne, sont cause que la nature de l'amour nous est difficile à connaître.' By the phrase 'when we first came into the world, Descartes has in mind the soul's first union with the body; hence he traces the causes of the passions back even prior to birth, to the experiences undergone inside the womb: ' . . . d'autant que l'amour n'était causée, avant la naissance, que par un aliment convenable qui, entrant abondamment dans le foie, dans le coeur et dans le poumon, y excitait plus de chaleur que de coutume, de là vient que maintenant cette chaleur accompagne toujours l'amour, encore qu'elle vienne d'autres causes fort différentes'. ('Before birth, love was caused only by suitable nourishment which, entering in abundance into the liver, heart and lungs, produced an increase of heat: this is the reason why similar heat still always accompanies love, even though it comes from other very different causes.') Letter to Chanut of 1 February 1647, AT iv 606: CSMK 308.

139 The Cartesian anticipation of Freud is, of course, only a partial one; though Descartes is alive to the distorting power of the past, his suggestions about the continuing influence of infantile experience fall considerably short of prefiguring the more complex psychoanalytic account of how we are affected by unconscious phantasies and projections. For the psychoanalytic development of the theme of recovering the significance of our past, see chapter 4, section 5, below.

140 To Mersenne, May 1637 (AT i 366: CSMK 56); cf. *Discourse*, part iii (AT vi 28: CSM i 125). In the *Conversation with Burman* (AT v 159:

CSMK 342), Descartes is reported as asserting that 'no one can pursue evil *qua* evil', a direct echo of Plato's claim οὐδεὶς βούλεται τὰ κακά (*Meno*, 78b1). See also chapter 2, above, sections 3 and 4.

141 Letter of 1 September 1645. Descartes goes on to say that the passions often 'represent the good to which they tend with greater splendour than they deserve' and they make us imagine pleasure to be much greater before we possess them than our subsequent experiences show them to be. He later observes that 'the true function of reason in the conduct of life is to examine and consider without passion the value of all the perfections, both of the body and of the soul, which can be acquired by our conduct, so that since we are commonly obliged to deprive ourselves of some good in order to acquire others, we shall always choose the better' (AT iv 284–5 and 286–7: CSMK 263–5).

142 AT vi 8: CSM i 114 (see further the comments by G. Rodis-Lewis in Descartes, *Passions of the Soul*, ed. Voss, p. xvi). Compare the following analysis by Zanta: 'Du stoïcisme, [Descartes] n'accepte point la théorie fondamentale de l'apathie, c'est-à-dire la suppression complète de toute passion. La passion, pour Descartes, participe de l'optimisme stoïcien; elle est par conséquent bonne, elle n'est nuisible que dans ses excès. Elle est bonne si l'on sait en faire un bon usage, c'est-à-dire, si la volonté sait s'en servir, et c'est alors que nous retrouvons le stoïcien. Descartes, lui aussi, ne voit dans l'âme qu'entendement et volonté; il sacrifie la sensibilité' (*La renaissance du stoïcisme au* xvie *siècle*, pp. 337–8). Much of this analysis seems sound, except for the final clause: as will be clear from much of the discussion of 'Cartesian anthropology' in this chapter, I would fundamentally reject the notion that the domain of the sensible is 'sacrificed' in Descartes' philosophical psychology.

143 See opening quotation of this section.

144 Sixth Meditation, AT vii 83: CSM ii 57. The question arises of why animals too would not benefit from such apparatus; Descartes (considering animals as purely mechanical automata) seems to believe that their avoidance of noxious stimuli arises entirely from mechanical instinct. Descartes' views on non-human animals are, however, complex and fraught with problems that have still not properly been sorted out by commentators. See further J. Cottingham, 'A Brute to the Brutes? Descartes' treatment of animals', and *A Descartes Dictionary*, s.v. 'animal'. For some useful references to the key texts, see *Passions of the Soul*, ed. Voss, part i, note 53. For a detailed discussion of the general role of sensory experience in Descartes' philosophy and science, see Ann MacKenzie, 'The Reconfiguration of Sensory Experience', in Cottingham (ed.), *Reason, Will, and Sensation*, pp. 251ff.

145 *Passions of the Soul*, art. 40. Descartes' preoccupation with the role of

the psycho-physical system in the preservation of life and health links up with his enduring interest in medicine, and in particular with the psycho-somatic causes of illness; cf. letter to Elizabeth of May or June 1645 (AT IV 218ff.: CSMK 249ff.).

146 Sixth Meditation, AT VII 89: CSM II 61.

147 The qualifications 'in general' and 'in the long run' are important; cf. Sixth Meditation, AT VII 88–8: CSM II 61.

148 Letter to Elizabeth of 1 September 1645 (AT IV 287: CSMK 265). Contrast the antihedonistic orientation of the Stoics: *vera voluptas voluptatum contemptio* (Seneca, *De vita beata*, IV, 2).

149 *Passions of the Soul*, art. 212.

150 Letter to Chanut of 15 June 1646 (AT IV 442: CSMK 289).

151 See G. Rodis-Lewis, 'Descartes' life and the development of his philosophy', in J. Cottingham (ed.), *The Cambridge Companion to Descartes*, pp. 40ff.; and S. Gaukroger, *Descartes, An Intellectual Biography*, pp. 294f.

152 See letter to Pollot of January 1641 (AT III 278ff.: CSMK 167–8); letters to Huygens of 20 May 1637 (AT I 631ff.: CSMK 54–5) and 10 October 1642 (AT III 796ff.: CSMK 215–6).

153 *De vita beata*, I, 4.

154 *Discourses* [*c.* AD 100], i. 1. 7–12 (in Long and Sedley (eds.), *The Hellenistic Philosophers*, 62K).

155 Cf. *Nicomachean Ethics*, 1122b29–33; 1124a1–4.

156 J. Casey, *Pagan Virtue*, p. 201.

157 Luke 21:4.

158 Michel de Montaigne, *Apology for Raymond Sebond* [1580]; quoted in J. B. Schneewind (ed.), *Moral Philosophy from Montaigne to Kant*, vol I, p. 39.

159 Indeed, his thinking is sufficiently rooted in the robust naturalism of traditional virtue-theory for him to acknowledge, in many places, the importance of good upbringing and above all training and habituation for the development of a worthwhile human life (*Passions of the Soul*, art. 50: AT XI 369–70: CSM I 348).

160 *Passions of the Soul*, art. 161.

161 'There is, it seems, no virtue so dependent on good birth as the virtue which causes us to esteem ourselves in accordance with our true value, and it is easy to believe that the souls God puts into our bodies are not equally noble and strong, and this is why, following the vernacular, I have called this virtue "generosity" rather than "magnanimity", a term used in the Schools' (*Passions*, art. 161). Descartes here makes explicit the 'genetic' link between this virtue and the ideal of noble birth. In fact, however, though his own vernacular term emphasizes the genetic connection more than the traditional Aristotelian term, the possession of Cartesian 'generosity', as we shall

see shortly, turns out to be far less dependent than its Aristotelian counterpart on the vicissitudes of birth and fortune.

162 *Passions of the Soul*, art. 153: AT xi 445–6: CSM i 384.

163 *Arete*, Aristotle's term for virtue or excellence, is etymologically connected with the adjective *aristos*, 'best'. Both terms seem to have been connected originally with pre-eminence on the battlefield (the same root being present in *Ares*, the Greek god of war).

164 *Discourse on the Method*, part i: AT vi 8: CSM i 114.

165 *Search for Truth*, AT x 500–3: CSM ii 402–3. See also the opening of the *Discourse*, AT vi 1: CSM i 111.

166 *Passions of the Soul*, art. 161: AT xi 453: CSM i 388.

167 *Passions of the Soul*, art. 153: AT xi 446: CSM i 384.

168 Ibid.

169 I say 'allegedly', since what Bernard Williams and Thomas Nagel have called 'constitutive luck' will inevitably play a role in determining the strength of will that each of us possesses. See T. Nagel, *Mortal Questions*, pp. 24ff., and B. Williams, *Moral Luck*, pp. 20–39. See further J. Cottingham, 'Partiality and the Virtues', in R. Crisp (ed.), *How Should One Live?*, pp. 67f.

170 *Passions, of the Soul*, art. 154 (AT xi 446–7: CSM i 384, emphasis supplied). For further discussion of Descartes' account of the virtue of *générosité* (in a rather different context), see Charles Taylor, *Sources of the Self*, ch. 8.

171 'Volumus enim qui beatus sit, tutum esse, inexpugnabilem, saeptum atque munitum'; Cicero, *Tusculan Disputations*, 5, 40–1 (in Long and Sedley, eds., *The Hellenistic Philosophers*, 63L).

172 *Passions of the Soul* , art. 148.

173 Compare the following reading of Descartes' account of 'generosity': '[Descartes la] définit en vrai stoïcien. Cette générosité ainsi définie nous apparaît vraiment comme la clé de voûte de la morale cartésienne aussi bien que de la morale stoïcienne. Etre maître de soi, ne dépendre que du dedans, ce dedans seul étant libre, tandis que les forces extérieures nous contraignent, attendre avant d'agir que la clarté se fasse en nous pour juger du meilleur, n'est-ce point là aussi tout l'essentiel d'une *morale intellectualiste*' (Zanta, *La renaissance du stoicisme*, p. 339, emphasis supplied). Compare Descartes' views on humility (*Passions of the Soul*, art. 155), which Zanta plausibly reads as having less in common with the Christian conception of that virtue than with the Stoic ideal of self esteem and human dignity: 'Or voir clair, pour Descartes comme pour les Stoïciens, c'est comprendre . . . qu'il faut . . . se soumettre aux décrets de la Providence, accepter en bonne part ce qui nous arrive, confiants dans l'ordre établi, dans cet ordre que proclame en tout lieu le monde infini. Voir clair . . . c'est

aussi et par-dessus tout avoir le sentiment de la dignité personelle, de la valeur infinie de cette âme dont la volonté est sans limite et qui participe avec elle de l'éternité' (ibid.). While I would agree that the Stoic influence can be clearly discerned in what I have called the 'resigned' mode of Descartes' ethics, it is important to see that this is only one aspect of a complex ethical outlook, and that it represents a striking retreat from the earlier (and more characteristically Cartesian) ideal of manipulative control over the environment and the workings of our human nature.

174 Letter to Elizabeth, October or November 1646 (AT IV 528–9: CSMK 296).

175 For some reservations about the inward turn, see J. Cottingham, 'Partiality and the Virtues', in R. Crisp (ed.), *How Should One Live?*, pp. 63 and 75.

176 *Passions of the Soul*, art. 153.

4 ETHICS AND THE CHALLENGE TO REASON

1 C. Jung, 'Die Probleme der modernen Psychotherapie', in *Seelenprobleme der Gegenwart* [1931], p. 21; trans. as 'Problems of Modern Psychotherapy', in *Modern Man in Search of a Soul*, chapter II, p. 48 (also in *Collected Works*, vol. 16).

2 *Le Mythe de Sisyphe* [1942], in A. Camus, *Essais*, p. 117; trans. J. O'Brien, p. 29.

3 For the term 'synoptic ethics', see chapter 1.

4 For more on this Nietzschean contrast, see above, Chapter 2, section 1.

5 Cf. Plato, *Crito*, 46a.

6 See F. Nietzsche, *The Twilight of the Gods* [*Die Götzen-Dämmerung*, 1889], trans. Kaufmann, pp. 475, 559, 571.

7 William Barrett, *Irrational Man, A Study in Existential Philosophy*. Though the label can be misleading, if it is taken to imply a wholesale rejection of reason, Barrett's plausible thesis is that the work of such writers as Kierkegaard, Nietzsche, Heidegger and Sartre centres around their rejection of the Aristotelian essentialist paradigm, their challenge to the traditional definition of man as *animal rationale* as providing the ultimate statement on the human condition.

8 See F. Nietzsche, *Also Sprach Zarathustra*, part 1 [1883]; cf. W. Kaufmann, *Nietzsche*, ch. 11.

9 *Lady Chatterley's Lover* [1928], ch. 4.

10 Bertrand Russell, *Autobiography*, vol. II, p. 22.

11 Russell provided an unequivocal statement of his attitude during the years following the second world war in a BBC television interview

in March 1959 (cited in R. W. Clark, *The Life of Bertrand Russell*, p. 659.

12 George Steiner, *Heidegger*, pp. 32–3.

13 *Discourse on the Method*, part vi (AT vi 62: CSM i 142).

14 Cf. Thomas Aquinas, *Summa Contra Gentiles* [1259–64], I, 2, 11.

15 Nothing is ever quite simple in philosophy: there are elements of the 'submissive' mode even in the most seemingly 'ratiocentric' of thinkers. Compare the striking devotional peroration at the end of Descartes' Third Meditation (AT vii 52: CSM ii 36). Cf. also the Stoic ideal of harmonious attunement (discussed in Chapter 2, section 1, above).

16 See M. Heidegger, 'What Thinking Signifies' ['Was Heisst Denken' 1951–2]; 'Letter on Humanism' ['Brief über den Humanismus', 1947].

17 See chapter 3, section 6, above.

18 Friedrich Hölderlin, 'Patmos' [1803]. See M. Heidegger, 'The Question concerning Technology' ['Die Frage Nach der Technik', 1953].

19 See Thomas Kuhn, *The Structure of Scientific Revolutions*. See also Paul Feyerabend, 'Explanation, Reduction and Empiricism' in Feigl and Maxwell (eds.), *Minnesota Studies in the Philosophy of Science* . There is no space here to evaluate such views, except perhaps to say that in the light of the spectacular predictive successes of science since the seventeenth century it is hard to give an unqualified acceptance to the claim of some of Kuhn's followers that the very idea of 'progress' in scientific knowledge is an illusion.

20 ' . . . there can be no philosophical science of ontology, no wellfounded attempt to see past our categories of expression and glimpse the way in which the world is truly furnished' (Crispin Wright, *Frege's Conception of Numbers as Objects*, p. 51).

21 See Richard Rorty, *Philosophy and the Mirror of Nature*, referred to in chapter 2, note 24, above.

22 Cf. L. Bonjour, *The Structure of Empirical Knowledge*.

23 For a fuller discussion of these themes, see J. Cottingham, 'The Cartesian Legacy'.

24 Compare the comment in G. Vesey & P. Foulkes, *Collins Dictionary of Philosophy*: 'Much of [Heidegger's] material is very obscure . . . and his philosophical import is slight'.

25 'My opponents have an interest in my refraining from publishing the principles of the philosophy I use. For these principles are so very simple and evident that in publishing them I should, as it were, be opening windows and admitting daylight into that cellar where they have gone down to fight'. *Discourse on the Method*, part vi (AT vi 71: CSM i 147).

26 For Hegel's concept of a dialectical opposition being 'superseded' (*aufgehoben*) by a synthesis which both negates elements of the orig-

inally conflicting elements and preserves what is true, see his *Phenomenology of Spirit*, trans. Baillie, pp. 163f. See also R. Norman, *Hegel's Phenomenology*, ch. 6, and J. Cottingham, *Rationalism*, pp. 95ff.

27 Though by no means all defences of the traditional claims of rationality have these vices; compare R. Trigg, *Rationality and Science*.

28 Compare ch. 3, section 2, above.

29 For the notion of *Zuhandenheit*, *see* Martin Heidegger, *Being and Time* [*Sein und Zeit*, 1927], section 15; for that of *Sorge*, *see* section 26.

30 See sections 6 and 8.

31 I should add that I shall not be discussing what might be called the 'technical' aspects of psychoanalytic theory – notions such as libido or the primary and secondary process in Freud, the theory of the archetypes in Jung, or the analysis of the role of language offered by Lacan. Interesting and important though these are, what follows will draw merely on those general aspects of psychoanalytic thought which are readily intelligible without technical training, since they have been more or less absorbed into our contemporary culture (for example the idea of the importance for our mental equilibrium and self-knowledge of the 'repressed' experiences of early childhood). Compare Thomas Nagel: 'For most of those who believe in the reality of repression and the unconscious, whether or not they have gone through psychoanalysis, the belief is based not on blind trust in the authority of analysts and their clinical observations but on the evident usefulness of a rudimentary Freudian outlook in understanding ourselves and other people, particularly erotic life, family dramas, and what Freud called the psychopathology of everyday life' ('Freud's Permanent Revolution', p. 35). For the growing interest among philosophers of mind in the more technical aspects of psychoanalytic thought, see, for example, S. Gardner, *Irrationality and the Philosophy of Psychoanalysis*, and M. Cavell, *The Psychoanalytic Mind: From Freud to Philosophy*. (It should be noticed incidentally that the terms 'psychoanalysis' and 'psychotherapy' are themselves sometimes used in quasi-technical senses, the former, for example, being restricted to approaches that adopt an explicitly Freudian framework. When I refer to 'psychoanalytic ideas' or 'psychoanalytic theory', however, I shall be using the terms in the broadest possible sense.)

32 'One of the Difficulties of Psychoanalysis' ['Einer Schwierigkeit der Psychoanalyse', 1917], in *Gesammelte Werke*, vol. XII, p. 11; trans. in J. Riviere (ed.), *Collected Papers*, vol. IV, p. 355.

33 See E. Gellner, *The Psychoanalytic Movement*, p. 99.

34 See David Sachs, 'On Grünbaum's critique of psychoanalysis' in J. Neu (ed.), *The Cambridge Companion to Freud*, p. 310.

35 See Sachs, 'On Grünbaum's critique of psychoanalysis'.

36 This approach was of course pioneered by Freud himself: it is when he is in the narrative mode that he is at his most sure-footed, and most persuasive. See, for example, *Introductory Lectures on Psychoanalysis*, chs. 16 and 17.

37 Thomas Nagel, 'Freud's Permanent Revolution', p. 38.

38 Nagel, 'Freud's Permanent Revolution', p. 36.

39 Gellner, *The Psychoanalytic Movement*, p. 64. In the preceding summary, I have sometimes reformulated Gellner's points in slightly different terms from those he uses himself.

40 See section 7 of the present chapter.

41 Gellner, *The Psychoanalytic Movement*, p. 65.

42 Gellner, *The Psychoanalytic Movement*, p. 57. Emphases supplied.

43 'Das Unbewusste' ('The Unconscious') [1915]; in Gesammelte Werke, vol. x, p. 270; trans. in Freud, *The Essentials of Psychoanalysis*, p. 147.

44 'The Unconscious' [1915]. Quoted in S. Gardner, 'The Unconscious', in J. Neu (ed.), *The Cambridge Companion to Freud*, p. 158, note 3.

45 AT VII 34: CSM II 2–3.

46 *Méditations chrétiennes et métaphysiques* [1683], ix, 15. See further J. Cottingham, *The Rationalists*, pp. 154–5 and p. 220, note 67.

47 The chief culprits here are E. Anscombe and P. T. Geach in their edition of Descartes, *Philosophical Writings*, Introduction. Cf. J. Cottingham, 'Descartes on Thought', *Philosophical Quarterly* vol. 28 (1978), pp. 208–14, reprinted in G. Moyal (ed.), *René Descartes, Critical Assessments*, vol. II, pp. 288ff.

48 Second Replies, AT VII 160: CSM II 113.

49 Descartes' own language is not always particularly helpful, since he sometimes uses 'idea' to refer to a simple 'mode of thought', thus employing the term in a psychological sense. But more often he uses the term to refer to the formal structure, or representational content of a thought (and indeed he explicitly distinguishes this second sense from the first in the Third Meditation, AT VII 40: CSM II 27–8). In this second sense (though not the first) it can be the case that two people have the same idea. For more on this, see J. Cottingham, *A Descartes Dictionary*, s. v. 'idea'. The distinction between psychology and logic is developed even more explicitly and carefully in the work of Descartes' successor Malebranche; see N. Jolley, *The Light of the Soul*, chs. 4 and 5.

50 Fifth Meditation, AT VII 67: CSM II 46–7.

51 'When we say that an idea is innate in us, we do not mean that it is always there before us – which would mean that no idea was innate.' Third Set of Objections and Replies, AT VII 189: CSM II 132. See further J. Cottingham, *The Rationalists*, pp. 70ff.; 153ff.

52 Letter to 'Hyperaspistes' of August 1641 (AT III 424: CSMK 190).
53 *Conversation with Burman* [1648], AT v 150: CSMK 336. See also *Principles of Philosophy*, part I, art. 47.
54 *Conversation with Burman*, AT v 150: CSMK 336.
55 See J. Cottingham, *A Descartes Dictionary*, s. v. 'angel'.
56 See above, chapter 3, sections 4 and 5, esp. pp. 93f.
57 Compare AT v 150: CSMK 336, and AT v 192: CSMK 354. Descartes goes on to suggest that our failure to remember such thoughts is due to their being too faint and indistinct to leave any trace in the memory. Locke seems to have been tempted to deny the highly plausible – one might almost say common-sense – view that there can be mental occurrences of which we are only very minimally aware, asserting that 'to suppose the Soul to think, and the Man not to perceive it, is to make two Persons in one man' (*Essay concerning Human Understanding*, Bk II, ch. i, section 19). It appears that he was led to that position by a theory of personal identity which (as is well known) leads to awkward consequences, and is arguably circular. For the circularity of the Lockean account, see the famous criticisms of Joseph Butler, *The Analogy of Religion* [1736], appendix 1. A good case has been made recently for the ultimate incoherence of memory and psychological continuity approaches to personal identity; see D. Oderberg, *The Metaphysics of Identity over Time*.

Descartes rightly incurs Locke's censure, however, for his notorious doctrine that the mind 'always thinks' – *anima semper cogitat* (letter to 'Hyperaspistes' of August 1641, AT III 423: CSMK 189). [The terms 'mind' (*esprit, mens*) and 'soul' (*âme, anima*) are often used interchangeably in Descartes; see J. Cottingham, 'Cartesian Dualism: Theology, Metaphysics and Science, in Cottingham (ed.), *The Cambridge Companion to Descartes*, p. 253, note 1.] Given the Cartesian definition of the mind as a thinking thing, Descartes could no more allow that the mind could exist without its essential attribute than he could allow that a body could exist without the defining attribute of extension: 'thought is not an attribute which can be present or absent, like motion in a body' (letter for Arnauld of 4 June 1648, AT v 193: CSMK 355). And hence he was obliged to maintain that the mind was continuously engaged in thinking, even in sleep: if it seems otherwise, that is just because we do not, on waking, remember the thoughts that occurred (letter for Arnauld of 29 July 1648, AT v 219ff.: CSMK 356ff.). Slating the doctrine of continuous thinking, Locke observed: 'methinks every drowsy Nod shakes their Doctrine, who teach That the Soul is always thinking. Those at least, who do at any time sleep without dreaming, can never be convinced That their Thoughts are sometimes for four hours busy without their knowing of it; and if they are taken in the very act, waked in the middle of that [alleged] sleeping contemplation, can give no manner of account of it' (*Essay*, II, i, 13). On the empirical question of whether there are, during the course of human life, gaps in consciousness, when there is nothing going on that is even minimally present to our awareness, Locke is surely right: there are indeed periods of totally dreamless sleep. For Descartes to have acknowledged this would have undermined his (in any case shaky) metaphysics of a continuously existing incorporeal soul; and it is no part of our present purpose to attempt any defence of that.

58 *Essay*, book I, ch. ii, section 5. Construed in terms of *propositions*, Locke's claim may seem highly plausible, since propositional content is evidently a function of what can be formulated in language, and this notion in turn seems to imply some implicit or explicit awareness on the part of the subject. Defenders of the psychoanalytic concept of unconscious mentality can argue, however, that where propositional content is attributed to the mind of a patient, this will hinge on the 'manifestability' of the relevant beliefs and desires. This notion will be discussed later on in the present chapter, section 4. See also S. Gardner, *Irrationality and the Philosophy of Psychoanalysis*, 153–6, 158–9, 189–91, 194–5.

59 *Essay*, book I, ch. ii, section 5.

60 *New Essays on Human Understanding* [*c.* 1704], in *Philosophical Writings*, ed. Parkinson, p. 151. Cf. J. Cottingham, *Rationalism*, p. 76.

61 *New Essays on Human Understanding*, in *Philosophical Writings*, ed. Parkinson, p. 154; *Monadology* [1714], para. 14, in Parkinson (ed.), p. 180.

62 Cf. Seventh Objections, AT VII 559: CSM II 382.

63 AT V 146: CSMK 332–3.

64 Cf. above, ch. I, note 26.

65 See however ch. 3, section 5, above, for some striking anticipations of Freudian ideas in Descartes. There is also something highly suggestive in Leibniz' remark (quoted in the previous paragraph) that the mind can 'let pass' certain impressions in such a way that they are lost to conscious awareness unless circumstances allow a special effort to be made to recall them.

66 I mean here simply a view which allows us to weaken the supposedly unbreakable link between mental processes and direct conscious awareness. If (as I argue both in this and in the following section) mentation below the threshold of conscious awareness is a notion which makes perfectly good sense, then the a major obstacle to the acceptance of psychoanalytic approaches to the mind is removed. I should add however that this is not of course supposed to constitute a vindication of all the complex structural and explanatory claims

which Freud and his successors make with respect to 'The Unconscious' with a capital 'U'.

67 Jacques Lacan, 'L'instance de la lettre dans l'inconscient ou la raison depuis Freud' [1957], in *Ecrits*, p. 517; trans. Sheridan, p. 165.

68 The case of non-human animals presents special problems which I cannot go into here. Some of these have to do with the difficulty of ascribing intentionality to the mental states of creatures that lack language. It could be maintained that exactly this difficulty precludes the attribution of genuine mental states to young infants. This issue is interestingly addressed, and a plausible solution proposed (invoking the notion of 'pre-intentionality') in Marcia Cavell, *The Psychoanalytic Mind: From Freud to Philosophy*. See also the review of Cavell by J. Cottingham, *Philosophical Quarterly*, 1995.

69 For an important caveat about the aims of this section, see above, note 66.

70 Among the problems concerning how far we should attribute mentality to animals, perhaps the principal one is that there seems to be no clear criterion for determining whether their 'experiences' might qualify as having reached the relevant threshold. For a fascinating account of the origins of the Western philosophical debate over animal mentality, see R. Sorabji, *Animal Minds and Human Morals*.

71 S. Gardner, 'The unconscious', in J. Neu (ed.), *The Cambridge Companion to Freud*, p. 147.

72 Gardner, in Neu (ed.), *The Cambridge Companion to Freud*, p. 156.

73 Ibid.

74 Freud, *Introductory Lectures on Psychoanalysis* [1916–17], Lecture XVIII, p. 239.

75 *Introductory Lectures on Psychoanalysis*, Lecture XVII, p. 223.

76 *Introductory Lectures on Psychoanalysis*, Lecture XVIII, p. 241.

77 Ibid.

78 See opening paragraph of ch. 2, section 3, above.

79 Iris Murdoch, *Metaphysics as a Guide to Morals* , ch. 10, p. 293.

80 'The unexamined life is not worth living'; Plato, *Apology*, 38A. Compare Socrates' allegiance to the ancient Delphic motto 'Know Thyself' (*Protagoras*, 343B).

81 Cf. Thomas Kuhn, *The Structure of Scientific Revolutions*.

82 See previous section.

83 Jacques Lacan, *L'éthique de la psychanalyse*, p. 71; cited in John Rajchman, *Truth and Eros*, p. 30. In the discussion of the Lacanian critique of Aristotle, Kant and Bentham which follows, I am greatly indebted to Rajchman's insightful analysis.

84 Rajchman, *Truth and Eros*, p. 36.

85 See M. Nussbaum, *The Fragility of Goodness*, ch. 1.

86 J. Rajchman, *Truth and Eros*, p. 39.

87 The German noun *Nachtrag* can mean a 'supplement, addendum or postscript', and this subtlety affects the sense of the corresponding temporal adverb *nachträglich* ('subsequently'), so that it can hint at the idea that what occurred is later added to or modified in the light of afterthought or further reflection. Among Freud's several discussions of *Nachträglichkeit*, the most striking occurs in connection with his account of the 'Wolfman' case: 'From the History of an Infantile Neurosis' [1918], Ch. 4 (*Gesammelte Werke*, XII, p. 72, note 1; *Standard Edition*, XVII, p. 45).

88 Malcolm Bowie, *Lacan*, pp. 180–1.

89 Cf. above, chapter 1, section 1, chapter 2, section 5, and chapter 3, section 5.

90 Jaques Lacan, *Ecrits*, trans. Sheridan, pp. 47–8 (modified). Cf. note 86, above. The Lacanian reflection on the future as well as the past, on the 'yet to be understood' that will retrospectively confer significance on the present, owes much to Heidegger. See Bowie, *Lacan*, p. 182.

91 Aeschylus, *Agamemnon* [458 BC], lines 160, 176–8, trans. J. C. For a brilliant discussion of the significance of the Greek proverb *pathei mathos* ('through suffering comes learning') see M. Nussbaum, *The Fragility of Goodness*, ch. 2, section 4.

92 The suggestive phrase occurs in the title of an insightful essay by Jennifer Church, 'Morality and the internalized other', in Neu (ed.), *The Cambridge Companion to Freud*, pp. 209ff.

93 Church, in Neu (ed.), *The Cambridge Companion to Freud*, p. 220.

94 For example, the fact that Kepler's approach to celestial motion was influenced by astrological and mystical considerations does not undermine the truth of his theory of the orbits of the planets. The question of the 'genetic fallacy' is, however, a highly complex one. It appears that, to count as knowledge, a belief must in some sense (difficult to specify precisely) 'track the truth'; and this in turn suggests that the epistemic status of a belief or theory is suspect when the objects to which it refers play no doxastic (belief-influencing) role. See further R. Nozick, *Philosophical Explanations*, part 3, section 1.

95 *Civilisation and its Discontents* (in Freud, *Standard Edition*, XXI, 123); quoted by Church in Neu (ed.), p. 218.

96 Here I follow Rajchman, *Truth and Eros*, p. 58.

97 Rajchman, *Truth and Eros*, p. 61.

98 M. Cavell, *The Psychoanalytic Mind*, p. 217.

99 One might add that the Kantian constraints are plausibly conceived as ground rules that must be presupposed in any society where cooperative enterprises are to be pursued subject to conditions of open debate. For more on various ways of developing this Kantian idea, see Onora O'Neill, *Constructions of Reason*, chapter 11.

100 'Morality lies in the relation of actions to the autonomy of the will . . . An action which is compatible with the autonomy of the will is *permitted*; one which does not harmonise with it is *forbidden*. A will whose maxims necessarily accord with the laws of autonomy is a *holy* or absolutely good will.' Immanuel Kant, *Grundlegung zur Metaphyik der Sitten* [1785], trans. Paton, *The Moral Law*, p. 101.

101 Immanuel Kant, *Grundlegung*, trans. Paton, p. 95 (emphasis supplied).

102 J. Cottingham, 'The Philosophy of Punishment', in G. H. R. Parkinson (ed.), *An Encyclopaedia of Philosophy*, p. 771.

103 *Truth and Eros*, pp. 66–7. In explicating Lacan's ideas, Rajchman here follows the persuasive analysis of Jaques-Alain Miller, 'Jeremy Bentham's Panoptic Device', *October*, vol. 41 (Summer 1987).

104 'Western Philosophers in a Nutshell'; series of talks by Miles Burnyeat, John Cottingham, David Pears, Onora O'Neill, Bernard Williams and Anthony Grayling, edited by David Edmonds, *BBC World Service*, 1993.

105 *Praeambula* [*c.* 1619], AT x 213: CSM I 2.

106 *L'éthique de la psychanalyse*; quoted in *Truth and Eros*, p. 32.

107 Friedrich Nietzsche, *Also Sprach Zarathustra*, part IV [1892], *The Drunken Song*, section 12 (trans. J. C.).

108 See above, chapter 1, section 4. I should perhaps add that the label is not in any way supposed to imply a downgrading or devaluing of this kind of ethics. Indeed, any model of the good life which allowed the project of psychological self-discovery to occupy *all* the space would rightly incur the charge of excessive self-absorption.

109 *Protagoras*, 358d. See above, chapter 2, section 3.

110 Aristotle, *Nicomachean Ethics*, book VII, ch. 3 (see chapter 2, section 3, above).

111 See above, chapter 2, section 4.

112 Spinoza, *Ethics* [1665]: 'An affect which is a passion ceases to be a passion when we form a clear and distinct idea of it' (part 5, prop. 3). For discussion of Spinoza's position, see J. Cottingham, *The Rationalists*, pp. 168ff.

113 There are parallels here with the idea of the 'remaking of the self' – a phrase which is, I think, Charles Taylor's though I have not been able to locate an exact reference. Taylor himself, it should be noted, is highly critical of what he calls the 'therapeutic turn' in our contemporary culture, but the main reason for his hostility seems to be that he associates it with a certain kind of ethical subjectivism (see *Sources of the Self*, pp. 507ff.).

114 The dictum (from Molière's *Le Médécin Malgré Lui* [1666], Act I, scene 5) is quoted by Freud in his *Introductory Lectures on Psychoanalysis*: 'It happens in analysis that an experienced practitioner can usually surmise very easily what those feelings are which have remained

unconscious in each individual patient. It should not therefore be a matter of great difficulty to cure the patient by imparting this knowledge to him . . . If only it were so! . . . There are various kinds of knowing, which psychologically are not by any means of equal value. *Il y a fagots et fagots*, as Molière says . . . When the physician conveys his knowledge to the patient by telling him what he knows . . . it does not have the effect of dispersing the symptoms' (Lecture XVIII). For more on the psychoanalytic process as involving far more than the imparting of new information, see section 7 of the present chapter.

115 Hug me till you drug me honey
Kiss me till I'm in a coma
Hug me honey, snuggly bunny,
Love's as good as *soma* !
Aldous Huxley, *Brave New World* [1932], ch. 11.

116 Rajchman, *Truth and Eros*, p. 47; cf. Lacan, *Four Fundamental Concepts*, p. 69.

117 William Shakespeare, *Sonnets* [1609], Sonnet CXXIX.

118 'Problems of Modern Psychotherapy' [1931], in *Modern Man in Search of a Soul*, ch. 11. For Jung's ecclecticism, see, pp. 53–4.

119 *Modern Man in Search of a Soul*, p. 40 (emphasis supplied).

120 See above, section 1. For an interesting exploration of some of the connections between Heidegger's philosophy and psychoanalytic ideas, see Charles Guignon, 'Authenticity, moral values and psychotherapy', in Guignon (ed.), *The Cambridge Companion to Heidegger*, pp. 215ff.

121 See above, section 2.

122 *Modern Man in Search of a Soul*, p. 49.

123 *Modern Man in Search of a Soul*, p. 51–2.

124 *Modern Man in Search of a Soul*, p. 53.

125 Cf. *Nicomachean Ethics*, 1114a15ff.

126 Indeed, Jung sometimes reserves the label 'transformation' for this last phase: *Modern Man in Search of a Soul*, p. 54.

127 *Modern Man in Search of a Soul*, p. 55.

128 *Modern Man in Search of a Soul*, p. 55.

129 Not untypical, I think, is the reply I once heard from a philosophical colleague to the suggestion that psychoanalytic ideas might be relevant to ethics: 'But surely ethics is concerned with *normal* people, not those who are bonkers!' The short answer is first (as even Plato saw) that psychic hygiene, the harmonious working of the constituents of the self, lies at the core of the good life; and second, that no such harmony is possible without the kind of self-awareness that involves an enriched understanding of the structure and genesis of the emotions. It is no doubt true that not everyone will need to be

psychoanalysed in order to reach such self-awareness; but many nonetheless seem to underestimate the complexities involved in rediscovering and reintegrating past experience into our understanding of our present selves. Some of these complexities will be explored in sections 7 and 8.

130 The principal thesis of Sebastian Gardner's illuminating study *Irrationality and the Philosophy of Psychoanalysis* is that psychoanalytic explanations are fundamentally continuous with the kinds of account that are available to deal with more 'normal' kinds of irrationality. The resources of ordinary psychology, for example notions such as those of mental conflict, and the power of desire to malform belief, are precisely those exploited by psychoanalytic theory, albeit with 'much greater intensity' (p. 36). And this leads to a general defence of the plausibility and coherence of psychoanalytic theory, showing that its concepts are 'natural extensions of the ways of thinking of ordinary psychology' (p. 87).

131 *Modern Man in Search of a Soul*, pp. 61–2.

132 *Modern Man in Search of a Soul*, p. 62.

133   The Child is father of the Man;
       And I could wish my days to be
       Bound each to each by natural piety.

William Wordsworth, 'Ode, Intimations of Immortality from Recollections of Early Childhood' [1815 version].

Although many have read the phrase 'natural piety' as painting a sentimental picture of idyllic childhood, discerning critics of Wordsworth's project in *The Prelude* (begun 1799) have plausibly seen it as describing the poet's struggle to understand the roots of his psyche – a struggle that in many respects prefigures the psychoanalytic quest for self-awareness. Cf. M. Baron, *Language and Relationship in Wordsworth's Writing*, ch. 4.

134 *Modern Man in Search of a Soul*, p. 44.

135 *A Treatise of Human Nature*, bk III, part 1, section 1 (ed. Selby-Bigge, p. 465).

136 I should stress that the case is an imaginary one. The name 'Cecil' is thought to be derived from the Latin word for 'blind'.

137 S. Freud, 'Notes upon a Case of Obsessional Neurosis' [1909], in *Standard Edition*, vol. 10, pp. 155ff. The case is discussed at length by Gardner in *Irrationality and the Philosophy of Psychoanalysis*, ch. 4.

138 'I find the world quite good enough for me: rather a jolly place, in fact' (George Bernard Shaw, 'John Bull's Other Island' [1904], Act IV).

139 Bernard Williams, *Shame and Necessity*, p. 45.

140 Descartes urges that no one should read his book except those who are prepared to meditate seriously along with him: Preface to *Meditations*, AT VII 9: CSM II 8.

141 See above, section 2.

142 Lacan, *Télévision*, p. 6.

143 Compare C. G. Jung, 'The Shadow', in *Collected Works*, vol. 6; also reproduced in *Selected Writings*, ed. Storr, pp. 91ff.

144 See Terence Wilkerson, 'Akrasia'.

145 Like that of Socrates, the Aristotelian analysis of *akrasia* (discussed in chapter 2, section 3, above) dimly prefigures the 'transformational account', since it sees akratic behaviour as due to some kind of failure of knowledge. It is, however, far superior to the Socratic account, since, first, it departs from the purely intellectual plane (by rejecting the Socratic idea that *akrasia* is simply an error of judgement), and, second, it provides the crucial insight that there are different grades of knowledge: the effect of the passions is to 'cloud' our grasp of the relevant syllogism (which would lead to our choosing the rationally desired good), thus rendering our knowledge inoperative. But what is lacking is, first, an awareness of the importance of the temporal dimension – the way in which any classification of an action as akratic must operate over a larger time-frame than that of the moment of action; and, second, any development of the idea that the true *significance* of much of our akratic behaviour must be sought through the investigation of mental processes whose operation lies beneath what is consciously accessible to the subject at the time of action.

146 For the stingray image, see Plato, *Meno*, 79e; for the gadfly, see *Apology*, 30e.

147 This is the typical result of the early Socratic dialogues; cf. *Euthyphro, Charmides, Laches*. Despite the frequently negative thrust of Socratic method, it should be noted that there are other passages where Socrates emerges in a more constructive role, awakening in those he questions the dormant knowledge which they can 'recollect' under the stimulus of his interrogation; cf. *Meno*, 84a.

148 William Blake, *Poems from the Notebook* [*c.* 1791–2], XXXIX ('Eternity').

149 'Wo Es war, soll Ich werden'; Sigmund Freud, *New Introductory Lectures on Psychoanalysis* [*Neue Folge der Vorlesungen zur Einführung in die Psychoanalyse*, 1933], Lecture XXXI, in *Standard Edition of Complete Works*, trans. J. Strachey, vol. XXII, p. 80.

150 'Préférer la raison à la félicité, c'est être très insensé': Voltaire, 'The Story of a Good Brahmin' ['L'histoire d'un bon brahmin', 1759], in *Œuvres Complètes*, vol. LX, p. 520; trans. Redman, p. 438.

151 *Conversation with Burman* [1648], AT v 179: CSMK 354.

152 In case of misunderstanding, I should make it clear that the term 'soul', like its Greek counterpart *psyche*, should not be construed here as having any dualist overtones (as implying the existence of a

non-physical substance apart from the biological complex that is the human individual).

153 Third Meditation (AT VII 49: CSM II 33).
154 Second Meditation (AT VII 27: CSM II 18).
155 *Philosophe en méditation* [1632]. Collection of Louis XVI, Musée du Louvre (see front cover of paperback edition of the present volume).
156 I develop this theme in the final section of 'Medicine, Virtues and Consequences', in Oderberg and Laing (eds.), *Human Lives*.
157 William Blake, *Jerusalem* [1805], f. 55, l. 54.
158 Compare Jacques Lacan, *The Four Fundamental Concepts of Psychoanalysis*, p. 263.
159 John Milton, *Paradise Lost* [1667], book XII, 645–6.

Bibliography

Ackrill, J., *Aristotle the Philosopher* (Oxford: Oxford University Press, 1981).
Altham, J. E. J. and Harrison, R. (eds.), *World, Mind, and Ethics: Essays on the ethical philosophy of Bernard Williams* (Cambridge: Cambridge University Press, 1995).
Annas, J., *Hellenistic Philosophy of Mind* (Berkeley and Los Angeles, Calif.: University of California Press, 1992).
Annas, J., *The Morality of Happiness* (New York: Oxford University Press, 1994).
Anscombe, G. E. M., 'Modern Moral Philosophy', *Philosophy*, 1 33 (1958), pp. 1–19.
Aristotle, *Nicomachean Ethics* [*c.* 325 BC]. translated by T. Irwin (Indianapolis: Hackett, 1985). Other translations include that by J. A. K. Thomson, rev. H. Tredennick (Harmondsworth: Penguin, 1976).
Aristotle, *Physics* [*c.* 325 BC], translated R. P. Hardie and R. K. Gaye (Oxford: Clarendon, 1930).
Augustine of Hippo, *De civitate Dei* [413–26]. Abridged English version, *The City of God*, trans. H. Bettenson (Harmondsworth: Penguin, 1973).
Aurelius, Marcus, *Meditations* [*Ta eis heauton, c.* AD 175], trans. in W. J. Oates (ed.), *The Stoic and Epicurean Philosophers* (New York: Random House, 1940), pp. 491–585.
Ayer, A. J., *Language, Truth and Logic* (London: Gollancz, 1936, 2nd edn, 1946).
Bacon, Francis, *The Works of Francis Bacon*, ed. J. Spedding and R. E. Ellis, abridged J. M. Robinson (London: Routledge, 1905).
Barnes, J. (ed.), *The Cambridge Companion to Aristotle* (Cambridge: Cambridge University Press, 1995).
Baron, M., *Language and Relationship in Wordsworth's Writing* (London: Longman, 1995).
Barrett, W., *Irrational Man. A Study in Existential Philosophy* (New York: Doubleday, 1958).

Barrett, W. and Aiken, H. D. (eds.), *Philosophy in the Twentieth Century: an anthology* (Random House: New York, 1962).

Becker, L. C. (ed.), *Encyclopedia of Ethics* (Garland: New York, 1992).

Bonjour, L., *The Structure of Empirical Knowledge* (Cambridge Mass.: Harvard University Press, 1985).

Broadie, S., *Ethics with Aristotle* (New York: Oxford University Press, 1991).

Bowie, M., *Lacan* (Cambridge, Mass.: Harvard University Press, 1991).

Boyle, Robert, *Selected Philosophical Papers of Robert Boyle*, ed. M. A. Stewart (Manchester: Manchester University Press, 1979).

Brandt, R. B., *A Theory of the Good and the Right* (Oxford: Oxford University Press, 1979).

Butler, J., *The Analogy of Religion* [1736], in *Works*, ed. W. E. Gladstone (Oxford: Oxford University Press, 1896).

Campbell, R., *Truth and Historicity* (Oxford: Clarendon, 1990).

Camus, Albert, *Le Mythe de Sisyphe* [1942], in *Essais*, ed. R. Quilliot and L. Faucon (Paris: Gallimard, 1965).

Camus, Albert, *Le Mythe de Sisyphe* [1942], trans. J. O'Brien (New York: Knopf, 1955).

Casey, J., *Pagan Virtue* (Oxford: Clarendon, 1990).

Cavell, M., *The Psychoanalytic Mind: From Freud to Philosophy.* (Cambridge, Mass.: Harvard University Press, 1993).

Cicero, *De Finibus* [45–44 BC]. Book III is translated in M. R. Wright, *Cicero on Stoic Good and Evil* (Warminster: Aris and Phillips, 1991).

Clark, R. W., *The Life of Bertrand Russell* (Harmondsworth: Penguin, 1978).

Coimbrian Commentators, *Commentarii in tres libros de anima Aristotelis* (Coimbra, 1598).

Cottingham, J., *A Descartes Dictionary* (Oxford: Blackwell, 1993).

Cottingham, J., 'A Brute to the Brutes? Descartes' treatment of animals', *Philosophy* vol. 53 (1978), pp. 551–9.

Cottingham, J., 'Cartesian Trialism', *Mind*, XCIV, 374 (1985), pp. 218–30.

Cottingham, J., *Descartes* (Oxford: Blackwell, 1986).

Cottingham, J., 'Descartes on Colour', *Proceedings of the Aristotelian Society*, XC, 3 (1989–90), pp. 231–46.

Cottingham, J., 'Neo-Naturalism and its Pitfalls', *Philosophy* (1983), pp. 445–70.

Cottingham, J., 'Partiality, Favouritism and Morality', *Philosophical Quarterly*, 36 (1986), pp. 357–73.

Cottingham, J., *Rationalism* (London: Granada, 1984. repr. Thoemmes: Bristol, 1997).

Cottingham, J., 'Religion, Virtue and Ethical Culture', *Philosophy* (1994), pp. 163–80.

Cottingham, J., 'The Cartesian Legacy', *Proceedings of the Aristotelian Society*, Sup. vol. LXVI (1992), pp. 1–21.

Cottingham, J., *The Rationalists* (Oxford: Oxford University Press, 1988).

Cottingham, J. (ed.), *Reason, Will, and Sensation: Studies in Descartes's Metaphysics* (Oxford: Clarendon, 1994).

Cottingham, J. (ed.), *The Cambridge Companion to Descartes* (Cambridge: Cambridge University Press, 1992).

Craig, E., *The Mind of God and the Works of Man* (Oxford: Oxford University Press, 1987).

Crisp, R. (ed.), *How Should One Live? Essays on the Virtues* (Oxford: Clarendon, 1995).

Daniels, N. (ed.), *Reading Rawls* (Oxford: Blackwell, 1975).

Dennett, D., *Consciousness Explained* (Harmondsworth: Allen Lane, 1992).

Descartes, René, *Conversation with Burman*, ed. and trans. J. Cottingham (Oxford: Clarendon, 1976).

Descartes, René, *La Morale*, textes choisis et presentés par N. Grimaldi (Paris: Vrin, 1992).

Descartes, René, *Les passions de l'âme*, ed. G. Rodis-Lewis (2nd edn, Paris: Vrin, 1970).

Descartes, René, *Œuvres de Descartes*, ed. C. Adam, and P. Tannery (12 vols., revised edn, Paris: Vrin/CNRS, 1964–76) [referred to as 'AT'].

Descartes, René, *Philosophical Writings*, ed. A. Anscombe and P. Geach (London: Nelson, 1969).

Descartes, René, *The Passions of the Soul*, [1649] trans. S. Voss (Indianapolis: Hackett, 1991).

Descartes, René, *The Philosophical Writings of Descartes*, vols. I and II, trans. J. Cottingham, R. Stoothoff and D. Murdoch (Cambridge: Cambridge University Press, 1985) [referred to as 'CSM']; vol. III, The Correspondence, by the same translators plus A. Kenny (Cambridge University Press, 1991) [referred to as 'CSMK'].

Dilman, I., *Freud and the Mind* (Oxford: Blackwell, 1984).

Dodds, E. R., *The Greeks and the Irrational* (Berkeley and Los Angeles: University of California Press, 1951).

Epictetus, *Discourses* [*c.* AD 100], trans. W. A. Oldfather, (Cambridge, Mass.: Harvard University Press, 1928). Also edited by C. Gill, translation revised by R. Hard (London: Dent, 1995).

Eustachius a Sancto Paulo, *Summa Philosophiae Quadripartita* (2 vols., Paris, 1609).

Feigl, H. and Maxwell, G. (eds.), *Minnesota Studies in the Philosophy of Science* (Minneapolis: University of Minnesota Press, 1962).

Foot, P. (ed.), *Theories of Ethics* (Oxford: Oxford University Press, 1997).

Fordham, F., *An Introduction to Jung's Psychology* (Harmondsworth: Penguin, 1953; 3rd edn, 1966).

Freud, Sigmund, *Collected Papers*, ed. J. Riviere (London: Hogarth Press, 1925).

Freud, Sigmund, *Gesammelte Werke*, ed. A. Freud (London: Imago, 1947).

Freud, Sigmund, *Introductory Lectures on Psychoanalysis* [1916–17], translated by J. Riviere (London: Routledge, 1922).

Freud, Sigmund, *Standard Edition of the Complete Psychological Works of Sigmund Freud*, ed. J. Strachey (London: Hogarth, 1953–74).

Freud, Sigmund, *The Essentials of Psychoanalysis*, ed. with introduction by Anna Freud (Harmondsworth: Penguin, 1986).

Galileo Galilei, *Le Opere*, ed. A. Favaro (Florence: Barbera, 1889–1901, repr. 1968).

Gardner, S., *Irrationality and the Philosophy of Psychoanalysis* (Cambridge: Cambridge University Press, 1993).

Gaukroger, S., *Cartesian Logic* (Oxford: Clarendon, 1989).

Gaukroger, S., *Descartes: An Intellectual Biography* (Oxford: Clarendon, 1995).

Gaukroger, S., 'Descartes' Methodology', in Parkinson (ed.), *The Renaissance and Seventeenth-Century Rationalism*, pp. 167ff.

Gellner, E., *The Psychoanalytic Movement* (London: Granada, 1985).

Gill, C. (ed.), *The Person and the Human Mind: Issues in Ancient and Modern Philosophy* (Oxford: Clarendon, 1991).

Gill, C., 'Did Chrysippus misunderstand the Medea?', *Phronesis*, vol. 28 (1983).

Gilson, E., *Index Scolastico-Cartésien* (Paris: Alcan, 1913; 2nd edn, Paris: Vrin, 1979).

Grice, P., *The Conception of Value* (Oxford: Clarendon, 1991).

Gueroult, M., *Descartes selon l'ordre des raisons* (Aubier: Paris, 1968).

Guignon, C., *The Cambridge Companion to Heidegger* (New York: Cambridge University Press, 1993).

Hare, R. M., *Moral Thinking* (Oxford: Oxford University Press, 1981).

Hegel, G. W. F., *Phenomenology of Mind* [*Phänomenologie des Geistes*, 1807], trans. J. B. Baillie (London: Sonnenschein, 1910; 2nd edn, 1931).

Heidegger, Martin, 'Brief über den Humanismus', translated as 'Letter on Humanism' by E. Lohner, in W. Barrett and H. D. Aiken (eds.), *Philosophy in the Twentieth Century*.

Heidegger, Martin, 'Die Frage Nach der Technik', translated by W. Lovitt in *The Question concerning Technology* (New York: Harper and Row, 1977).

Heidegger, Martin, *Being and Time* [*Sein und Zeit*, 1927], section 15 trans. J. Macquarrie and E. Robinson (New York: Harper and Row, 1962).

Heidegger, Martin, 'Was Heisst Denken' [1951–2], translated by F. Wieck and J. Gray as *What is Called Thinking?* (New York: Harper & Row, 1968).

Hicks, R. D., *Stoic and Epicurean* (New York: Russell, 1962).

Hobbes, Thomas, *Leviathan* [1651], ed. C. B. Macpherson (Harmondsworth: Penguin, 1951).

Hook, S. (ed.), *Psychoanalysis, Scientific Method and Philosophy* (New York: New York University Press, 1959).

Hudson, W. D., *The Is/Ought Question* (London: Macmillan, 1969).

Hume, David, *A Treatise of Human Nature* [1739–40], ed. L. A. Selby-Bigge, rev. P. H. Niddich (Oxford: Clarendon, 1978).

Hume, David, *An Enquiry concerning Human Understanding* [1748], ed. L. A. Selby-Bigge, rev. P. H. Nidditch (Oxford: Clarendon, 1975).

Hurka, T., *Perfectionism* (New York: Oxford University Press, 1993).

Hutchison, K., 'What Happened to Occult Qualities in the Scientific Revolution', *ISIS* vol. 73 (1982), pp. 233ff.

Huxley, Aldous, *Brave New World* [1932] (Harmondsworth: Penguin, 1955).

Inwood, B., *Ethics and Human Action in Early Stoicism* (Oxford: Clarendon, 1985).

Irwin, T. H., *Plato's Ethics* (Oxford: Oxford University Press, 1995).

Irwin, T. H., *Plato's Moral Theory* (Oxford: Oxford University Press, 1977).

Irwin, T. H. and Nussbaum, M. C. (eds.), *Virtue, Love and Form: Essays in Memory of Gregory Vlastos* (Edmonton, Alberta: Academic Printing and Publishing, 1993).

Jolley, N., *The Light of the Soul: Theories of Ideas in Leibniz, Malebranche and Descartes* (Oxford: Clarendon, 1990).

Jones, H., *The Epicurean Tradition* (London: Routledge, 1989).

Jung, Carl G., *Modern Man in Search of a Soul*. Essays from the 1920s and 1930s, translated C. F. Baynes (London: Routledge, 1933).

Jung, Carl G., *Collected Works* (revised edition, London: Routledge, 1967–77).

Jung, Carl G., *Seelenprobleme der Gegenwart* (Rascher: Zurich, 1931).

Jung, Carl G., *Selected Writings*, ed. A. Storr (London: Harper Collins, 1983).

Kant, Immanuel, *Critique of Pure Reason* [*Kritik der Reinen Vernunft*, 1781; 2nd edn, 1787], trans. N. Kemp-Smith (London: Macmillan, 1929).

Kant, Immanuel, *Grundlegung zur Metaphysik der Sitten* [1785], translated as *The Moral Law*, ed. H. J. Paton (London: Hutchinson, 1948).

Kaufmann, W., *Nietzsche: Philosopher, Psychologist, Antichrist* (Princeton: Princeton University Press, 1950).

Kekes, J., *Moral Wisdom and Good Lives* (Ithaca: Cornell University Press, 1995).

Kierkegaard, Søren, *Journals* [1834–55], ed. and trans. A. Dru (London: Oxford University Press, 1938).

Kraut, R. (ed.), *The Cambridge Companion to Plato* (Cambridge: Cambridge University Press, 1992).

Kuhn, T. S., *The Structure of Scientific Revolutions* [1962] (2nd edn, Chicago: University of Chicago Press, 1970).

Kymlika, W., 'Liberal Individualism and Liberal Neutrality', *Ethics* 99 (July 1989) 883–905.

Lacan, Jacques, *Ecrits* (Paris: Seuil, 1966); translated by A. Sheridan in *Ecrits, A Selection* (London: Tavistock/Routledge, 1977).

Lacan, Jacques, *L'éthique de la psychanalyse* (Paris: Seuil, 1986).

Lacan, Jacques, *Télévision* (Paris: Seuie,1974).

Lacan, Jacques, *The Four Fundamental Concepts of Psychoanalysis* [1973], trans. A. Sheridan (Harmondsworth: Penguin, 1979)

Leibniz, Gottfried Wilhelm, *Philosophical Writings*, ed. G. H. R. Parkinson (London: Dent, 1973).

Leishman, J. B., *Themes and Variations in Shakespeare's Sonnets* (London: Hutchinson, 1961).

Locke, John, *An Essay concerning Human Understanding* [1689], ed. P. H. Nidditch (Oxford: Clarendon, 1975; repr. 1984).

Long, A. A. and Sedley, D. N. (eds.), *The Hellenistic philosophers* (Cambridge: Cambridge University Press, 1987).

Long, A. A., *Hellenistic Philosophy* (London: Duckworth, 1974; 2nd edn. 1986).

Lucretius, *De rerum natura* [*c.* 60 BC], trans. W. H. D. Rouse (Loeb Classical Library, Cambridge Mass.: Harvard University Press, 1966).

Lyotard, Jean-François, *La Condition-postmoderne* [1979], translated by G. Bennington and B. Massumi as *The Postmodern Condition: A Report on Knowledge* (Manchester: Manchester University Press, 1984).

MacIntyre, Alasdair, *A Short History of Ethics* (New York: Macmillan, 1966).

MacIntyre, Alasdair, *After Virtue* [1981], 2nd edn (London: Duckworth, 1985).

McGinn, C., *The Subjective View* (Oxford: Oxford University Press, 1983).

Malebranche, Nicolas, *Méditations chrétiennes et métaphysiques* [1683], in A. Robinet (ed.) *Œuvres complètes de Malebranche* (Paris: Vrin, 1958–67).

Matthews, E., *Twentieth-Century French Philosophy* (Oxford: Oxford University Press, 1996).

Midgley, M., *Beast and Man* (Sussex: Harvester, 1978).

Mill, J. S., *Collected Works* (London: Routledge, 1965–86).

Moore, G. E., *Principia Ethica* [1903] (Cambridge: Cambridge University Press, 1959).

Moyal, G. (ed.), *René Descartes: Critical Assessments* (4 vols., London: Routledte, 1991).

Murdoch, I., *Metaphysics as a Guide to Morals* (Harmondsworth: Penguin, 1992).

Nagel, T., 'Freud's Permanent Revolution', *New York Review of Books*, XLI, 9 (12 May, 1994), pp. 34–8.

Nagel, T., *Mortal Questions* (Cambridge: Cambridge University Press, 1979).

Neu, J. (ed.), *The Cambridge Companion to Freud* (New York: Cambridge University Press, 1991).

Nietzsche, Friedrich, *The Birth of Tragedy* [*Die Geburt der Tragödie*, 1872], trans. W. Kaufmann (New York: Random House, 1967).

Nietzsche, Friedrich, *The Twilight of the Gods* [*Die Götzen-Dämmerung*, 1889], and *Also Sprach Zarathustra*, [1883–92], trans. in W. Kaufmann (ed.), *The Portable Nietzsche* (New York: Viking, 1954).

Nietzsche, Friedrich, *Unzeitgemässe Betrachtungen* [1873], translated as *Unmodern Observations*, ed. W. Arrowsmith (New Haven, Conn: Yale University Press, 1990).

Norman, R., *Hegel's Phenomenology* (London: Sussex University Press, 1976).

Nozick, R., *Philosophical Explanations* (Oxford: Oxford University Press, 1981).

Nussbaum, M., *The Fragility of Goodness* (Cambridge: Cambridge University Press, 1986).

Nussbaum, M. (ed.), *The Poetics of Therapy* (Edmonton, Alberta: Academic Printing and Publishing, 1990).

O'Neill, O., *Constructions of Reason* (Cambridge: Cambridge University Press, 1989).

Oderberg, D., *The Metaphysics of Identity over Time* (London: Macmillan, 1993).

Oderberg, D. and Laing, L. (eds.), *Human Lives* (London: Macmillan, 1996).

Paracelsus, Theophrastus, *Sämtliche Werke*, ed. K. Sudhoff and W. Matthiessen (Munich: Marth, 1922–5, and Berlin: Oldebourg, 1928–33).

Paracelsus, Theophrastus, *Selected Writings* ed. J. Jacobi (London: Routledge, 1951).

Parkinson, G. H. R. (ed.), *An Encyclopaedia of Philosophy* (London: Routledge, 1988).

Parkinson, G. H. R. (ed.), *The Renaissance and Seventeenth-Century Rationalism*. Routledge History of Philosophy, volume IV (London: Routledge, 1993).

Pascal, Blaise, *Œuvres* (3 vols., Paris: Hachette, 1904).

Pascal, Blaise, *Pensées* [c. 1660], ed. L. Lafuma (Paris: Editions du Seuil, 1962).

Penrose, R., *The Emperor's New Mind* (New York: Oxford University Press, 1989).

Phillips Griffiths, A. (ed.), *Ethics*. Royal Institute of Philosophy Supplement: 35 (Cambridge: Cambridge University Press, 1993).

Plato, *Protagoras and Meno* [c. 385 BC], trans. W. K. C. Guthrie (Harmondsworth: Penguin, 1956).

Plato, *Republic* [*c.* 380 BC], trans. H. D. P. Lee (Harmondsworth: Penguin, 1955).

Plumwood, V., *Feminism and the Mastery of Nature* (London: Routledge, 1993).

Popper, Karl, *Conjectures and Refutations* (London: Routledge, 1963; 3rd edn, 1969).

Price, A. W., *Mental Conflict* (London: Routledge, 1995).

Price, C., 'Functional Explanations and Natural Norms', *Ratio*, vol. VIII (1995), pp. 143ff.

Rajchman, J., *Truth and Eros: Foucault, Lacan, and the question of ethics* (New York: Routledge, 1991).

Raphael, D. D. (ed.), *British Moralists 1650–1800*, 2 vols., (Oxford: Clarendon, 1969).

Rawls, J., *A Theory of Justice* (Cambridge, Mass.: Harvard University Press, 1971).

Rawls, J., 'On the idea of an Overlapping Consensus', *Oxford Journal for Legal Studies* (1987), pp. 1–25.

Raz, J., *The Morality of Freedom* (Oxford: Clarendon, 1986).

Rist, J. M., *Stoic Philosophy* (Cambridge: Cambridge University Press, 1969).

Rodis-Lewis, G., *La Morale de Descartes* (Paris: Presses Universitaires de France, 1957).

Rodis-Lewis, G., *L'anthropologie cartésienne* (Paris: Presses Universitaires de France, 1990).

Rogers, J. and Vienne, J-M. (eds.), *The Cambridge Platonists in Philosophical Context* (Dordrecht: Kluwer, 1997).

Rorty, A. (ed.), *Essays on Aristotle's Ethics* (Berkeley: University of California Press, 1980).

Rorty, R., *Philosophy and the Mirror of Nature* (Oxford : Blackwell, 1980).

Russell, Bertrand, *The Autobiography of Bertrand Russell* (London: Allen & Unwin, 1968).

Sandbach, F. H., *The Stoics* (London: Chatto & Windus, 1975).

Sartre, Jean-Paul, *Critique de la raison dialectique* (Paris: Gallimard, 1960).

Sartre, Jean-Paul, 'Question de méthode' [1957], trans. H. Barnes, *The Problem of Method* (London: Methuen, 1963).

Scheffler, S., 'Against the System', *Times Literary Supplement*, 16 February, 1996.

Schneewind, J. B. (ed.), *Moral philosophy from Montaigne to Kant*, 2 vols. (Cambridge: Cambridge University Press, 1990).

Sen A. and Williams B. (eds), *Utilitarianism and Beyond* (Cambridge: Cambridge University Press, 1982).

Seneca, *De Vita Beata* ('On the Blessed Life') [*c.* AD 58], in *Moral Essays*, vol. II, trans. for Loeb Classical Library by J. W. Basore (Cambridge Mass.: Harvard University Press, 1932).

Seneca, *Moral Essays [Epistulae Morales, c.* AD 64], trans. for Loeb Classical Library by J. W. Basore (Cambridge Mass.: Harvard University Press, 1932).

Singer, P. (ed.), *Ethics* (Oxford: Oxford University Press, 1994).

Skorupski, J., *English-Language Philosophy 1750–1945* (Oxford: Oxford University Press, 1993).

Skorupski, J., *John Stuart Mill* (London: Routledge, 1989).

Smith, M., *The Moral Problem* (Oxford: Blackwell, 1994).

Sorabji, R., *Animal Minds and Human Morals* (London: Duckworth, 1993).

Spinoza, Benedict, *Ethics* [c.1665], in *Opera,* ed. C. Gebhardt, 3 vols. (Heidelberg: Winters, 1925, repr. 1972). English translation, *The Collected Works of Spinoza,* ed. E. Curley, vol. 1 (Princeton: Princeton University Press, 1985).

Steiner, G., *Heidegger* [1978] (2nd edn, London: Fontana, 1992).

Taylor, C., *Sources of the Self: the making of the modern identity* (Cambridge: Cambridge University Press, 1989).

Trigg, R., *Rationality and Science* (Oxford: Blackwell, 1993).

Vesey, G. and Foulkes, P., *Collins Dictionary of Philosophy* (London: Collins, 1990).

Voltaire, *Œuvres Complètes* (Paris: Baudouin, 1826).

Voltaire, *The Portable Voltaire* (New York: Viking Press, 1963).

Wilkerson, T., 'Akrasia', *Ratio,* VIII (1992), pp. 164ff.

Williams, B., *Descartes, The Project of Pure Inquiry* (Harmondsworth: Penguin, 1978).

Williams, B., *Moral Luck* (Cambridge: Cambridge University Press, 1981).

Williams, B., *Shame and Necessity* (Berkeley and Los Angeles: University of California Press, 1993).

Wilson, M., *Descartes* (London: Routledge, 1978).

Wittgenstein, Ludwig, *Tractatus Logico-Philosophicus* [1921], ed. D. F. Pears and B. F. McGuinness (Oxford: Blackwell, 1961).

Wittgenstein, Ludwig, *The Blue and Brown Books* (Oxford: Blackwell, 1958).

Wolf, S., ' Moral Saints', *Journal of Philosophy,* 79 (1982) 419–39.

Wollheim, R., *The Thread of Life* (Cambridge Mass.: Harvard University Press, 1984).

Wollheim, R. and Hopkins, J. (eds.), *Philosophical Essays on Freud* (Cambridge: Cambridge University Press, 1982).

Woodfield, A., *Teleology* (Cambridge: Cambridge University Press, 1976).

Wright, C., *Frege's Conception of Numbers as Objects* (Aberdeen: Aberdeen University Press, 1983).

Wright, J., *The Sceptical Realism of David Hume* (Cambridge, Cambridge University Press, 1983).

Zanta, L., *La renaissance du stoïcisme au xvie siècle* (Paris: Champion, 1914).

Index

Printed in the United Kingdom
by Lightning Source UK Ltd.
109904UKS00001B/150